# AIR FORCE

PAGE 1: A modern F-15 Strike Eagle (top) flies above a venerable P-51 Mustang from World War II during an October 2, 2007 air show.

THIS PAGE: An A/OA-10 Thunderbolt II is surrounded by a plume of gun smoke while firing its 30mm seven-barrel GAU-8 Avenger Gatling gun.

# AIR FORCE
## An Illustrated History
### The U.S. Air Force from the 1910s to the 21st Century

# Chester G. Hearn

ZENITH PRESS

Project manager: Ray Bonds
Design: Mark Tennent/Compendium Design
Maps: Mike Marino


ISBN 13: 978-0-7603-3308-2
ISBN 10: 0-7603-3308-4

Printed in China

Acknowledgments
Thanks to all those who helped by providing photographs for this book. Most of the images come from the Library of Congress (LoC), Defense Visual Information Center (DVIC), or Air Force Link (AFL, official web site of the United States Air Force). Others are from private collections (PC). Specifics are as follows: Pages 1-5 DVIC; 6-7 AFL; 8-9 DVIC; 10-11 LoC; 12 LoC; 13 LoC; 14-15 AFL; 16-17 AFL; 18-19 AFL; 20 AFL; 21 LoC; 22-23 AFL; 24 AFL; 25 (top left and bottom) LoC, top right AFL; 26-27 (posters) LoC, others AFL; 28-29 (left and center) AFL, others LoC; 30-31 AFL; 32-33 LoC; 34 AFL; 35 LoC; 37 AFL; 38 AFL; 39 LoC; 40 LoC; 41 AFL; 42, left top and bottom, AFL; right LoC; 43 LoC; 44 leftLoC; right AFL; 45 AFL; 46 AFL; 47 top LoC, bottom AFL; 48-49 AFL;  50-51 left and center AFL, right PC; 52 AFL; 54 left AFL, right LoC; 55 top PC, bottom LoC; 56 top AFL, bottom PC; 57 LoC; 58 AFL; 59 PC; 60 PC; 61 AFL; 62 PC; 64 top PC, bottom LoC; 65 PC; 66 ttop AFL, bottom PC; 68 left LoC, right AFL; 70 AFL; 71 PC;  72 left AFL, others PC; 74-75 main pic LoC, others AFL; 76 PC; 77 AFL; 78-79 AFL; 80 PC; 81 far left LoC, others AFL; 82 PC; 83 AFL; 84 PC; 85 AFL; 86 AFL; 88 LoC; 89 top PC, bottom AFL; 91 AFL; 92 left AFL, right PC; 94-95 bottom right LoC, others AFL;  96 top left AFL, others LoC; 97 PC; 98 left LoC, others PC; 98 AFL; 100 left AFL, right  PC; 101 left LoC, right PC; 102-103 left AFL, center PC, right AFL; 104 LoC; 105 left and bottom right LoC, top PC; 106 top PC, bottom LoC; 107 PC; 108 AFL; 109 LoC; 110 LoC; 111 top PC, bottom AFL; 112-113 LoC; 114 LoC; 115 AFL; 116-117 left AFL, right PC; 118 top left AFL, top cente and right PC, bottom right AFL; 119 AFL;120 AFL; 122 AFL; 123 PC; 124-125 AFL; 127 AFL; 128-129 PC; 130 PC;  132 AFL; 133 LoC 134-135 AFL;  136 PC; 137 top and bottom left AFL, bottom right PC; 138 top AFL, bottom PC; 139 top PC, bottom AFL; 140-141 far right PC, others AFL;  142 AFL; 144-145 CVIC; 146 top AFL, bottom PC; 147 AFL; 148 DVIC; 149 AFL; 150-151 LoC; 152-153 DVIC; 154-155 DVIC; 156-157 DVIC; 158-159; 160-161 DVIC; 162-163 DVIC; 164-165 DVIC: 166-16 DVIC; 168 DVIC; 169 AFL; 170-171 AFL; 172-187 DVIC.

*RIGHT: A Boeing B-52H Stratofortress waits on the flightline to be prepped by its crew for a mission during a period of low visibility, sub-zero temperatures, and wind gusts of over fifty knots.*

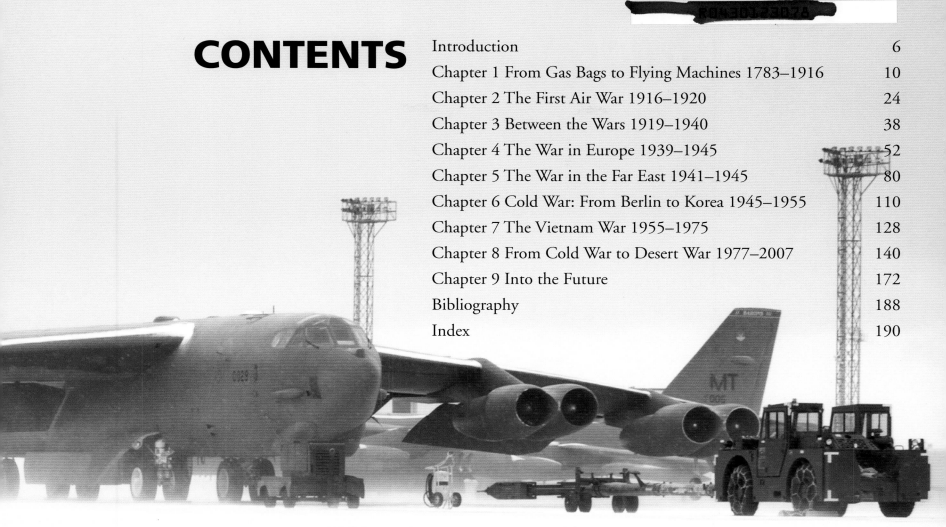

# CONTENTS

# INTRODUCTION

The United States Air Force (USAF) celebrated its sixtieth birthday on September 18, 2007, but its roots reach back to August 1, 1907, when the U.S. Army Signal Corps formed the Aeronautical Division to "take charge of all matters pertaining to military ballooning, air machines, and all kindred matters." As better aircraft became available, American pilots who participated in World War I quickly recognized the potential of airpower and began lobbying for independence from the army. Forty years passed before the air force became, in 1947, the manager of its own destiny. During the intervening years, the army general staff suppressed the careers of air advocates because of major differences in warfighting philosophies. Senior army officers gave way grudgingly, forming the Air Service during World War I, the Air Corps during the 1920s, and the Army Air Force during World War II. Each step led to the eventual formation of the USAF, which after World War II could no longer justifiably be denied. Though often without sufficient funding, the early leaders who believed in

RIGHT: *In an era of gas bags and flying machines, on February 10, 1908, following a lengthy series of tests at Fort Myer, Virginia, Orville Wright (in suit) succeeded in persuading the U.S. Army to accept the Wright Model A biplane as its first military aeroplane.*

LEFT: The Eighth Air Force, operating out of England during World War II, fills the skies with hundreds of Boeing B-17 Flying Fortresses, which during the bombing of Germany became part of the greatest aerial armada in history.

airpower tenaciously drove the technology of flight and the development of weaponry that eventually shaped the most capable and powerful air force in the world.

From its beginnings in 1907, the heart and soul of the air force has been its people, their dedication to excellence, their technological resourcefulness, and their vision. From the very beginning of powered flight in 1903, men like the Wright brothers and Glenn Curtiss predicted the importance of aviation to armies and navies at a time when militarists could not see beyond fortifications and the perpetuity of conventional ground wars. The Wrights and Curtiss trained the first pilots, and in 1911 those same men began test-firing machine guns from a Wright *Flyer* and experimenting with aerial bombing from a Curtiss pusher.

The U.S. Army took little interest in aviation until the waning months of World War I. The young pilots who earned their wings and the few producers who designed and manufactured the aircraft created a new science called aeronautics. During the twentieth century, the knowledge of flight evolved from rickety biplanes made from wood, fabric, wire, and bicycle engines to Mach-3 jet aircraft, jump jets, stealth technology, helicopters, intercontinental ballistic missiles, anti-ballistic weapons, precision-guided weapons, information gathering satellites, space shuttles, and an array of avionics and targeting technology unimaginable during World War I.

With the development of better aircraft and better weapons came new methods for waging war. One of the most remarkable aspects of this phenomenon was the ability of men like Billy Mitchell, Benny Foulois, and Henry "Hap" Arnold to foresee what aircraft and weapons would be needed one to two decades in advance. Walter J. Boyne, one of America's leading authorities on the U. S. Air Force, summed it up in *Beyond the Wild Blue*, writing: "The successes attained in World War II might be attributed to a specialized leadership, trained for twenty years with but a single goal, that of establishing air superiority with conventional weapons of the times."

The advent of medium-range V-2 rockets, jet engines, Boeing B-29 bombers, and nuclear explosive devices set the world on another course. In 1945 the air age of unconditional surrender in which Mitchell, Foulois, Arnold, and millions of others had participated came to an end. On September 18, 1947, with the formation of the United States Air Force, a new air age began, soon to usher in a strategy of Soviet containment by using an arsenal of aircraft and weapons far beyond the vision of the founding air strategists.

After World War II, President Harry S. Truman gutted the military. At the time of the Berlin blockade the air force had a few nuclear bombs but little else with which to respond to the immense standing armies of the U.S.S.R. American pilots fought the early months of the Korean War with World War II aircraft. During the Vietnam War, operations were micro-managed from the White House and the Pentagon, which shackled the USAF from unleashing its airpower. During the later 1970s, President Jimmy Carter cut air strength at a time when the Soviet economy was straining to remain competitive in the development of arms. In 1981 President Ronald Reagan reversed Carter's policies, poured money into air superiority, and announced the Strategic Defense Initiative (SDI),

8

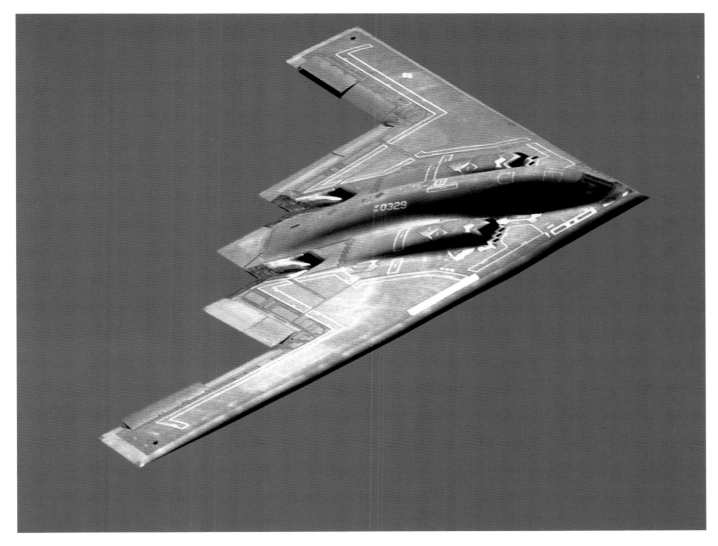

LEFT: *Northrop Grumman's B-2 Spirit, a multi-role bomber capable of delivering both conventional and nuclear munitions, provides a strong, effective deterrent and combat force well into the 21st century. Although operating from Whiteman, Missouri, the versatile stealth bomber has carried payloads of 40,000 pounds of munitions on non-stop missions to Serbia, Afghanistan, and Iraq.*

ABOVE: *The U.S. Air Force wings were originally adopted by General Henry "Hap" Arnold during the 1940s and are often referred to as the "Arnold" wings. The symbol represents the many different aspects of the service's proud heritage, which bridges the purchase of the first aircraft in 1908 to the magnificent aerospace force of today and tomorrow. The angularity of the wings emphasizes swiftness and power, which symbolizes the air superiority of the USAF in 2008, one hundred years after the first purchase of a rickety biplane made from wood and canvas.*

mirthfully known as Stars Wars. The Soviets bankrupted their economy attempting to keep pace with the United States, and dissolved, and the USAF became the most powerful air force in the world.

The USAF never looked back. During the Persian Gulf War the air force showcased an arsenal of weapons the world had never seen or imagined. Despite "peace dividends" during the administration of President William J. Clinton, the USAF continued to expand technology through research and development, produced aircraft and weapons of greater accuracy and capability, and in 2003 applied them against Saddam Hussein's standing army during Operation Iraqi Freedom.

Becoming the foremost airpower in the world during the early years of the twenty-first century has not created complacency within the USAF. Like the nearly forgotten airmen of vision in the far distant past, today's leaders are still looking two decades into the future, reshaping the USAF into the most powerful deterrent- and offensive-capable force in a constantly changing world of new threats.

Unlike the roots of the army and the navy, which trace back through centuries, the history of the air force is unique in its rapid development. Man's first powered flight in 1903 set the stage. And then the journey began.

# FROM GAS BAGS TO FLYING MACHINES 1783–1916

> The Atlantic Ocean, one of these days, will be no more difficult to cross by air than a fish pond. *Glenn Curtiss in the* Curtiss Aviation Book.

Although the concept of mechanical flight can be traced back to Leonardo de Vinci (circa 1500), dozens of scientists and hacks spent another three centuries attempting to become airborne. Lured by the mysteries of flight, many self-proclaimed *aérostiers* suffered injury or death trying to conquer the sky. Finally on November 21, 1783, Frenchman Michael Montgolfier and his brother Jacques persuaded two friends to step into a basket and, together, became the first successful balloonists. The day marked the beginning of ballooning. It also marked the birth of aviation.

Despite the dangers, the new hot-air technology attracted hundreds of balloonists. Creative minds in Europe began contemplating aerial voyages from one town to another. This required getting airborne at point A, reliance on a favorable wind, and then the tricky process of landing in one piece at point B without steerage.

**LEFT: Ballooning in the 1780s was very risky, usually when trying to land in a tree-lined field in the face of an oncoming storm. August 27, 1783, marked the first year that balloonist began using hydrogen, which made the balloon more manageable, instead of hot air, which quickly decayed.**

**RIGHT: An imaginative artist added wings and a tail to Jean-Pierre François Blanchard's balloon commemorating the first air crossing of the English Channel in 1785. By the early 1800s, more than 450 aeronauts had taken to the skies, including forty-nine women.**

## An American in Paris

Benjamin Franklin spent much of his time in Paris during the American Revolution, and in 1783 he became intrigued by the aerial endeavors of the Montgolfiers. In 1785, Franklin was again in France when his friend, Dr. John Jeffries, a Massachusetts physician, made the first balloon crossing of the English Channel with Jean-Pierre François Blanchard, who had financed the enterprise.

## The First American Balloonists

In 1840, Colonel John H. Sherburne requisitioned several $900 balloons for reconnaissance during the Seminole War to aid in locating the Indians, but the war department rejected his request.

Six years later, during the Mexican War, John Wise of Lancaster, Pennsylvania, offered to provide the army with enough balloons to reconnoiter enemy positions in Mexico City and annoy them by dropping explosives. He never received an answer. Undaunted by indifference, Wise continued to develop balloon technology, and on July 1, 1859, established a world distance record by flying 809 miles from St. Louis to Jefferson County, New York, in 19 hours and 40 minutes.

## Ballooning in the Civil War

Even during the Civil War, the war department showed modest interest in vertical maneuver. One week after the surrender of Fort Sumter, James Allen arrived in Washington, D.C, with two balloons and offered his services to the war department. In July 1861 he attempted to spy on Confederate positions near Manassas. The portable gas generator failed, and Allen never got off the ground. Further mishaps ended Allen's efforts to support the Union cause.

John LaMountain, who attempted to cross the Atlantic carried aloft by a balloon, wrote the war department offering to become a balloonist but never received a response. Several weeks later Major General

*ABOVE: At Fair Oaks, Virginia, on May 30, 1862, Thaddeus Lowe begins to inflate the balloon Intrepid from two bulky, hydrogen-generating machines. These had to accompany the aerial observation team wherever they went.*

Benjamin F. Butler, headquartered at Fort Monroe, Virginia, offered LaMountain a job as aerial observer. LaMountain packed up his balloon and ascended over Hampton Roads on July 25, 1861. By mid-August he had made six ascents, one of 2,000 feet from the stern of the armed transport *Fanny* and another of 3,500 feet from land. While airborne, he spotted and sketched artillery and enemy positions unknown to Butler.

LaMountain eventually took leave to obtain a larger balloon and his own gas generator. After returning to Fort Monroe and finding that a disinterested general had replaced Butler, LaMountain obtained a transfer to the Army of the Potomac, commanded by Major General George B. McClellan. There he encountered his primary rival, Thaddeus S. C. Lowe, the civilian chief of army aeronautics.

## Thaddeus Sobieski Constantine Lowe (1832–1913)

Born on August 20, 1832, at Jefferson Mills, New Hampshire, Lowe received a very limited education but grew up fascinated with science. He developed an interest in upper air currents during his early twenties and adopted aeronautics as his profession. In 1858 he built the first of many balloons and became an exhibitionist. In August he celebrated the laying of the Atlantic cable by making an ascent in Ottawa, Ontario. A year later, using donations and profits from traveling exhibitions, Lowe built a huge airship, the *City of New York*, to use in competition against Wise and LaMountain's challenge to balloon across the Atlantic. In 1859, "Professor" Lowe's aspirations failed when handlers damaged the airship's gas envelope during inflation. By 1861 neither the partners LaMountain and Wise, nor Lowe, had succeeded in making a trans-Atlantic voyage, but they knew each other as bitter rivals.

During April 19-20, 1861, Lowe made an untimely nine-hour, 900-mile flight from Cincinnati, Ohio, to Unionville, South Carolina, and landed five days after the surrender of Fort Sumter. Captured as a Union spy, Lowe spent time in prison. When released, he hastened to Washington and offered his services to the war department. Impressed by the balloonist's accomplishments, which included sending telegraphic messages while airborne, Abraham Lincoln named him civilian chief of army aeronautics with the pay of colonel and a modest appropriation for running the operation. Lowe began building the 25,000-cubic-foot *Union* and on August 29 ascended outside Washington. A month later he established an airborne first by directing artillery fire at Confederate targets in the Falls Church area.

In the spring of 1862, Lowe transported his balloons and portable coal-gas generators to Virginia to serve with General McClellan and the Army of the Potomac during the Peninsular Campaign. Lowe conducted both aerial observation and photographic reconnaissance, and McClellan awarded him with an additional appropriation of $8,600. Lowe used the funds to enlarge his fleet to seven airships ranging in capacity from 15,000 cubic feet to the 32,000-cubic-foot *Intrepid*.

During the Peninsular Campaign, Lowe and LaMountain each attempted to diminish the efforts and accomplishments of the other. Brigadier General Fitz John Porter convinced McClellan that the two civilians could best serve the army if they worked together. The two men agreed to cooperate, and LaMountain went on the payroll at the same daily $10 rate as Lowe. Both men were great innovators. LaMountain's lower altitude flights took him over Confederate lines, after which he ascended to 18,000 ft to catch upper prevailing winds that carried him back to Union lines. His aerial reconnaissance forced the Confederate army to resort to camouflage.

One of Lowe's aeronauts, William Paullin, operated from the flat deck of a remodeled coal barge that resembled a mini-aircraft carrier. The barge had been modified for balloon operations and carried its own windlass, restraining lines, gas generator, spare parts, and used a tug for maneuvering.

Cooperation between Lowe and LaMountain could not last, mainly because Lowe had all the balloons. LaMountain went to Washington to request one of Lowe's balloons but made the mistake of denouncing his rival. McClellan discharged LaMountain for insubordination.

Lowe could be equally as feisty and during the Chancellorsville campaign (May 1–4, 1863) ran afoul of Major General Joseph Hooker, who reduced the balloonist's pay, pruned his staff, and obstructed his work. On May 9, Lowe resigned after he and his aeronauts had completed more than 3,000 ascents. It would not be the last time that flyers would make major but unrecognized contributions while supporting the army.

*LEFT: The durability of Thaddeus Lowe's **Intrepid** made it the most famous airship of the Civil War. Retained by three ground ropes, the balloon allowed observation from 1,000 ft.*

## San Juan Hill (1898)

After the Civil War, and without support from the army, ballooning reverted to the public sector. During the post-war years creative minds worked on controllable flight, but when the Spanish-American War erupted during April 1898, small engines were not quite ready for adaptation to airships.

Brigadier General Adolphus W. Greeley reorganized the Signal Corps on July 1, 1891, and created the first purely military balloon section. Seven years later, at the outbreak of war, the corps' only balloon lay in dead storage at Denver without a single soldier capable of restoring or operating it. With civilian help, a work party resurrected the gasbag, made three trials, and in June 1898 shipped it off to Daiquiri, Cuba.

On July 29 the balloon detachment made its first ascent and reported the Spanish fleet in Santiago harbor, confirming what the U.S. Navy already suspected. Two days later Lieutenant Colonels Joseph E. Maxfield and George McC. Derby ascended from El Poso Hill and witnessed the American advance, but could not see the enemy because of thick woods. After moving the balloon to San Juan Hill, trees fouled the maneuvering lines, but Maxfield and Derby attained enough altitude to spot the Spanish entrenchments and redirect artillery fire. The Spaniards, however, assumed that the Americans would be in the vicinity of their balloon and sprayed the area with shells. They also peppered the balloon with bullets and perforated the envelope, forcing the ground crew to lower it for repairs. Colonel Leonard Wood, while maneuvering to avoid Spanish artillery, derided Maxfield's and Derby's ballooning escapade as "one of the most ill-judged and idiotic acts" he had ever witnessed.

Although ballooning on San Juan Hill had been an almost impossible task from the start, Major General

William Shafter, commanding American ground forces, issued a favorable report. After the war, the army established a Balloon Detachment at Fort Myer, Virginia. The war department authorized funds for new airships and more aeronauts to fly them, and encouraged army officers to participate in some of the great early twentieth century international balloon races.

### Dirigible No. 1

During the early 1900s, the search for controllable flight continued apace. After Brigadier General James Allen, the new chief signal officer, witnessed dirigible competition during the international balloon race at St. Louis, he spoke with daredevil Thomas S. Baldwin, an entrant, and asked for assistance in developing specifications for the army. Baldwin not only agreed, but he added several novel concepts he believed would

work. The specifications called for a 1,350-pound dirigible capable of carrying two persons, plus gear and 100 pounds of ballast, up to 20 miles per hour. Baldwin specified a fabric of silk laminated with rubber for the envelope, a composition no American manufacturer had ever made. Hydrogen served as the lifting gas, and Glenn Curtiss, who had already taken an interest in heavier-than-air flight, provided lightweight engines similar to those Baldwin had used in the past. Having developed the design, Baldwin also became the low bidder at $6,750 and agreed to deliver the army's first dirigible in 150 days.

Baldwin's pint-sized airship had characteristics in common with German Zeppelins, which first appeared in July 1900. The operator's nacelle lay under a cylindrical gasbag having pointed ends. Curtiss, who manufactured lightweight motorcycle engines, began work on a new, water-cooled, four-cylinder combustion engine capable of delivering 20 horsepower. He mounted the engine near the forward section of the nacelle and connected it to a twenty-two-foot-long shaft driving the propeller. For flight control, one pilot sat behind the engine and steered the airship in the vertical plane using a set of short-span wings as stabilizers. A second pilot stationed aft managed the rudder to provide directional control.

In late July 1908, Baldwin delivered *Dirigible No. 1* to Fort Myer and on August 4 performed the first flight test. After ascending to 250 ft, Baldwin and Curtiss made several adjustments to correct the steerage. On August 14 they successfully completed the test course and logged a speed of 19.61 mph, which the Signal Corps ruled close enough. Acid used in the hydrogen gas process eventually penetrated the envelope and created small perforations, but by then Baldwin had trained three pilots—Lieutenants Frank P. Lahm, Benjamin D. Foulois, and Thomas E. Selfridge—all of whom would soon become engaged in the development of aircraft.

**LEFT:** *Frank P. Lahm became one of the pioneers in the formation of the Air Service and worked closely with Orville Wright in the development of aircraft. While serving as Orville's passenger on July 27, 1909, Lahm participated in the first official test flight conducted for the army, establishing a world record of one hour, twelve minutes, and forty seconds for a two-man flight. Three months later Lahm soloed on "Aeroplane No. 1" and became the Signal Corps' first official pilot.*

*ABOVE: On December 17, 1903, at Kitty Hawk, North Carolina, Orville Wright made the first successful powered flight. It lasted twelve seconds and covered a distance of 120 ft. His fourth flight lasted fifty-nine seconds and covered 852 ft.*

*ABOVE: Within a few years, other airplane developers entered the field of aviation, and air shows in the United States and Europe began attracting large crowds of spectators, including military personnel. Here, enthusiasts watch an Aero Club of America fly-past at Belmont Park, New York, October 30, 1910.*

## The Wright Brothers

Wilbur and Orville Wright, two bicycle mechanics from Dayton, Ohio, became interested in the early science of aerodynamics in 1896 after Dr. Samuel Pierpont Langley of the Smithsonian Institution built an "aerodrome" having a one horsepower engine and attempted to catapult it over the Potomac. The powered glider failed because it struck its launching post and toppled into the river. The exact experiment, repeated successfully years later, proved the aerodrome would have flown but for the accident. Langley was not alone in his efforts to fly. Glider enthusiasts were springing up everywhere, including the Wrights, who in 1899 built a large kite to study the dynamics of flying.

The Wrights were not geniuses, but they knew something about chains, sprockets, and motive power. They were also extremely methodical, patient, skillful, and persistent experimenters. They built homemade gliders to learn how they fly,

and they built a small wind tunnel to study wind lift. When they decided to emulate Langley by adding a small engine to a glider, they realized that neither steam nor electric power would work, and built their own ultra-light combustion engine.

Having chosen a glider, they packed it up, transported it to Kill Devil Hill near Kitty Hawk, North Carolina, and fitted it with their pusher engine. On December 17, 1903, with thirty-six-year-old Wilbur at the controls, the first powered flight struggled aloft for 59 seconds and changed the world forever.

The British approached the Wrights in 1904 and offered to buy their contraption, but were politely rebuffed. Wilbur and Orville believed that Americans should benefit from the invention and on three separate occasions attempted to interest the war department's Board of Ordnance and Fortification but in 1905 were told by an

ignorant, bureaucratic respondent that the army would not take action "until a machine is produced which by actual operation is shown to produce horizontal flight and carry an operator." The Wrights were stupefied. By then they had made more than 150 flights observed by spectators and reporters.

The Wrights continued to experiment and improved their design with better controls and a better pusher engine. In 1907, the Aero Club of America began enjoying the fruits of heavier-than-air machines and urged President Theodore Roosevelt to acquire the Wrights' invention and develop the aircraft as a weapon. Roosevelt referred the Wrights, who had drawn up new plans for an improved aircraft, back to the stodgy Board of Ordnance, which again balked and said the matter must be referred to Congress. Wilbur Wright ignored the advice and went back to the board and convinced them that operational flying

machines were already being built in America as well as in Europe.

The Aeronautical Division drafted specifications based on Wilbur Wright's estimates of performance and on December 23, 1907, asked for competitive bids. Forty-one firms responded with bids ranging from $500 to $10,000,000. Of three contracts issued by the government, only two made sense. Augustus M. Herring, who in 1908 went into partnership with Glenn Curtiss, asked $20,000 and 180 days. The other contract went to the Wrights for $25,000 and 200 days. On August 20, 1908, the Ohio brothers delivered the first Wright Type A *Flyer*, a biplane with a pusher engine. During the same period, Curtiss produced the *June Bug*, a bi-winged pusher that became the first plane in the world to fly a kilometer before judges. Curtiss, however, was more interested in developing planes than wasting all his efforts on the army.

## Development of Flying Machines

In 1907, while the Wrights were developing specifications for their *Flyer*, Alexander Graham Bell, the inventor of the telephone and a proponent of flying machines, formed the Aerial Experiment Association (AEA) with Douglas McCurdy, Glenn Curtiss, Thomas Scott Baldwin, and Lieutenant Selfridge of the Army Signal Corps. Thirty-year-old Curtiss became interested in flying machines while working with Baldwin. The AEA named him director of experiments with an annual salary of $5,000. Curtiss attempted to establish a working relationship between the AEA and the Wrights but was rebuffed. The Wrights underestimated the AEA, and Curtiss in particular, whose engines and flight controls were superior to theirs. They viewed Curtiss as a rival and patent usurper the day he entered the *June Bug* in competition and won the coveted *Scientific American* trophy. The Wrights had no one to blame but themselves when their competitor formed the Curtiss Aeroplane Company.

The Wrights suffered embarrassment in September 1908 while performing trials with the *Flyer*. One propeller cracked and deflected, sliced a bracing attached to the rudder frame, and fractured the skull of Lieutenant Selfridge, who was acting as Orville's passenger. Selfridge died the following day, and Orville spent several days in the hospital with a broken left thigh and cracked ribs. During another trial, the *Flyer*'s engine failed to reach maximum speed on takeoff and the biplane nose-dived off the end of its launch rail.

The [fifty-nine] seconds during which it [*Kitty Hawk*] had remained in the air were long enough to shrivel the globe and present a future still uncertain for mankind.
*Emile Gauvreau,* The Wild Blue Yonder.

ABOVE: Glenn Curtiss entered aircraft competition on July 4, 1908, with the epochal June Bug during trials over Hammondsport, New York. Curtiss won the coveted Scientific American trophy by designing the first airplane to fly a kilometer before judges.

ABOVE: A photographer captures the scene immediately after the crash of a Wright Type A during air trials on September 17, 1908, at Fort Myer, Virginia. The accident killed Lieutenant Thomas E. Selfridge and seriously injured Orville Wright.

The Wrights deservedly had the advantage of being in the aircraft business first. During the first endurance test of the Type A *Flyer* on July 27, 1909, Orville flew the plane with Lieutenant Lahm as passenger. The plane stayed aloft for more than seventy-two minutes and established a new endurance record for airplanes. Three days later Lieutenant Foulois acted as passenger when Orville flew a measured course between Fort Myer and Alexandria, Virginia, at an average speed of 42 mph. Orville preferred flying with Foulois, who weighed less than other pilots. On returning to Fort Myer, Orville climbed to 410 ft, tipped over gently, and spiraled down in view of an enthusiastic crowd that included President William Howard Taft.

One problem with the *Flyer* involved steerage, which the Wrights accomplished by using pulleys and cable to warp the wings. Once again, the Wrights missed the opportunity to partner with Curtiss, who later eliminated wing-warping by developing ailerons (wing flaps).

Nevertheless, on August 2, 1909, the war department accepted the Wright *Flyer* as Aeroplane No. 1 of the Heavier-than-air Division, United States Aerial Fleet.

By 1910, the Wrights and Curtiss shared a common vision: they believed in the future of the airplane as a war machine. While Orville and Wilbur advocated the deployment of aircraft for observation, Curtiss dropped bombs from one of his biplanes on a dummy battleship outlined on the surface of Lake Keuka, New York. Lieutenant Jacob Earl Fickel jumped into a passenger seat of a Curtiss machine and when airborne fired his rifle at ground targets. In 1911, the army began dropping live bombs from a Wright Model B, and in 1912 used the same biplane to test fire a machine gun. Dropping bombs from aircraft was not new. In October 1911 Italian flyer Giulio Gavotti became the first to perform an act of war by flying a Blériot monoplane over Turkish positions in North Africa and dropping hand-held bombs.

first to perform an act of war by flying a Blériot monoplane over Turkish positions in North Africa and dropping hand-held bombs.

## Organizing the Air Arm

On August 2, 1909, the army officially had an aerial fleet of one Wright Type A *Flyer* but no officially commissioned pilots. In October, Wilbur Wright trained Lieutenants Frederic E. Humphreys and Frank Lahm. After soloing for three hours at College Park, Maryland, Humphreys and Lahm became military aviators numbers one and two, respectively. Lieutenant Foulois returned from France to be trained by Wright and Humphreys, but on November 5 Aeroplane No. 1 crashed, and the army lost its total air strength. Because planes were made of wood and cloth and held together by wire, they were readily repaired, but during the interval the army sent Lahm back to the cavalry and Humphreys back to the engineers, from which they

had been previously detached on temporary duty to become flyers. This left Foulois, who had not yet soloed. He obtained the balance of his flight instruction from the Wrights by mail after the Signal Corps moved him with flight operations to Fort Sam Houston, Texas. As military aviator number three, Foulois became the first correspondence-school pilot in history, and he remained the only pilot until 1911 because the Signal Corps had only one plane. By then, Aeroplane No. 1 could no longer be repaired. One might wonder what would have become of military air if publisher Robert F. Collier had not purchased a Wright Type B Flyer in early 1911 and donated it to the war department.

Until 1911, Congress had not appropriated a single dollar for aviation. Foulois paid some of the expenses for gasoline and repairs out of his salary. Although the Signal Corps had been requesting $200,000 a year for aviation since 1908, senior army officers remained

*ABOVE: Purchased by the army in 1914, the Curtiss R-3 tractor plane, with the engine mounted in front of the aircraft, became the first of its kind produced in the United States and soon eclipsed the capabilities of Wright Flyers.*

ABOVE: The Wrights designed the Type B specifically as a two-seater for training pilots, and the army provided a field for that purpose at College Park, Maryland. The Signal Corps also opened the flying program to enlisted men, and Corporal Vernon L. Burge, seated in the aircraft, volunteered for flight training.

RIGHT: Orville Wright and Lieutenant Lahm of the Signal Corps established a world record flight at Fort Myer on July 27, 1910. The Wright Type A flew a distance of fifty miles at a speed of about 40 mph. At the time, the Wright biplane was still more advanced than most aircraft built in Europe.

indifferent about aeronautics and ignored the request. In March, Chief Signal Officer James Allen finally obtained an appropriation of $125,000 and used it to order five new planes—four Wright Type Bs and a Curtiss pusher.

Much to the annoyance of the Wrights, Glenn Curtiss had been aggressively developing planes and improving technology. Much of his work had been done for the navy in single-seat machines, some of which were fitted with both landing gear and pontoons. In 1910–11 he moved his operation to San Diego, California, to capitalize on more favorable flying conditions. To promote flying, Curtiss invited the army and navy to send candidates for free instruction. Thirty officers applied, but the army sent only Lieutenants Paul W. Beck, G.E.M. Kelly, and

John C. Walker for flight instruction. They learned to fly in a single-seater, their first solo being a ten-foot hop off the ground. After training, they joined Foulois in Texas and began training on Wright Type Bs. Kelly crashed and lost his life. The base commander at Fort Sam Houston promptly suspended flying, and the Signal Corps moved men and planes back to College Park to continue training.

### The New Flying Schools
In June 1911, after resuming his position as chief of the army's Aeronautical Division, Captain Charles Chandler, acting as commandant, began expanding operations at College Park. During the summer, Lieutenants Henry H. "Hap" Arnold, Thomas D. Milling, and Roy C. Kirtland, all of whom had been trained at the Wright School, arrived after completing their instruction at Dayton. Chandler had no guidance from the army for qualifying pilots and adopted the French regulations used by the Aero Flying Club. In 1912, pilots were awarded a badge with two bars that said "Military Aviator" above an eagle with outstretched wings. A year later Congress authorized thirty-five percent extra pay for a maximum of thirty officers assigned to flying duty. Chandler used the bonus to attract volunteers.

With a flying school to develop air tactics, good things began to happen. Arnold made record-breaking altitude flights to 4,167 ft. Flyers performed aerial photography experiments. Pilots tested a bombsight invented by former army officer Riley E. Scott, although the army refused to purchase it. Scott took his invention to Europe and collected a $5,000 prize.

During 1912, more than a dozen officers entered the flying school and some learned to fly at night as well as during daytime. Chandler took aviation to the next step and in June began the experimental firing of a low-recoil machine gun mounted in a plane flown by Lieutenant Milling. The army balked because retired army Colonel

LEFT: *Rockwell Field Air Service Flying School, San Diego, California, became one of twenty-seven flying fields used for training U.S. pilots during World War I. Most of the fields were built in southern states, where better year-round flying conditions occurred.*

aerial reconnaissance maneuvers with the army. The weather turned bad and pilots lost sight of ground movements. When Foulois, acting for the Red team, landed to send a telegram warning of an imminent attack, the Blue team captured him.

By the end of 1912 College Park had grown to fourteen flying officers, thirty-nine enlisted men, and nine airplanes. The Burgess Company provided the first hydroplane with a tractor power train, so-called because the propeller spun from the front of the aircraft and pulled it through the air instead of pushing it from the rear. Because of operational advantages of having the propeller in front of the plane, Curtiss promptly changed his designs and produced the JN-1, the first in a series of two-seater training planes that evolved into aircraft affectionately known by student pilots as the "Jenny."

When winter weather shut down operations at College Park, Wright planes and pilots moved to Augusta, Georgia, and Curtiss planes and pilots went back to San Diego. The JN-1, coupled with Glenn L. Martin's dual-controlled sports planes from Los Angeles, ended the use of pusher-type aircraft. San Diego eventually grew into the army's first permanent aviation school.

Although the army had transferred Lahm (now a captain) back to the cavalry and shipped him off to Fort William McKinley in the Philippines, he did not stop flying. He opened his own school under the auspices of the army and offered flying lessons to enlisted personnel. Corporal Vernon L. Burge volunteered for pilot's training and became the army's first noncommissioned pilot.

## The Awakening of Congress

By 1911, eight years after the Wrights proved that machines could fly, the United States had lost its leadership in aviation to Europe. Of twenty-six pilots in the United States, only eight flew for the army, contrasted with 353 certified pilots in France. During 1914, the U.S. Army had no more than twenty serviceable aircraft at any time while the British Royal Flying Corps operated more than a hundred. European

| International Expenditures for Aviation, 1908–1913 | |
|---|---:|
| Germany | $22,000,000 |
| France | $22,000,000 |
| Great Britain | $14,000,000 |
| Russia | $12,000,000 |
| Belgium | $2,000,000 |
| United States | $430,000 |

ABOVE: *During the 1916 punitive expedition into Mexico, pilots from the 1st Aero Squadron took Curtiss JN-2s and JN-3s, better known as "Jennies," into a campaign mode for the first time, but the aircraft soon proved too under-powered and flimsy for observation assignments and spent most of the time delivering mail and messages.*

of numerous fatalities that had occurred. The Aviation Section's charter included the use and development of balloons, aeroplanes, signaling apparatus, and other related appliances. Congress also established aeronautical ratings of "Military Aviator" and "Junior Military Aviator," and increased flying pay. American aviation was finally off and running, but not very fast.

### The 1st Aero Squadron

In September 1914, the Signal Corps reorganized the 1st Aero Squadron, which had existed since 1913 in one form or another, and based it in San Diego. By then, pusher-type airplanes had been condemned, and the only aircraft that could meet the corps' specifications were Curtiss Jennies. With a new congressional appropriation in his pocket, Brigadier General George P. Scriven, Chief Signal Officer, asked the army for four squadrons of eight planes each, another sixteen planes in reserve, and twenty officers and ninety enlisted men for each squadron. Scriven soon realized that his request for forty-eight planes fell far short of Europe's air arsenal and in 1915 he raised the ante to eighteen squadrons of twelve planes each. The request, though clearly necessary, exceeded the war department's most liberal expectations, so little happened until 1917.

Meanwhile, Foulois went to San Diego and concentrated on preparing sixteen officers, seventy-seven enlisted men, and eight airplanes of the 1st Aero Squadron for possible combat duty. The problem with American aircraft became manifest in 1914 and 1915 when Foulois sent a plane piloted by Lieutenants Milling and Byron Q. Jones to Brownsville, Texas, to assist the army in suppressing Pancho Villa's raids along the Mexican border. Milling and Jones flew a number of reconnaissance missions and reported that they were unable to work effectively with artillery. Difficulties with the Jennies, compounded by pilots having to depend on watches, compasses, and aneroid barometers for navigation, limited

planes were not only more numerous, they were technically superior. Because an ocean separated the United States from Europe's frequent disruptions, Congress adopted a policy of not preparing for war until after it began.

On July 18, 1914, ten days before the outbreak of war in Europe, Congress passed legislation giving statutory recognition to army aviation. The bill had been under discussion since 1913. Some proponents, including Lieutenant Beck, wanted aviation removed from the Signal Corps, but flyers like Lieutenants William "Billy" Mitchell and Benjamin Foulois argued that the time for change would come later because aviation in America was still in its infancy. During World War I, the opinions of Mitchell and Foulois radically changed.

The new legislation officially created the Signal Corps' Aviation Section, with an authorized strength of 60 officers and 260 enlisted men. Pilots' commissions, however, were restricted to unmarried lieutenants because

the effectiveness of the effort. Late in 1915 the entire squadron, including Milling and Jones, flew to Fort Sam Houston to winter at San Antonio, Texas.

**Jennies in Action**

On March 9, 1916, Villa's revolutionaries crossed the border and raided Columbus, New Mexico, killing seventeen Americans. Brigadier General John J. Pershing organized a force of 15,000 men to pursue the guerrillas into Mexico and take Villa, dead or alive. Ordered to Columbus, Foulois arrived with ten pilots, eighty-four enlisted men, and eight Curtiss JN-3 Jennies in the first real test of American aircraft collaborating with the army in combat. When Pershing ordered the planes to Casas Grandes, Mexico, one turned back with mechanical trouble, one crashed at night, and only four of the remaining six stayed together until forced down by darkness. The squadron's planes never had a chance. The flimsy aircraft could not ascend the area's 12,000-foot mountain ranges during reconnaissance missions.

Nor could they battle the fierce air currents, whirlwinds, dust storms, and snow blizzards that buffeted the area. Pilots could make short reconnaissance flights in good weather but spent most of their time transporting the mail. If a plane landed near a Mexican town, the inhabitants would burn holes in the fuselage with cigars, or slash the fabric with knives. By April 1916, only two planes remained operational. Foulois ordered them back to Columbus, where they were condemned and destroyed as unserviceable.

Although the 1st Aero Squadron began receiving new and better aircraft, the failure of operations in Mexico testified to the shortcomings of army aviation when compared with the military aircraft of Europe. By then, it became a question of how much longer the United States could avoid joining in the war. In August 1916, Congress stunned the Signal Corps by appropriating $13,282,000 for aeronautical development. How to spend the money became a staggering issue for the Aviation Section, and one without a simple solution.

*ABOVE: Lieutenant George Boyle gets ready to fly a modified Curtiss JN4-H Jenny during the inauguration of U.S. airmail service in Washington, D.C. on May 15, 1918. Unfortunately, Lieutenant Boyle got lost and never reached his intended destination.*

# THE FIRST AIR WAR 1916–1920

> Whoever will be master of the sky will be master of the world.
> *Clement Ader, French aviation pioneer, 1909.*

*RIGHT: On April 27, 1916, a Curtiss Jenny conked out over Mexico while searching for Pancho Villa's insurgents, and pilots Captain Benjamin D. Foulois and Lieutenant J. E. Carberry somewhat sheepishly secured transportation back to the airfield by hiring a ranchero with a wagon. This incident during the Mexican revolution served as a demonstration, among others, of the inability of American aircraft to perform to the standards of European aircraft.*

The 1st Aero Squadron's shoddy performance in Mexico, coupled with the tremendous war-induced advancements in European aviation, finally brought home to Congress what warnings from the chief signal officer and other army officers had failed to do. In addition to the $13.3 million appropriation for more pilots and better planes, the National Defense Act of 1916 also established a reserve corps of officers and enlisted men. The legislation poured money into the National Advisory Committee for Aeronautics (NACA), established in March 1915 for the promotion of "scientific study of the problems of flight" with the objective of finding solutions through "research and experiment in aeronautics." Congress simply acted too late. Neither the NACA nor the National Defense Act came in time to create American combat aircraft capable of competing with European planes. The NACA remained handicapped by the lack of a research facility until after the war, when the unit moved into Langley Memorial Aeronautical Laboratory at Langley Field, Virginia. The organization eventually evolved to become the National Aeronautic and Space Administration (NASA), America's greatest incubator for aeronautical research and development.

## The Aviation Section

The $13.3 million appropriated by Congress in August

ABOVE: Balloons played an important, but unspectacular, role in World War I by flying over territory near the front lines. Balloonist training remained separate from the basic Air Service program. Those who first went aloft to perform observation did so without parachutes, a practice later changed.

Fokkers, Rumplers, and Albatrosses; France also flew sixteen models, including SPADs, Nieuports, and Bréguets; and Great Britain produced thirty-four models, including Sopwiths, Bristols, and de Havillands.

ABOVE: The only American-built combat plane to see service at the front was the British-designed de Havilland DH.4, powered by a 400-horsepower Liberty engine. Over time, more than 4,000 DH.4 "Liberties" were built.

## Pre-World War I Preparedness

In 1916, America's aerial arm consisted of 125 communication, reconnaissance, and training planes comprised of Curtiss JN-4s and JN-4Bs, a few R-2s and R-4s (larger and more powerful Jennies), and five experimental trainers built by five different companies. None of the aircraft prepared flyers for combat. Conspicuously absent were Wright planes.

The Aviation Section did expand flight schools, beginning with San Diego, where in late 1916 about forty-five officers a month received flight training. In 1916 Major "Billy" Mitchell, who learned to fly at his own expense at a Curtiss school, became assistant chief of the Aviation Section and things started to happen. Civilian schools began assisting the army, and a new flight school to train reservists and National Guard volunteers opened at Mineola, New York. In anticipation of more planes and instructors, the Aviation Section opened another flight school at Essington, Pennsylvania.

1916 landed squarely on the Aviation Section of the Signal Corps, which had neither the staff nor the ability to cope with it. Had civilian air units not been organized by flying enthusiasts associated with the Aero Club of America, there would not have been pilots or planes available for training recruits. During 1917 these voluntary air units, some of which became affiliated with the Reserve Corps and others with the newly formed National Guard, eventually formed most of the Aviation Section's manpower.

By the end of 1916, German Zeppelins had bombed London, European pursuit planes had become active in combat, synchronized machine guns were firing through propellers, and large German Gotha bombers were already in production for operations in 1917. Germany operated an air fleet of sixteen models, including

ABOVE: Following the early air battles over France, the Air Service quickly discovered the importance of advertising and began producing thousands of posters to attract recruits.

ABOVE: Posters were not issued just for recruitment. Some, like this one issued in 1916/1917, urged workers in manufacturing industries to consider the effects on the boys at the front of carelessness in the factories at home.

With authorization from the war department, the Aviation Section formed seven twelve-plane aero squadrons—three for overseas duty and four for domestic service. The 2nd Aero Squadron went to the Philippines; the 6th to Hawaii; the 7th to Panama; and the 1st, 3rd, 4th, and 5th remained in the United States. Only the 1st Aero Squadron had been fully organized and equipped—though inadequately—and plans to increase the air service to twenty squadrons were still a matter of paperwork when on April 6, 1917, Congress declared war on Germany. At the time, the Aviation Section had 131 officers (most of them pilots), 1,087 enlisted men, and about 250 training aircraft.

Until 1917 the American aircraft industry, which consisted of nine small factories, had no reason to mobilize. When in 1916 the Aviation Section suddenly ordered 366 planes, the entire aircraft industry could deliver only sixty-four. Because the war department had never sent trained observers abroad to study European aircraft development, American military aviation suffered technically and operationally. Because the war department was concerned only with the mobilization of ground forces, the Aviation Section had no insight into what planes to build to fight a modern war. Blame fell on Congress, which had now thrown money at the problem, for allowing the United States to rank fourteenth among the air powers of the world, but blame must also be shared by the army because the general staff never considered aviation important. The same problem would fester for another twenty years.

## Requests from Abroad

Once Congress declared war on Germany, Great Britain and France sent delegations to Washington to appeal for troops and offer technical assistance for building aircraft. In May 1917, Premier Alexandre Ribot of France asked the United States for 4,500 planes, 5,000 pilots, and 50,000 mechanics for operations in 1918, and another 12,000 planes and 24,000 engines during the first six months of

ABOVE: An observer in the rear cockpit of a DH.4 uses the aircraft's rudimentary Wimperis bombsight to locate worthwhile targets on the ground. The army copied the Wimperis and developed the Mark I. The accuracy of both bombsights suffered from erratic movements of the aircraft.

1919. At the time, France had no more than 1,700 planes at the front and 3,000 trainers in the rear. The request stunned the Signal Corps' small Aviation Section. Congress responded with an appropriation of $10.8 million in May and another $43.4 million in June, far too little to satisfy Ribot's request but reflective of the war department's disinterest in aviation. Congress upped the ante and in July rushed through an appropriation of $640 million, which was supposedly the first installment for an air force consisting of 22,625 planes, 44,000 engines, and enough spare parts to build another 17,600 planes. Twelve thousand of the aircraft were to be used in France, but which models to build remained a mystery. Nor had any consideration been given to American industrial capacity.

Only Germany, France, Great Britain, and Italy were building state-of-the-art aircraft. When European Allies offered to share their designs, fifty different models clouded the choices. Nobody had the answers.

**ABOVE: At the Dayton-Wright aircraft plant at Dayton, Ohio, assemblers celebrated on July 25, 1918, by applying a special paint job to a particular DH.4's fuselage, which read: "I am ship No. 1000. Will leave for France July 31st – 4.30 P.M."**

## A Choice of Designs

In June 1917, Brigadier General George O. Squier, Chief Signal Officer, sent Major Raynal C. Bolling and a group of aviation officers to Europe to negotiate with the British, French, and Italians and recommend what aircraft to build in America. The trip might have been more useful had it included aircraft manufacturers. Bolling's August 17, 1917, report recommended Bristol scouts for advanced training; Bristol F.2B fighters for combat; de Havilland DH.4s for long-range reconnaissance and bombing; two SPAD designs as fighters; and the Caproni triplane for night bombing.

Meanwhile, aircraft design improved another notch and the DH.9 replaced the DH.4; a new, smaller biplane design replaced the Caproni; the British Handley Page 0/400 became the night bomber; and the latest SPAD design failed in service in France. By then, the Curtiss Aeroplane Company had already started

**LEFT: Major Henry H. "Hap" Arnold stands beside a 12-cylinder Liberty engine produced in 1917. The engine, designed in six days and developed for the interchangeability of parts and ease of production, was America's greatest industrial contribution to the Allied effort in World War I.**

## The Liberty Engine and the Liberty DH.4

In the field of aeronautical development during World War I, the Liberty engine probably represented America's greatest contribution to flying. The engine was denigrated by detractors as being too heavy, too unreliable, and too costly to operate, but most of the complaints were disingenuous. On May 29, 1917, Colonel Edwin Deeds took Jesse G. Vincent and Elbert J. Hall, two engineers in the business, and their designers to the Willard Hotel, Washington, D.C., and in two days created the Liberty engine.

They produced design concepts for four standard "Liberty engines" ranging from 100 to 400 horsepower with 4, 6- 8, and 12 cylinders. Many of the ideas going into the finished product came from Mercedes engines used by the Germans.

Congress appropriated $640 million to produce the engine, and on August 29, 1917, three months after the design conference, Packard made the first flight test of a 12-cylinder Liberty engine. Manufactured with either eight or twelve cylinders, the Liberty became the American engine of the Air Service and remained in use through the early 1930s. By October 1918, some 46,000 engines were being produced annually for aircraft. In 1918, a pair of 410-horsepower Liberty engines powered America's first twin-engined bomber, the Martin MB-1. The same engine was eventually adapted for powerboats and wind machines. During World War II, 6,500 Liberties went into British tanks.

Not all aircraft were built with Liberties. Curtiss produced OX-5 engines for trainers; Hall-Scott continued to produce engines of greater horsepower; and a few Spanish and French engines made inroads into the American aviation market.

Flyers gave the two-seat DH.4 high marks for observation, but day bombing pilots hated the aircraft. Loaded with 500 pounds of bombs, it took the plane an hour to climb to 10,000 ft. With a top speed under 100 mph, the DH.4 became a sitting duck for German fighters. The 2nd Day Bombardment Group complained, "For a bombing plane, it carries to any altitude an inferior quality of bombs. The fuel tank between the pilot and observer is the target of every pursuit plane that attacks it. The fuel tank is unsupported, works by pressure, and explodes when shot-up. When the plane crashes, the tank leaves its bedding, having nothing to keep it there, and crushes the pilot against the motor."

The "Liberty De Havilland" produced in the United States, however, became a hit with pilots, although the first American-made model did not arrive in France until May 17, 1918. Powered by an American 410-horsepower "Liberty" engine, the aircraft had a service ceiling of 16,000 ft, but flyers sitting in the open cockpits had neither oxygen nor heat. They did wear seat belts, which consisted of a canvas and leather harness. Liberty DH.4s came with a top rated air speed of 124 mph, which was probably exaggerated. The DH.4's 42 ft 5 in wingspan and empty weight of 2,732 pounds made it one of the largest aircraft that operated in World War I.

| Annual Aircraft Production Rates (1918) | |
|---|---|
| Great Britain | 41,000 |
| France | 31,000 |
| United States | 23,000 |

*RIGHT: The 1st Pursuit Group flew a variety of French planes, including this grotesquely decorated Nieuport 17. In addition to the flying-fish paint job, the top of the upper wing and the underside of the lower wing also carried a star, which became the emblem for American flyers in France.*

gearing up to build 3,000 SPAD fighters, 500 Caproni bombers, and 1,000 Bristol F.2Bs. The Dayton-Wright Airplane Company also contracted to produce 2,000 DH.4 day bombers, and the Fisher Body Company agreed to build 3,000 more. Trouble followed when the Italians began redesigning the Caproni at the Curtiss company; the British refused to send a sample of the Handley Page; and the French decided to build all SPADs themselves, thus interrupting Curtiss's efforts to understand new technologies related to fighters.

The confusion resulted in only one European plane being built in America, the de Havilland DH.4, which was becoming obsolete and known by its pilots as the "Flaming Coffin" because of exposed and unshielded fuel tanks. Although production was stepped up from fifteen in April 1918 to 1,100 a month by October, only 1,213 DH.4s reached France, and only 417 ever participated in combat operations.

During the entire war, not one American-designed aircraft logged a single hour over the front lines. The United States did produce about a thousand balloons, some 650 of which served in observation.

### Cost of Aircraft, 1918

| Plane | Cost ($) |
|---|---|
| Curtiss JN-4A | 5,550 |
| Curtiss JN-4H | 8,043 |
| Dayton-Wright DH.4 | 10,350 |
| Curtiss S.E. 5 | 7,443 |
| Handley Page | 51,600 |
| Martin Bomber MB-1 | 50,600 |
| Caproni | 30,900 |
| Curtiss R-4 | 19,149 |
| SPAD | 10,243 |

Source: Alfred Goldberg, *History of the United States Air Force*

*LEFT: On the 148th Aero Squadron's airfield at Petite Sythe, France, pilots and mechanics test their planes as preparations begin for an August 6, 1918, daylight raid on German trenches and cities.*

*LEFT: On the French airfield at Issoudon, twenty-six American-piloted pursuit and observation planes line up for a routine mechanical and equipment inspection during operations in April 1918.*

### Emergence of the Air Service

Problems of getting aviation on a war footing became manifest the day Congress declared war on Germany. Neither the war department nor the general staff understood airpower, nor did the miniscule Aviation Section of the Signal Corps when it was established on July 18, 1914. Chief Signal Officer Squier found himself in charge of several new divisions he knew nothing about. Aircraft production remained unsynchronized for months. By January 1918 a monthly rate of 800 planes, mostly trainers, were being manufactured as opposed to 700 engines. Not one combat plane had been produced and shipped to France. Disturbed by poor progress, President Wilson transferred aviation from the Signal Corps to two agencies under the secretary of war: the Bureau of Aircraft Production, which was not meeting its targets, and the Division of Military Aeronautics, commanded by Major General William L. Kenly. Separating two divisions that should have been working together merely led to more problems, so on May 24, 1918, both units became part of the Air Service.

## The AEF Air Service—France

In March 1917 the Aviation Section of the Signal Corps sent five officers to Europe: three to attend French flying school, one as assistant military attaché in London, and one as an air observer in, of all places, Spain. The latter, Major Billy Mitchell, said he was wasting time in Spain and obtained permission to visit the front in northern Europe. For ten days he prowled French airfields and flew observation planes over the battlefield to study German dispositions. On his own initiative, and with help from French advisors, he drew up a plan for the organization of an American air force in France and sent it to the war department. Having put the process in motion, he continued to send reports to Washington on every aspect of the air war.

After General Pershing arrived in France to head the AEF, Mitchell presented a two-pronged plan for air operations in France. The first force consisted of air squadrons attached to infantry units and under the direct control of ground commanders. The second force consisted of strategic operations against enemy lines and sources of supply, which involved "independent" bombing missions against German factories and resources deep beyond the battlefield. Mitchell's second proposal reflected many of the controversial opinions of Major General Hugh M. "Boom" Trenchard, commander of the British Royal Flying Corps, who advocated strategic bombardment and unified air command.

Pershing formed a board of officers to recommend the structure of the AEF's Air Service. Because Mitchell was the only officer on the board who had witnessed and studied aerial tactics in France, he convinced the others that the Air Service should consist of a strategic force of thirty bombing and thirty fighter groups, plus a second air division geared to the size of the AEF's anticipated ground force. Pershing rejected the board's recommendations, perhaps doubting the availability of planes and pilots. He also disagreed with the formation

*ABOVE: In an effort to accelerate mobilization for the Air Service, on August 27, 1918, President Wilson appointed John D. Ryan, former president of the Anaconda Copper Company, as Director of Air Service and Second Assistant Secretary of War.*

The Air Service already existed, having been formed by General Pershing on April 24, 1918, as part of the American Expeditionary Force (AEF). The earliest components consisted of four squadrons from the 1st Pursuit Group, which arrived in France in early 1918 with pilots full of enthusiasm but without planes. They flew flashy French Nieuport 28 biplanes, which looked sleek and clean, but the French had pulled them out of front-line service because the aircraft tended to shed its upper-wing fabric when diving. Loss of control usually killed the pilot.

On August 27, 1918, during the last weeks of the war, President Wilson finally combined all the loose divisions of the Air Service under John D. Ryan and made him director and second assistant secretary of war. During the war, American pilots flew foreign planes with either foreign insignia or no insignia, and it was not until the organization of the Air Service that a star was adopted for American planes. The organization did not officially become the Army Air Service until July 4, 1920.

**FOR ACTION**

**ENLIST IN THE AIR SERVICE**

*ABOVE: Trench warfare in France did not appeal to the average American draftee, and the Air Service drew thousands of volunteers who preferred flying to dying in ditches.*

ABOVE: Some of the men who pioneered flying posed for this photograph in 1911 at College Park, Maryland— (standing, left to right) Capt. Hennessy, Lt. Henry H. Arnold, Lt. Roy C. Kirtland, Capt. Frank N. Kennedy, Lt. McLeary, and Lt. Harold Geiger; (kneeling, left to right) Lt. Louis C. Rockwell and Lt. Thomas D. Milling.

ABOVE: Major Raoul Lufbery, commander of the 94th Aero Squadron, became an ace with the Lafayette Escadrille before joining the Air Service. Lufbery's Hat-in-the-Ring outfit scored the first Air Service victories in France. After notching seventeen victories, he died in combat in May 1918 while flying his Nieuport 28.

of strategic bombing groups and agreed to only four air groups to support ground troops. Mitchell felt frustrated by Pershing's failure to grasp the importance of airpower. Though he accepted the general's decision, he waited until the final battles of the war to prove his point. Thus began a three-decade battle by the advocates of airpower for self-determination and separation from the army.

On April 24, 1918, Pershing terminated the Signal Corps' responsibility for the Aviation Section and created the Army Air Service, AEF.

## The Escadrille Américaine

In April 1916, seven American citizens ignored United States neutrality and founded the *Escadrille Américaine* to fight Germany. Six men were already veterans, having joined the French Foreign Legion in 1914. Many of the volunteers had not learned to fly, but soon did. The membership included Gervais Raoul Lufbery, pioneer flyer William Thaw, daredevil Bert Hall, and a trio of aristocratic young idealists, Victor Chapman and the brothers Paul and Kiffin Rockwell.

On April 18 the French army authorized the unit and sent Captain George Thenault to command the squadron and teach the men how to fly Nieuport 11 fighters. During the outfit's first patrol on May 13, Kiffin Rockwell scored the first victory, shooting down a German observation plane. More Americans wanting to save the world joined the squadron, including barnstormers, exhibitionists, racecar drivers, and a sailor. In September 1916 the unit officially became the Lafayette Escadrille, the most famous American squadron in World War I. When the German ambassador in Washington accused the United States of violating neutrality by sending American flyers to France, the army dodged the complaint because of a potential need for combat pilots in a war against Mexico.

During twenty-two months of combat under the French flag, the prestigious Lafayette Escadrille grew to 209 Americans, of which thirty-eight became pilots. While shooting down fifty-seven enemy planes, they lost nine pilots killed in action. The squadron used an American Indian head painted on the fuselage for an insignia, and owned two lions as mascots, which they named Whiskey and Soda. On December 17, 1917, the Lafayettes discontinued their relationship with France and became the nucleus of the AEF's 103rd Aero Squadron, commanded by Major William Thaw, a war-weary aristocrat who became an ace.

## Sky Kings in the RAF

More American volunteers served in British squadrons and scored more victories with less notoriety than those flying in France. When U.S. recruitment began in 1917, the first air cadets, who eventually grew to 542 men, went to England to be trained and equipped to serve in the Royal Flying Corps, which on April 1, 1918, was incorporated along with the Royal Naval Air Service into the Royal Air Force. About half the pilots later became members of the U.S. 17th or 148th, which were actually RAF squadrons flown entirely by Americans.

Eleven of America's sixteen top aces obtained some or all of their victories flying for the RFC/RAF. The training was superior, and so were British Sopwith Camels. After U.S. aero squadrons began forming in France, a number of British-trained American pilots transferred to the AEF Air Service. Many of the pilots, some of them already aces, promptly returned to England and rejoined the RFC/RAF because the Air Service bureaucracy insisted they go to flight school and learn from some lieutenant how to fly.

LEFT: Although not a pilot, Major General Mason M. Patrick became chief of the Air Service in May 1918, reorganized the unit as part of the American Expeditionary Force (AEF), and promoted the addition of night bombing in conjunction with Great Britain.

## Major General Mason M. Patrick (1863–1942)

In 1886, Mason Patrick graduated from West Point with John "Black Jack" Pershing. Patrick chose the engineers: Pershing chose the cavalry. After Pershing arrived in France and established the Air Service, he observed there were "a lot of good men running around in circles" and transferred Brigadier General Patrick out of the engineers to organize the unit. Although Patrick had never become a pilot, Pershing believed a good, well-structured engineer could get the best out of ambitious young air officers like Foulois, Lahm, and Mitchell, who had their own ideas about air operations.

Fifty-five-year-old Patrick took control of the Air Service, adopted some of the ideas of Foulois and Mitchell, rejected others, and eventually agreed to participate in the night-bombing program initiated by the RAF. Patrick replaced General Kenly, a former artillery officer who in 1917 had become the AEF's air officer, with Foulois as Chief of Air Service, First Army, and Lahm, Chief of Air Service, Second Army. Annoyed by being overlooked and upset by having to report to Foulois, with whom he habitually disagreed, Mitchell continued to work around the system in an effort to expand combat operations. Foulois became frustrated and asked Patrick to name him Assistant Chief of Air Service and replace him with Mitchell. After making the change, Pershing promoted Mitchell to brigadier general and put him in charge of all combat operations at the front, where he became the outstanding American air commander of the war. Patrick then promoted another pioneer flyer, Colonel Thomas D. Milling, to fill Mitchell's vacancy at the Air Service, First Army.

By August 1918, Patrick had twenty-four American squadrons in Europe. For every plane, he needed from thirty-five to forty men on the ground. He believed the war would continue for at least another year and asked for 202 American squadrons by June 1919. Building another 178 squadrons in ten months would have been an impossible strain on American industry, which had not produced its first combat pursuit plane. However, by November 11, 1918, Patrick had 58,000 officers and men in the Air Service in France, and another 20,000 training or operating in Great Britain and Italy, while simultaneously building another wing for the Third Army.

Patrick remained in the Air Service after the war, and in 1923, at the age of sixty, he finally learned to fly. By then he agreed with Mitchell on the future of airpower, and said, "The next war will be decided in the air." Patrick remained in office to nurture and build the Air Service, which on July 2, 1926, become the Army Air Corps. Though he retired in 1927, Patrick continued to promote the cause of air superiority. He died in 1942, confident that men like Henry "Hap" Arnold would finish the work that he and men like Billy Mitchell and Ben Foulois had started.

**RIGHT: Attraction to flying continued to grow throughout the war. By 1918, with new aviation schools established throughout the country and with the development of better aircraft, Air Service posters began emphasizing the Learn-and-Earn aspects of enlisting.**

**FAR RIGHT: The star with the bulls-eye in the center became the new insignia for the Air Service. It was not unusual in France to find Nieuports and SPADs with French colors on the tail, American stars on the wings, and an eagle or hat on the fuselage.**

Like the acrobatic and madcap "Sky Kings" of Europe, American aces such as Captains Warren Gillette and John W. Malone each registered twenty victories flying for the British, and Captain Alan Wilkenson added nineteen more. In all, eighteen American aces served with the RFC/RAF and refused to transfer to the U.S. Air Service.

### The 1st Pursuit Group

On September 3, 1917, Major Ralph Royce brought the 1st Aero Squadron (recently on the Mexican border) to France. Although the unit could claim to be the first U.S. squadron in Europe, it spent the next several months learning to fly French planes. After training as an observation squadron, the unit moved in March 1918 to the Toul area, a relatively quiet sector on the Eastern Front

where in February and March the American build-up of the 94th and 95th Aero Squadrons had commenced. Pilots flew fast and maneuverable Nieuport N28C-1s, which had dangerous design problems. The vibration of the Gnome rotary engines had a tendency to crack the copper fuel lines and set the plane on fire. A further problem occurred when fabric peeled off the upper wing during a steep dive and sent the plane crashing to the ground. The French would not use the plane but had no compunctions about loaning them to American pilots until SPADs became available. Nevertheless, on March 15 the 94th and 95th began flying missions over enemy lines, although machine guns had not arrived. After the guns came, the 94th and 95th were still restrained from going into combat because pilots had to attend a French gunnery school before using the weapons.

Military Aviation is apparently the most dangerous sport man has discovered since the contests of the Gladiators.

*Quoted in General James P. McCarthy, ed.,* The Air Force.

The 94th and 95th became the two leading squadrons in the formation of the 1st Pursuit Group, which soon included the 27th and 147th Aero Squadrons. Two new units also joined 1st Aero Squadron to become the I Corps Observation Group, which flew two-seater SPADs and remained under French tactical control. Several American pilots in the 1st Pursuit Group came from French squadrons, and though seasoned flyers, few had any leadership training. The exception was the 94th Aero Squadron's commander Major Raoul Lufbery, who had become the first American ace while flying with the Lafayette Escadrille.

On April 3, after the 94th completed gunnery school, Lufbery unleashed his soon-to-be-vaunted "Hat-in-the-Ring" squadron for combat operations. Eleven days later, Lieutenants Alan F. Winslow and Douglas Campbell were on duty when German aircraft approached the field. Winslow shot down a German Albatross crossing one end of the field, and Campbell downed a Pfalz D-III, even though the Nieuports had been fitted with only one gun instead of two. Lufbery scored seventeen victories before being shot down and killed on May 17, 1918, by the rear cockpit gunner in a German Rumpler. Men who flew with Lufbery claimed that he never kept score and may well have shot down as many as seventy enemy planes. Captain Edward V. Rickenbacker assumed command of the "Hat-in-the-Ring" squadron and made it famous.

Every pilot in the Toul sector chafed to go into action against the enemy, but the quiet area offered few opportunities until April, after Germany launched its spring campaign. In July, First Air Brigade commander Billy Mitchell moved the 1st Pursuit Group and the 1st Observation Group to the Marne sector, where the Germans had their best pilots and fighters (Fokker D.VIIs), and 4:1 air supremacy.

During the next several months, no air group would account for destroying more German aircraft or creating more American aces than the 1st Pursuit Group.

### Captain Edward Vernon Rickenbacker (1890–1973)

Born October 8, 1890, at Columbus, Ohio, Eddie Rickenbacker became one of America's top racecar drivers. In 1917 he established a world speed record of 134 mph, after which he enlisted as a sergeant and became one of General Pershing's drivers. Bored by the routine, he transferred to the AEF Air Service at Tours, France, and on March 4, 1918, joined the 94th (Hat-in-the-Ring) Squadron.

On April 29, at the age of thirty-seven, Rickenbacker shot down his first enemy plane and within two weeks became an ace. He also survived a close brush with death. Though separated from his wingman, Rickenbacker attacked three German planes and shot one down. As he dived at high speed to escape the others, the fabric on the top right wing of his Nieuport 28 tore off in the slipstream. With the plane in a spin over German lines, he idled the engine, brought the nose up, leveled into a glide, conned the plane toward French lines, survived a spatter of antiaircraft fire, opened the throttle, and landed safely in friendly territory. He claimed that everything he knew about flying he learned from Raoul Lufbery.

Promoted to command the 94th in June, Rickenbacker switched to a SPAD XIII. Using his knowledge of mechanics, he kept the plane in top condition and the twin machine guns clean and in perfect working order. Despite being sidelined for several weeks by a severe mastoid operation, Rickenbacker returned to the air and became America's leading ace, scoring twenty-six victories and earning the Medal of Honor.

After the war, Rickenbacker operated his own automobile company, but his national reputation as a flyer brought him to Eastern Air Lines as general manager. A year later, Eastern named him chairman of the board. From 1939 to 1945, Rickenbacker served in World War II as a representative of the secretary of war, but in 1946 he returned to Eastern Air Lines to build the company into one of the largest commercial airlines in the world.

***ABOVE LEFT: First Lieutenant Eddie Rickenbacker in the cockpit of his French-built SPAD XIII, one of the war's most formidable pursuit planes. Rickenbacker, a trained mechanic, took exceptional care of his SPAD. Unlike Nieuports flown by some pilots, the SPAD never failed Rickenbacker.***

***ABOVE RIGHT: Medal of Honor recipient Eddie Rickenbacker came out of World War I as America's top ace, having scored twenty-six victories. His closest competitor, Lieutenant Frank Luke, was killed in September 1918 after scoring eighteen victories.***

ABOVE: The Curtiss SE-5 pursuit plane did not come off production lines in time to fight in Europe. By 1921 the SE-5 became obsolete, but the Air Service continued to use the aircraft despite its poor serviceability.

Newspaper clippings from home proclaim thousands of American planes in France…. There is not a single plane of American make on the Western Front.
*John Pershing* Diary, *April 1917.*

## Château-Thierry

On June 28, 1918, the four squadrons of the 1st Pursuit Group and the three squadrons of the I Corps Observation Group moved north to Touquin with the 1st and 2nd Balloon Companies to help gain air superiority in the vicinity of Château-Thierry, where Germans had collapsed Allied lines and established a huge bulge. Amalgamation of the air groups, together with several French squadrons, formed Colonel Billy Mitchell's First Air Brigade.

During March, the German army had commenced its spring campaign. After being temporarily stopped at the Marne River, the kaiser's generals began massing troops for a breakthrough at Château-Thierry, some fifty miles from Paris. Château-Thierry would become the first of three major battles in which American flyers would play an increasingly important role in gaining air control.

Opposing the Allied air groups were forty-six German fighter squadrons, including three crack units from the "Flying Circuses," so-called because of their brightly colored aircraft. During the June offensive, the Germans used massed airpower for the first time—300 planes to seize control of the air and disrupt Allied troop movements. Against such tactics, the Allies required vastly more planes. The ensuing air battles provided generals on both sides lessons on the growing importance of airpower.

Billy Mitchell still had much to learn himself. While flying reconnaissance on the morning of July 15, he observed long columns of German infantry crossing five pontoon bridges slung across the Marne River. A few weeks later he would have dispatched bombers to blow up the bridges, but Mitchell was still in the learning curve and the orders he had been given were to perform observation. As a consequence, he merely reported the enemy movement and urged headquarters to shift forces to meet the attack.

During the six-week battle, German flyers maintained air superiority mainly because of greater

numbers and the quality of their *Jagdstaffeln* pursuit squadrons. American pilots, because they were mostly inexperienced, found themselves outmatched and on the defensive when dueling with Fokker pursuit planes. Because American pilots had been instructed to protect observation planes, they did not fight aggressively. The experience at Château-Thierry cost Mitchell all his balloons and thirty-six pilots from the 1st Pursuit Group, but the action prepared American flyers for the next campaign.

### The St. Mihiel Salient

Perhaps as a reward for smashing the German base at Fere-en-Tardenois with five RAF squadrons and the 1st Pursuit Group, General Patrick put Billy Mitchell in charge of all air groups assigned to the First Army. The promotion gave Mitchell command of ninety-eight American, British, and French squadrons, half of which he arranged into pursuit, bomber, and observation wings and massed them for operations against the St.

Mihiel salient. From behind the salient—a triangular protrusion with its tip at St. Mihiel on the Meuse River and its base stretching thirty miles from Freses to Pont-à-Mousson—the Germans had been mining ore for four years in the Briey Iron Basin to feed the kaiser's arms industry without ever being bombed or bothered by French aircraft. After carefully guarded reconnaissance by ground commanders and the 1st Corps Observation Group, which included the 1st, 12th, and 88th Aero Squadrons, Mitchell prepared his first demonstration of tactical airpower. He organized

The French Independent Air Force was at my disposal which, together with the British bombing squadrons and our own air force, gave us the largest assembly of aviation that had ever been engaged in one operation.
*General Pershing, September 12, 1918.*

**TOP: During the battle for the St. Mihiel Salient, a U.S. observation plane flew over Thiaucourt, France, and photographed the ground situation before the American onslaught on September 12–13, 1918.**

**ABOVE: A low-flying observation plane passed at treetop level over Limy, France, and photographed the route American forces used to cut off the St. Mihiel Salient during operations in September 1918.**

RIGHT: THE French Front. Colonel Billy Mitchell became Chief of Air Service, First Army, in August 1918. After failing for eighteen months to convince the French on the merits of strategic bombing, he finally obtained permission from General Pershing to launch the first mass coordinated air strike on the German stronghold at St. Mihiel. On September 26, more than 800 pursuit planes and bombers, 600 of which were flown by Americans, plastered the salient and local airfields in the first combined strategic bombing operation ever and established permanent air superiority over the battle area.

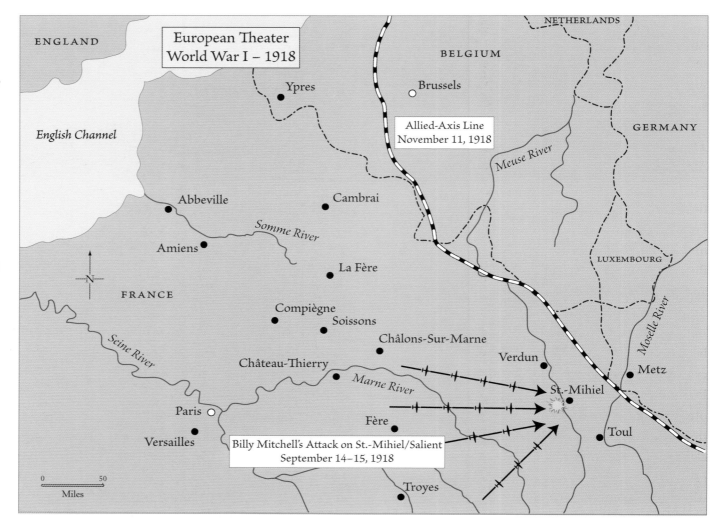

the greatest aggregation of aircraft that had ever been dedicated to a single operation on the Western Front. With 1,481 Allied planes available, opposed to 295 German aircraft, he planned to throw 959 aircraft against the salient while reserving about 500 observation and pursuit planes for ground support.

During the first two days of battle, bad weather kept planes on the ground, but with better weather on September 14-15, bombers and pursuit planes flew over the salient, bombing and strafing German communications, military installations, and infantry positions. The air assault, though met with fierce resistance by enemy pursuit squadrons from other parts of the front, completely disrupted German defensive efforts.

September 14 marked the first time the 20th Aero Squadron, flying DH.4s with Liberty engines, joined the 1st Day Bombardment Group and participated in bombing missions. Most pilots had never flown over enemy lines, some had never flown a DH.4 Liberty plane, and few of them had ever dropped a bomb. Despite several accidents during the first day, the squadron flew eight missions in three days and dropped more than eight tons of explosives during operations against Etain and other targets within the salient. The 1st Day Bombardment Group, flying at 10,000 to 15,000 ft with no oxygen or heat, dropped another twenty-two tons. The biggest air battles occurred during bombing raids, which were always escorted by squadrons of pursuit planes.

During the four-day operation, twenty-nine squadrons from the First Army Air Service flew 3,300 sorties and for the first time in the war gained air superiority over the strike zone, destroying twelve enemy balloons and more than sixty planes.

## The Last Campaign

After reducing the salient at St. Mihiel, the Germans began the long retreat across the Meuse River and into the forested Argonne. Mitchell released most of the French squadrons for service elsewhere, retaining only night bombardment and observation units. The 1st Pursuit Group still flew mostly Nieuports, but the 2nd and 3rd Pursuit Groups flew SPADs armed with 25-pound bombs for harassing infantry.

On September 25 the Meuse-Argonne offensive began, but the weather turned bad, and with the exception of ten days remained bad until the armistice. Pursuit planes saw most of the action during the offensive, flying low-level intercepts under clouds and through rain and overcast. The 1st Pursuit Group alone claimed 101 victories at the cost of fifteen pilots. The green 2nd and 3rd Pursuit Groups never got into the war soon enough to establish a notable record.

On November 11, 1918, when Germany surrendered, the United States had only 740 planes at the front, most of them French. They represented about ten percent of the Allies' total air strength. American pilots flew 150 separate bombing missions and dropped more than 140 tons of bombs as deep as 160 miles behind German lines. American combat losses included forty-eight balloons and 289 planes, which included fifty-seven planes piloted by officers flying for England, France, and Italy. The Air Service did not supply parachutes; had they done so, some of the 237 American flyers killed in battle could have been saved.

World War I became the first era of aerial combat, during which Americans shot down 781 enemy planes and 73 balloons. It also marked the beginning of the

glorification of the fighter ace, and pilots earned that distinction by shooting down five or more enemy planes. Eddie Rickenbacker topped the list with twenty-six. Captains Warren Gillette and John W. Malone flew Sopwith Dolphins for the RAF and scored twenty victories. Lieutenant Frank Luke of the 103rd Aero Squadron shot down eighteen before being killed in September 1918. Major Raoul Lufbery never kept count and jumped to his death from a flaming plane after tallying seventeen. Captains Elliot Spring and Lieutenant George Vaughn each shot down twelve. Sergeant Frank Bayliss, flying for France, shot down twelve enemy planes and became the only enlisted man to ace. Altogether, America's seventy-one aces shot down 450 planes and fifty balloons.

The war made Billy Mitchell and Benjamin Foulois brigadier generals, the first true airmen to earn a star. Both men held strong feelings about airpower, yet they were archenemies with a common goal. After the war ended, their strong views regarding airpower may have garnered more support had they joined hands and worked together.

*ABOVE: Second Lieutenant Frank Luke shot down eighteen German planes before losing his life on September 29, 1918. Luke earned the reputation of fighting a one-man war. During a seventeen-day period he downed four planes and fourteen balloons. Of the fifty balloons shot down by American pilots, Luke scored the most, including the one in the photo. For his services, twenty-one-year-old Luke was awarded two Distinguished Service Crosses, one Purple Heart, and in 1919 the Medal of Honor, posthumously.*

# BETWEEN THE WARS 1919–1940

| Planes fielded in World War I | |
|---|---|
| France | 4,500 |
| Great Britain | 3,300 |
| Germany | 2,400 |
| Italy | 1,200 |
| United States | 740 |

At the conclusion of World War I, which had placed 65 million men under arms, the United States leaped in two years from 14th to 5th place in the acquisition of air power. Throughout the war the German air service had out-performed all other nations by providing better pilots, aircraft, weaponry, leadership, and tactics, and simply lost control of the skies by being overwhelmed by the sheer number of Allied planes. Had it not been for war, one might wonder where aviation aircraft and engines would be today.

American flyers came home heroes because of the vast publicity showered on aces and air battles, but aviation became the greatest winner because of its

If we should ever have to depend upon our generals I hope they will not be the type that is now laughing at the airplane.
*Henry T. Rainey, Speaker of the House, 1934.*

development. Flyers were convinced that airpower would be the dominant weapon of the next war. Men like Billy Mitchell and Benny Foulois, two of the most determined apostles of airpower, fought to have the weapons to prove their theories, but would they get them?

*RIGHT: Post-World War I, two men in a DH.4 demonstrate the use of Lewis machine guns installed in the forward and rear cockpits. The Lewis was simple and weighed about half as much as other medium machine guns of the era.*

*FAR RIGHT: An unidentified officer poses beside a Liberty-engined Martin MB-2, the Air Service's first heavy bomber, whose design reflected conventional features of the time, including internal wood structure and fabric covering.*

## The Air Prophets

Technology stood on the side of Mitchell and Foulois, but their ideas met resistance from the army general staff. The two outspoken air prophets believed that the development of American aviation could only move ahead of Europe if removed from the army and made an independent service. On June 4, 1920, the general staff quashed the effort to create a separate arm commanded by air generals, and created the Army Air Service. Despite the determining role played by bombers and pursuit planes in ending the war a year sooner than anyone predicted, the general staff clung to the opinion that the sole purpose of aircraft was to make observations and provide ground troops with intelligence. They protected their position by naming Major General Charles T. Menoher, an artilleryman opposed to a separate air force, chief of the Air Service.

Congress followed the wishes of Secretary of War Newton D. Baker, Pershing, and Menoher and passed the Army Reorganization Act of 1920, setting the authorized strength of the Air Service at 1,516 officers, 16,000 enlisted, and 2,500 cadets, which represented about seven per cent of the 280,000 men authorized for the army. Although the legislation unified control of aviation by doing away with the dual-control organization imposed on the Air Service during the war, Congress failed to provide funds for aircraft, research and development, procurement, or pay for the authorized force. Cadets continued to fly old trainers, and with the exception of a few new Martin bombers, pilots continued to fly obsolescent DH.4s and wartime relics.

The fallout from having too many planes after the war worked wonders for civilian aviation. Barnstormers,

> …an air force acting independently can of its own account neither win a war at the present time nor, so far as we can tell, at any time in the future.
> *General Pershing's statement to Congress, 1920.*

LEFT: Brigadier General William "Billy" Mitchell risked his career to promote his vision of airpower against a military bureaucracy focused on ground wars. In the early 1920s he predicted that some Sunday morning the Japanese would launch a surprise attack on Pearl Harbor. He died five years before it happened.

exhibitionists, veterans of the war, and a growing wave of hobbyist flyers bought more than a thousand surplus aircraft, some still in crates, for a few hundred dollars. Despite the absence of purchases from the Air Service, public interest in aviation kept several aircraft plants in business, but technology stagnated. Germany's armed forces had never been physically defeated, and the oppressive reparation clause in the Treaty of Versailles touched off a slow fuse that would explode with greater catastrophic consequences twenty-one years later.

| The Air Service (1921) | |
|---|---|
| Curtiss Jennies for training | 1,500 |
| DH.4Bs for observation | 1,100* |
| S.E. 5 Pursuit planes | 175* |
| Martin MB-2 bombers | 12 |
| *British designs* | |

LEFT: Billy Mitchell used the Martin MB-2 heavy bomber to prove the viability of air power at sea. During trials on September 27, 1921, pilots from his provisional air brigade hit the obsolete battleship USS Alabama with a phosphorus bomb before sinking it.

**LEFT:** *The surrendered German battleship Ostfriesland, once considered unsinkable, staggers under the impact of 2,000-pound bombs dropped from Mitchell's Martin MB-2 bombers during demonstration trials in 1921.*

**ABOVE:** *Billy Mitchell, standing and in uniform, is flanked by his advisors and supporters during his 1925 court martial, which resulted from insubordinately disagreeing with his superiors on the importance of airpower.*

## Billy Mitchell and Airpower

Born in France in 1879, Billy Mitchell served as an infantryman during the Spanish-American War before receiving his commission in the U.S. Army. In 1915 his interest in aircraft drew him into the Aviation Section of the Signal Corps, where he became one of five observers sent to Europe to study air operations. Mitchell made his own observations from aloft and immediately became infatuated with the potential of airpower. After becoming colonel and commander of 1,500 Allied aircraft assigned to the First Army, he demonstrated, as no man before, the impact of massed air power during the 1918 Meuse-Argonne campaign.

After being promoted to brigadier general on the last day of the war, Mitchell almost immediately reverted to colonel and served as assistant chief of the Air Service under Major General Charles T. Menoher, an officer with whom he seldom agreed. Mitchell's enormous public popularity kept him in office and, with the passage of the National Defense Act of 1920, he once again became a brigadier general despite his constant agitation for an independent air force and a larger share of funds from the military pot. Mitchell was not alone in his quest for air independence. His allies included Henry H. "Hap" Arnold, Lewis H. Brereton, Ira C. Eaker, James H. Doolittle, George C. Kenney, Joseph T. McNarney, Carl Spaatz, Claire Chennault, and many others, all of whom had served in France and participated in the air war. They all agreed with Mitchell but were more temperate in expressing their views.

In 1921, after the United States received a small share of the warships surrendered by Germany, Mitchell touched off his crusade by insinuating that airpower trumped naval power as defender of the American seaboard. In July, he cajoled the admirals into a live bombing competition between the Air Service and the navy on three German surface ships, including the heavy battleship *Ostfriesland*. Although the navy made the rules and restricted bomb weights, Mitchell ignored the agreement and prodded the Ordnance Corps to develop a 2,000-pound concussion bomb. After the *Ostfriesland* survived the lighter bombs, Mitchell loaded the 2,000-pounders on Martin MB-2s. The concussion bombs sank the drifting battleship by exploding beneath the surface alongside the ship, fracturing her unarmored hull. Admirals confounded by the unexpected yelled, "Foul!" Mitchell proved his point but failed to displace the navy in protecting America's seaboard.

Frustrated by inaction, Mitchell became more outspoken. When his term as assistant chief of the Air Service expired in 1925, his one-time ally, General Pershing, reduced Mitchell to the permanent grade of lieutenant colonel and sent him to San Antonio, Texas. Later that year Mitchell accused military leaders of incompetence and criminal negligence over, among several issues, the mismanagement of national defense. Court-martialed for insubordination, Mitchell lost his case and drew a five-year suspension from the army. General Douglas MacArthur, who chaired the court, later claimed to have been the only member who voted for Mitchell's acquittal.

In 1926 Mitchell resigned his commission and returned to public life, but he never stopped campaigning for airpower until his death in 1936. Men like Arnold, Spaatz, Doolittle, and Kenney suffered slow promotion because they agreed with Mitchell. Those same men became the leaders of air operations in World War II.

In 1946, Congress posthumously awarded Mitchell a gold medal for his dedication to the advancement of airpower, and for the sacrifice of his professional career to drive home a point that an old army hierarchy failed to accept.

## Bombers and Pursuit Planes—The 1920s

With inadequate funds and mixed results, the small Engineering Division of the Air Service began building experimental airplanes at McCook Field in Ohio, and the learning curve began. With an appropriation of $3 million in 1924, they could put resources only into articles such as bombsights, aircraft weapons, more efficient engines, light metals to replace fabric for covering aircraft, and specification writing. Producing the plane remained with commercial manufacturers. From this combined effort came an abundance of failures, a few successes, and a great deal of knowledge.

The experimental 42,000-pound Barling XNBL-1 triplane bomber could not generate enough power from six Liberty 420-horsepower 12-cylinder engines to attain 100 mph or lift the aircraft over the Appalachian Mountains. The smaller, two-engined Curtiss B-2 Condor could reach 100 mph loaded with 2,500 pounds of bombs but had an unacceptable cruising radius of only 300 miles. The army thought the price too high and purchased only twelve. In the 1920s, neither the Air Service nor the manufacturers knew how to build a bomber.

Pursuit aircraft made slightly better progress, but they were all biplanes. The Curtiss PW-8 Hawk recorded a speed of 178 mph and could attain an altitude of 22,000 ft and a range of 335 miles. The Curtiss A-3 Falcon, the army's first attack plane, could carry 600 pounds of bombs 630 miles at 140 mph.

The Air Service continued to wither. By mid-1924 there were only 754 planes in commission, which included a mixture of 457 observation aircraft, fifty-nine bombers, seventy-eight pursuit planes, eight attack planes, and trainers. The combined force equaled one pursuit, one attack, and one bombardment group. No wonder Mitchell lost his temper.

Lack of interest in bombers emanated from military ignorance. The sinking of the *Ostfriesland* in 1921, coupled with the development of the aircraft carrier,

actually signaled the first steps in the subordination of battleships to airpower. Tactical exercises during the 1920s highlighted biplane bomber inefficiencies, which when compared with European models included a lack of speed, poor maneuverability, inadequate range, bad targeting, and excessive accidents. Something clearly needed to be done, but what?

## Record Setters of the Early Twenties

Throughout the 1920s, Congress and the general staff juggled funds and wondered what to do about the Air Service while a small band of flyers and mechanics began pointing the way. Mitchell stimulated the cause by encouraging Air Service officers to set world records for altitude, speed, and distance, thereby attracting publicity. Major "Hap" Arnold became a newsmaker in 1921 when he won a race against pigeons between Portland, Oregon, and San Francisco. On June 23, 1924, Lieutenant Russell L. Maugham flew a PW-8 from New York to San Francisco in less than twenty-two hours, but made five fueling stops. The Air Service had been working on aerial refueling, and in August Lieutenants Lowell Smith and John Richter set a world

*ABOVE: Boeing P-12Es from the 27th Pursuit Squadron roar across the sky over Selfridge Field, Michigan. The aircraft came with modified headrests containing life rafts, giving them a horizontal line behind the cockpit. P-12Es of the early 1930s were among the last of the helmet-and-goggles era.*

*ABOVE: Eight Air Service flyers took off from Seattle, Washington, on April 4, 1924, for the first round-the-world flight in four Douglas World Cruisers. The Chicago (shown here) and another aircraft completed the 26,000-mile route, returning to Seattle on September 28.*

*ABOVE: Captain Lowell H. Smith and Lieutenant John P. Richter, flying a DH.4 out of Rockwell Field, California, set a world endurance record in June 1923 by remaining in flight for four days by utilizing another DH.4 for first-ever aerial refueling.*

*RIGHT: Captain Lowell Smith and Lieutenant John Richter pause to be photographed having stepped from their DH.4 at Rockwell Field, California, after breaking the world's endurance record in June 1923.*

endurance record of 37 hours 15 minutes in their DH.4 by refueling from a hose draped from another DH.4. A year later Lieutenants Cy Bettis and Jimmy Doolittle set new speed records, winning the Pulitzer and Schneider Cup.

On April 4, 1924, eight flyers in four specially built Douglas World Cruisers took off from Seattle, Washington, in an attempt to make the first round-the-world flight. The single-engine biplane weighed more than 4,000 pounds, had a 50 ft wingspan, and could land on wheels or floats. A 420-horsepower Liberty engine provided the thrust but could generate only about 80 mph. On September 28, only two planes flown by Lieutenants Lowell Smith and Erik Nelson made the 27,500-mile flight back to Seattle. Major Frederick L. Martin, leader of the flight, struck a hill in Alaska, and Lieutenant Leigh Wade suffered mechanical trouble, rendering both crews incapable of continuing.

Other flyers began compiling data for systematically locating airfields across the continent. Improved day and night aerial photography made spotting more efficient, as did the use of radios in cockpits for communicating between planes and the ground. With new airfields scattered at strategic locations around the country, bombers and transports began moving men and supplies by air. The pioneering work of the Air Service demonstrated how aircraft could be used for commercial purposes.

## Air Corps Act of July 2, 1926

While he was still serving as assistant chief of the Air Service, Billy Mitchell's unrelenting agitation led to the formation of several committees to study the question of airpower, which resulted in months of hearings and discussions without any progress. President Calvin Coolidge became frustrated over the delays and in September 1925 created another board headed by Dwight W. Morrow to investigate the "best means of developing and applying aircraft in national defense." A House of Representatives proposal by the Lampert Committee pleased Mitchell because it provided for separate air, army, and navy organizations responsible to a department of defense. The Lampert committee went a step beyond General Patrick's request for a separate air service responsible to the secretary of war. The Morrow Board, however, issued its report first and upstaged the Lampert Committee by two weeks. As a consequence, neither a department of defense nor an independent air force emerged from the study.

The Morrow Board did make recommendations that won the approval of Congress and went part way in assuaging Patrick and Mitchell. On July 2, 1926, Congress passed an act replacing the name Air Service with Air Corps and made provision for acts of heroism to be awarded with the Distinguished Flying Cross. The legislation also strengthened the Air Corps by creating an assistant secretary of war to advance military aeronautics and gave representatives from each air section access to the general staff. Coolidge, however, did the Air Corps no favor by naming F. Trubee Davison, who knew nothing about airpower, assistant secretary of war for air.

ABOVE: The famous transatlantic flight of Charles Lindbergh in May 1927 came at exactly the right time to reestablish in the minds of Americans the importance of aviation. Lindbergh's non-stop flight to Europe also established a new benchmark for aircraft engine reliability and performance.

The Air Corps Act provided a five-year expansion program that in 1927 began to slowly correct the funding problems enacted in 1920. Because of Davison's apathetic approach to budgetary matters, the new program evolved slowly during his six years in office. Goals were not met, but progress was made.

During the Davison years, Brigadier General Frank P. Lahm took over the newly created Air Corps Training Center at San Antonio and by the 1930s had turned Randolph Field into the "West Point of the Air" and nearby Kelly Field into the nation's advanced training

| 1926–1932 Expansion | | | |
|---|---|---|---|
| | 1926 | 1932 Actual | 1932 Goal |
| Aircraft | 1,000 | 1,709 | 1,800 |
| Officers | 919 | 1,305 | 1,650 |
| Enlisted | 8,725 | 13,400 | 15,000 |

ABOVE: After returning to the United States in June 1927, Charles Lindbergh (right) chats with Major John F. Curry (center), and Orville Wright (left) during a stop at Wright Field, Dayton, Ohio.

RIGHT: During an air strategy conference in 1927, Brigadier General Benjamin D. Foulois (left) meets with Major General James E. Fechet (center), chief of the Air Corps, and Brigadier General H. C. Pratt (right), of the U.S. Army.

The bomber clan took notice a month later when Lieutenants Lester J. Maitland and Albert F. Hegenberger flew a trimotor Fokker C-2 2,418 miles non-stop from Oakland, California, to Hawaii in less than twenty-six hours. Then, in January 1929, Major Carl "Tooey" Spaatz, Captain Ira C. Eaker, and Lieutenants Elwood R. Quesada and Harry Halvorsen, four officers who believed in the concept of strategic bombing, stayed aloft for more than 150 hours over Los Angeles by using refueling techniques developed in 1923.

During the record-breaking, five-day experiment, they received 5,500 gallons of fuel, 250 gallons of oil, and a ton of food and supplies from Douglas C-1C tankers before being forced down by engine trouble. Long-distance flights made in the late 1920s, coupled with the development of refueling techniques, led to the idea of reinforcing distant bases by air, but Major General James E. Fechet, chief of the Air Corps from 1927 to 1931, was still not able to convince the general staff that an air force could be used for something other than supporting the army.

school. Brigadier General William E. Gillmore also moved into new facilities at Wright Field in Dayton, Ohio, and with engineers and specialists reorganized Air Corps logistics. Between the efforts of Lahm and Gillmore, thirty regular bases and depots sprang up around the country, plus sixteen bases for reservists and the National Guard. For the first time since the invention of the airplane, the Air Corps had the nucleus of an organization for growth.

## Pushing the Envelope

To focus attention on aviation, air officers took the initiative. In May 1927 25-year-old Charles Lindbergh, a former Air Service pilot and reserve officer, won world recognition by being the first to fly solo from New York to Paris in 33½ hours. Promoted to colonel and awarded the Medal of Honor, though in violation of the army's combat-only policy, "Lindy" became the most famous pilot on the planet. Overnight, a new generation of young men became fascinated with flying and overwhelmed Air Corps recruiters with applications.

## Building the Bomber

In 1931, General Foulois became chief of the Air Corps and for the next four years relentlessly lobbied for bigger bombers. He set out to prove the validity of airpower to members of the general staff who had traditionally suppressed the development of aircraft. With Foulois at the helm, a new era began.

After a decade of false starts, bomber technology began turning the corner after the Air Corps distributed a circular to aircraft manufacturers inviting innovative designs. In response, Boeing produced the B-9 in 1931, and Glenn L. Martin Company produced the B-10. The sleek, under-wing B-9 with twin-engines provided the first "big-bomber" look of the 1930s, but had open cockpits. Martin's swift and compact B-10, flown on February 18, 1932, became an instant success, and the army ordered its first "modern" bomber, an aircraft technically superior and faster than most contemporary fighters.

"Hap" Arnold proved a point in 1934 when he led an air expedition consisting of ten Martin B-10s and thirty officers and enlisted men on an 8,290-mile flight to Alaska and back. The new, all-metal B-10s came with twin 775-horsepower Wright engines, retractable landing gear, and glaze-enclosed cockpits and turrets. The 5-ton bomber (empty weight) flew at 210 mph, which equaled the speed of most Depression-era fighter planes, and attained a ceiling of 28,000 feet.

The success of the B-10 motivated Foulois to press for more improvements. He endorsed Project A, a 1933 extrapolation made by Material Division engineers at Wright Field showing that a bomber could theoretically be built to carry a ton of bombs 5,000 miles at 200 mph. In response, Boeing produced the experimental XB-15. While it fell short of expectations by being structurally and aerodynamically problematical and underpowered, the XB-15 gave Boeing and the Air Corps a great deal of knowledge about building big bombers.

ABOVE: The big bomber look began evolving in the early 1930s with the Boeing B-9, a low wing, all-metal, cantilever monoplane with retractable landing gear, but with open cockpits.

LEFT: After experimenting with the B-9 and B-10, Air Corps planners set specifications for the XB-15, a gigantic aircraft weighing five times more and with twice the wingspan. However, engine development lagged behind.

In May 1934, the Air Corps once again circulated requests and specifications for new multi-engined bombers. Every aircraft producer except Boeing assumed "multi-engined" meant two engines. On August 20, 1935, Boeing revolutionized bomber technology for the second time in five years by demonstrating Model 299, a four-engine heavyweight, to a small crowd of astounded airmen and generals at Wright Field during official flight tests. To complete the test, pilots flew the big bomber 2,000 miles back to Seattle at an average speed of 252 mph. Billy Mitchell died the following year, but he lived long enough to see this prototype of the B-17 validate his decades-old campaign for airpower. In a small twist of irony, Mitchell's old rival, Benny Foulois, became the impetus for making it happen.

ABOVE: In May 1937 the war department made the decision to order 133 obsolete Douglas B-18s instead of purchasing sixty-five Boeing B-17s because the smaller bomber cost fifty percent less than a B-17.

## The B-17 Flying Fortress

Billy Mitchell did not live to experience his dream of a seeing a modern bomber wing roaring across the skies, but the bright aluminum-skinned B-17s developed from Boeing's Model 299 were on the way. Thirteen pre-production aircraft followed, beginning with the Y1B-17s and followed by the B-17B, C, and D. The models were not completely successful because of trouble with superchargers and oxygen delivery systems at high altitudes.

In May 1937, thirteen Boeing Y1B-17s participated in joint army-navy maneuvers off the Pacific coast. The performance of the big Boeings, with their top-secret Norden bombsights, made an enormous impression, but when the Air Corps attempted to make the aircraft its standard bomber, the war department balked and ruled that it would be cheaper to purchase 133 obsolete Douglas B-18s instead of sixty-five B-17s. Airmen disagreed and quietly continued with their plans to make the B-17 an offensive weapon.

During World War II, several aircraft plants became involved in producing more than 12,700 B-17s. The B-17E became the first to go to Europe. The Eighth Air Force eventually replaced the Es with Fs and finally the ten-man-crew G series, which had grown from an empty weight of twelve to eighteen tons. The powerplant had also been boosted with four 1200hp 9-cylinder turbo-charged radial piston engines. With a maximum speed of 295 mph, a service ceiling of 35,600 ft, and a range of 3,160 miles, the all-metal 74 ft 9 in long bomber had a wingspan of 103 ft 9 in. The plane weighed 65,500 pounds when loaded with equipment, 13,600 pounds of bombs, and ammunition for thirteen 12.7mm turreted machine guns. Billy Mitchell could not have imagined such an aircraft back in the early 1920s, when the best bomber in America was a Martin MB-2 biplane with open cockpits.

*ABOVE LEFT: By 1937 the XB-15 had evolved through a series of design changes into the venerable, four-engined Boeing B-17 Flying Fortress, which in 1942 began flying missions over Europe.*

*ABOVE: During pre-war operations in the United States, a Boeing Model 299, precursor to the B-17, after crash landing in an open field.*

*ABOVE: Brigadier General Frank M. Andrews, a member of the General Staff and one of aviation's ablest officers, became the first commander of General Headquarters, Air Force.*

## Broadening Responsibilities

In 1931, Foulois also accomplished another of Mitchell's objectives when he convinced General MacArthur, Chief of Staff of the U.S. Army, and Admiral William V. Pratt, Chief of Naval Operations, to turn the responsibility for coastal defense over to the Air Corps. Two years later the corps assumed responsibility for long-range reconnaissance to the limits of their aircraft, all of which prepared flyers for protecting convoys and defending America from seaborne attack during World War II.

In 1918, Mitchell had been among the first to suggest that the Air Service carry the nation's mail. At the time, Mitchell was merely seeking ways to promote flying.

After a three-month trial, the flights were transferred to the Post Office Department. Nine years elapsed before the government transferred all airmail business to commercial air carriers. Postmaster General James A. Farley remembered that the Air Service once carried mail.

On February 9, 1934, Foulois received an urgent inquiry from Farley asking if the Air Corps could carry airmail if commercial contracts were canceled. Foulois replied that he would be ready, if necessary, in four to six weeks. Farley ignored the general's reply, voided the government's contracts, and left Foulois with just ten days to prepare for flying the mail. What followed became one of most hectic peacetime ventures in the history of the Air Corps.

Commercial airlines used 500 planes to move three million pounds of mail a year over a network of 25,000 miles. In 1934 the Air Corps had about 250 planes, including obsolete aircraft. Its pilots had never received training in foul weather or night flying, and their aircraft were not all equipped with proper instruments. Because of a long spell of bad weather in February, several crashes occurred. Despite criticism from the press and a series of congressional investigations, the Air Corps, with half the number of planes flown by commercial airlines, logged 14,109 flying hours transporting more than 777,000 pounds of mail over 1.6 million route miles up to June 1, when commercial flights resumed.

Because of the Air Corps' loss of fifty-seven planes and a dozen lives, what appeared to the public as an operational fiasco resulted in fringe benefits for the corps, which had actually fulfilled its mission under the most adverse conditions and deserved high marks for responsiveness. The unplanned exercise highlighted several deficiencies, and Foulois wasted no time demanding better planes and better instruments for navigation and all-weather flying. Even the Joint Board of the Army and the Navy, which contained few air enthusiasts, agreed that something had to be done.

## General Headquarters, Air Force (GHQAF)

Demands for a general headquarters for the air force resonated back to the early 1920s during General Patrick's term as chief of the Air Service. General Fechet also tried to establish a GHQ, but the general staff could not envision any mission for an air force other than army support. When in 1933 the army began reorganizing its ground forces into four field armies, Foulois took advantage of the shuffling and proposed a general headquarters so that the Air Corps could maintain overall control of bombardment, attack, and pursuit planes. The sticking point was Foulois' request for 2,320 planes. The war department cringed because the increased expenditures would have to come from the army budget.

The 1934 mail-flying episode, coupled with the loss of aircraft, led to a study by the war department to define the relationship between the Air Corps and civilian aviation. Former Secretary of War Baker, who had never taken airpower seriously, headed the board. Although Baker's board rejected most of the efforts by Air Corps officers for greater expansion, it did recommend the creation of a general headquarters made up of combat units capable of operating independently or in cooperation with ground forces. Although the recommendation came somewhat as a surprise to the general staff, the war department ordered the creation of the GHQAF as of March 1, 1935, and placed Brigadier General Frank M. Andrews in charge. One of the most able officers of the Air Corps, Andrews organized his 1,000 planes into three pursuit, four bombardment, two attack, and four reconnaissance squadrons. Then in 1936, when Andrews asked for more money, the general staff cut back air expenditures for research and development, and reverted the funds to the army.

*ABOVE: During the early 1930s, while the Air Corps was attracted to U.S. Mail delivery, Charles Lindbergh, in a Boeing P-12. set about pioneering and establishing mail-carrying routes to South America.*

*ABOVE: Henry H. "Hap" Arnold believed as strongly as Billy Mitchell in the future of airpower but, unlike Mitchell, he wisely nurtured the process by setting an example.*

*ABOVE: Impressed by the performance of the new Curtiss P-36A during trials in 1937, the Army Air Corps placed an order for 210 of the planes, at the time the largest-ever peacetime order for fighters. With rapid advancement in technology, the aircraft quickly became obsolete.*

*ABOVE CENTER: With the scarcity of fighter aircraft in 1941, the upgraded P-36Cs lined up for the Cleveland National Air Races in 1939 found their way into the Pacific and in December became part of the Army Air Force's fighter squadrons posted at Pearl Harbor and on the Philippines.*

Disconnects also existed between GHQAF and Major General Oscar Westover, who in 1935 replaced Foulois as chief of the Air Corps, because GHQAF reported to the general staff. The awkward situation remained uncorrected until March 1, 1939, when Andrews stepped down. Thereafter, GHQAF reported to "Hap" Arnold, who on September 29, 1938, as major general, had become chief of the Air Corps after a plane crash had taken the life of Westover.

## Aircraft in Transition

Unlike the quantum leap in bombers marked by the B-17, the development of pursuit and attack aircraft came slowly, even though Germany had entered a new phase of military mobilization and was experimenting with Stukas and Messerschmitts in Spain's civil war. Boeing P-26 Peashooters and Curtiss A-12s, the last of the open cockpit fighters from the early 1930s, were already obsolete though still in service in 1941.

In the mid-1930s, the first of the future transitional fighters with closed cockpits began appearing. In 1935

the two-seater PB-2A proved to be faster at 274 mph than any other fighter-bomber in the Air Corps' arsenal, but lacked the dogfighting capability of single-seaters. In 1936 the Air Corps purchased seventy-seven P-35 pursuit planes from the Seversky Aero Corporation. P-35s came with retractable gear and a variable-pitch propeller, but without armor, adequate firepower, or self-sealing fuel tanks. Curtiss responded and in 1937 sold the Air Corps 210 P-36s, which, though still not comparable to the latest European fighters, overcame the deficiencies of Seversky P-35s and eventually led to the development of the immortal P-40. France bought hundreds of P-36s and during the early days of World War II used them successfully against German Messerschmitts.

In 1937 the two-man Northrop A-17 entered the Air Corps inventory and became one of the first modern attack planes with bomb racks. Douglas Aircraft modified the design and produced the first modern torpedo-planes and dive-bombers, the TBD Devastator and the SBD Dauntless, both of which

ABOVE: *The twin-engined Douglas B-18 quickly gave way to the Boeing B-17. Nor could the B-18 compete with designs for medium bombers, which were then in the development stage.*

went into the navy's air arsenal. By then, General Andrews had become almost as persistent as Mitchell had been in his demands for more money. When Andrews' term ended, the army reduced him to the permanent rank of colonel and assigned him to the same post where Mitchell had been banished in 1925.

In 1938, after Adolf Hitler attacked Czechoslovakia and exposed the *Luftwaffe's* air arsenal, President Franklin D. Roosevelt anticipated another war in Europe and took steps to boost aircraft production. He expected Great Britain and France to ask for help, which would mobilize American industry and boost the nation out of the nagging after-effects of the Depression.

The Air Corps, now in the capable hands of General Arnold, asked for 7,000 aircraft, including 3,500 combat planes. On April 3, 1939, Congress authorized $300 million to purchase 5,500 planes and enough gear to support 48,000 officers and enlisted men. General George C. Marshall, chief of staff, concurred with the plan and began broadening the national defense strategy to include the entire Western Hemisphere. The Air

Corps now had a specific mission that required the fullest development of long-range bombers and fighter planes. The aircraft industry, which had survived through the years because of commercial demand, was suddenly swamped by government contracts for aircraft still in the design and experimental stages.

In January 1940, American airpower was placed sixth in the world. The Air Corps' standard bomber, the two-engined B-18, could not compare with the B-17, but there were only two dozen of the bigger bombers in inventory, while the Consolidated B-24 was just coming off the drawing boards. The Northrop A-17 served as the standard attack plane, and the Curtiss P-36 the standard fighter. By the end of 1940, the B-10, A-17, and P-36 were all obsolete.

| On the Eve of War | | |
|---|---|---|
| *January 1939* | *Air Personnel* | *First-line Aircraft* |
| German Luftwaffe | 500,000 | 4,100 |
| British RAF | 100,000 | 1,900 |
| U.S. Air Corps | 26,000 | 800 |

*ABOVE: Republic's P-47 Thunderbolts went through numerous design changes after reaching England, where the fighter entered combat on April 8, 1943. The fighter eventually clocked 473 mph with a service ceiling of 42,000 ft. The aircraft carried six to eight 12.7mm machine guns and two 1,000-pound bombs or ten rockets. Its huge size led to it being christened the "Juggernaut," or "Jug," and it was easily out-turned and out-climbed by the agile German single-seaters, although it displayed good high-altitude performance and superb roll capability.*

## Mobilization

Alarms rang in early 1940 when General Arnold informed General Marshall and President Roosevelt that the Air Corps was at "zero strength," providing facts and figures to support his statement. Had it not been for foreign orders during the 1930s, the aircraft industry would have been in no position to respond to Roosevelt's request for 50,000 planes. In December 1939, Great Britain and France placed orders for 2,500 military aircraft, and by March 1940 had ordered 8,200 planes. Foreign demands quickly consumed the capacity of American aircraft plants, creating an unexpected problem for aircraft manufacturers Curtiss, Douglas, Martin, and North American, and engine producers Wright Aeronautical and Pratt & Whitney.

Despite these capacity problems, foreign money accelerated design improvements. Douglas A-20 Bostons, sold to France and England, developed into one of the Air Corps' best light bombers. The British were responsible for getting P-40 "Hawks" into the production lines at North American after Curtiss ran out of capacity. After the fall of France in June 1940, most of the aircraft went to Great Britain, but the Air Corps took possession of about 10,000 of the 22,000 planes then on order. Had it not been for foreign sales, which also accelerated technological improvements, the Air Corps might have been without a modern fighter plane.

LEFT: The Lockheed P-38 Lightning was designed to meet the Air Corps' requirement for a high altitude interceptor capable of 360 mph at 20,000 ft. By November 1941, the P-38E appeared with heavier armament and a new power plant that eventually increased the aircraft's speed to 414 mph with a service ceiling of 44,000 ft.

ABOVE: The Republic P-47 Thunderbolt rapidly replaced Republic's P-43s. The Thunderbolt prototype flew for the first time on May 6, 1941.

When in 1938 Congress authorized the Air Corps to spend $8 billion for aircraft (enough for 37,500 planes) over the next several years, the money might well have been partly wasted had it not been for B-17s and the rapid learning curve imposed by foreign aircraft orders. Out of this maze came bombers like North American's B-25 Mitchell (1939), Consolidated's B-24 Liberator (1940), and Martin's B-26 Marauder (1941). Fighters such as Lockheed's P-38 Lightning, Bell's P-39 Airacobra, and Curtiss's P-40 Kittyhawk all went into production during 1940, followed by Republic's P-47 Thunderbolt in 1941. The aircraft came with armored cockpits, self-sealing fuel tanks, increased engine horsepower, improved navigation avionics, and radio communication systems. Armaments also changed. The .30-caliber Browning machine gun gave way to the .50-caliber, the 20mm cannon, and the 37mm cannon.

The Air Corps still had much more to learn about aircraft technology, but by the beginning of 1941, the journey had begun.

# THE WAR IN EUROPE 1939–1945

RIGHT: Above the USAAF advanced flying school at Moore Field, near Mission, Texas, the lead ship in a formation of P-40s peels off for a mock attack during a practice maneuver. Aviation cadets received transition training in Tomahawk fighters before receiving their wings as pilots.

The United States had slumbered through two decades of peace and was ill-prepared on September 1, 1939, when Germany attacked Poland without formally declaring war. Two days later Britain and France declared war on Germany, marking the failure of British Prime Minister Neville Chamberlain's appeasement policy. On September 4 the *Luftwaffe* struck Poland's airfields, wiped out hundreds of antiquated planes parked on the ground, and established air superiority. Resistance ebbed away. Germany and the Soviet Union began partitioning Poland, and on October 4 Polish pilots flew their last sorties before taking refuge in the west.

## Rearming

General Arnold went before Congress during the summer of 1939 to request more aircraft. "I want to ask you," one congressman inquired acerbically, "who[m] are we going to fight?" Arnold could not answer the question. At the time, the U.S. Army consisted of about 200,000 men, including 26,000 in the Air Corps.

After the fall of France in June 1940, Arnold returned to Congress. By then defense had become a national concern. The air war in Europe, with screaming Stukas and dramatic dogfights between Messerschmitts and Spitfires, had elevated the public's awareness to the importance of airpower. Before Arnold laid out his proposal, members of Congress informed him that any appropriation request would be approved. "All you have to do is ask for it," declared Senator

Henry Cabot Lodge, Jr. Arnold asked for 18,000 planes by April 1, 1942, and President Roosevelt approved the request. General Marshall backed off the number to 12,835 planes (4,000 for combat), fifty-four combat groups, and 220,000 officers and men. Arnold parlayed and in July 1942 asked for eighty-four combat groups with 7,800 planes and 400,000 officers and enlisted. Congress approved the appropriation, and Arnold began the task of reorganizing the Air Corps, which in 1945 would reach peak strength at 2,400,000 men, 243 combat groups, and 80,000 aircraft.

> You can't build an Air Force overnight.
> *General Harold H. Arnold in* Global Mission.

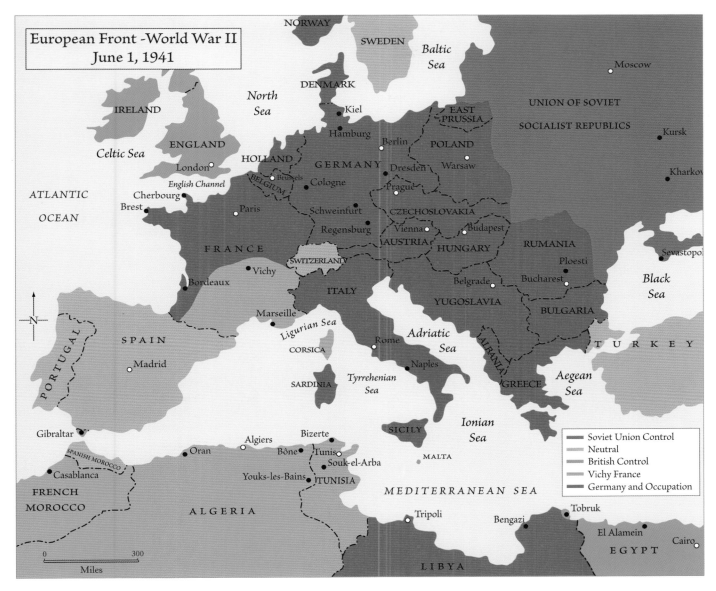

European Front – World War II
June 1, 1941

Soviet Union Control
Neutral
British Control
Vichy France
Germany and Occupation

**LEFT: By June 1940, the Axis controlled most of Europe and, with Vichy France, most of North Africa. The United States could not avoid war much longer and time was running out for Great Britain. President Roosevelt called for 50,000 military planes a year. Four years passed before the Army Air Forces reached its full strength of 80,000 aircraft and 2,400,000 personnel.**

## Reorganizing for War

In March 1941 Robert A. Lovett, a former World War I navy pilot, became assistant secretary of war for air. He understood the importance of airpower and was instrumental in naming Arnold chief of the AAF, making him responsible for designing and implementing plans and policies for aviation. Arnold wasted no time placing his best men in key positions, and the short list included a handful of officers devoted to airpower.

The AAF needed more than planes and manpower. It needed flight schools, air bases, runways, barracks, mechanics, ordnance specialists, and engineers. Pilots and planes alone could not create an air force.

In 1939 the Air Corps graduated 1,500 mechanics and technicians. By March 1941, to keep pace with anticipated aircraft production and pilot availability, the requirement for mechanics and technicians leaped to 110,000.

The Air Corps operated seventeen airbases in 1939, and four depots, some from World War I. By December 1941 the number of bases increased to 114 in the United States, with more on the way. By V-J Day, there would be 670.

| Pilot Training Projections | |
|---|---|
| Year | Per year |
| 1938 (actual) | 300 |
| 1939 | 1,200 |
| June 1940 | 7,000 |
| July 1940 | 12,000 |
| February 1941 | 30,000 |

RIGHT: In a move to bolster manpower, 1,500 mechanics and technicians graduated from Air Corps schools in 1939and made major contributions in Europe. The P-47 is that of top-scoring ace, Francis Gabreski.

## The Air Intelligence Section

During 1940, Arnold established the Air Intelligence Section and engaged bankers, diplomats, and businessmen to obtain information on the location of Germany's and Italy's petroleum industries, power grids, manufacturing plants, and synthetic oil operations, many of which could be accessed by the Americans who had financed them. After Arnold's intelligence operatives collected the information, the United States exchanged it with Great Britain for

### General Henry Harley "Hap" Arnold (1886–1950)

Born in Gladwyne, Pennsylvania, "Hap" Arnold graduated from West Point in 1907 and took his commission in the infantry. After serving in the Philippines (1907–1909), he transferred to the aeronautical section of the Signal Corps in 1911 and learned to fly from the Wright brothers. Promoted to captain in 1916, he supervised the army's aviation training schools during World War I. Major Arnold did not reach France until October 1918, but he arrived in time to observe the last days of the air war and become a disciple of Billy Mitchell.

Arnold never stopped preparing for the next war. Promotions did not come quickly because he persistently advocated airpower. He kept the cause alive by promoting aeronautical technology and put aviation before the public by setting records and writing books for the young men who one day would become pilots. In 1935, as war clouds collected over Europe, Arnold became a brigadier general, commanded the 1st Wing, GHQ, and in the

same year became assistant chief of staff of the Air Corps. Upon the death of General Westover in 1938, Arnold assumed the temporary rank of major general, chief of staff, and began devoting all his energy to improving the combat readiness of the Air Corps. Preparing for global war soon absorbed his life.

Boosted to the rank of temporary lieutenant general in 1941, Arnold was instrumental in changing the name of the Air Corps to the U.S. Army Air Forces (USAAF). In March 1942 he became commanding general and in 1943 received

his fourth star. As a member of the Joint Chiefs of Staff, he participated in the planning of Allied strategy in Europe and the Pacific.

Arnold eventually rose to the highest rank in the army, wearing the same five stars as Eisenhower, MacArthur, and Marshall. Though he retired in 1946, he lived to see Mitchell's dream become a reality when on September 18, 1947, the United States Air Force became a separate service, independent of the army. Three years later he died in Sonoma, California, a master strategist, tactician, and the air force's first great general.

**ABOVE: Hap Arnold became committed to air power after learning to fly with the Wright brothers in 1911. He steadily promoted his beliefs, became chief of staff of the USAAF during World War II, and served on the Joint Chiefs of Staff from 1941 to 1946.**

massive amounts of data on the *Luftwaffe's* aircraft and engine industries.

The working relationship between Great Britain and the United States led to the ABC-1 Staff Agreement on March 27, 1941, and established the basis for Anglo-American cooperation should America enter the war. Both nations agreed to concentrate their collective power on defeating Germany, with chiefs of staff from both countries working together as the combined chiefs of staff. From this agreement a working arrangement evolved between the RAF and the AAF for defeating Germany.

With the ABC-1 agreement activated, Arnold organized the Air War Plans Division under Colonel Harold L. George and filled the staff with devoted air advocates from the Air Tactical School, his personal brain trust. Using information obtained through the Air Intelligence Section and the RAF, George's tacticians identified targets and on August 11, 1941, after seven-days of intense labor, determined the amount and types of aircraft, ordnance, and personnel required to execute the plan. The war department approved the plan without noticing that the air force had independently put the entire strategy together without any input from the army or navy.

All the AAF needed now were lots of planes, personnel, and a declaration of war.

## The Day of Infamy

On the quiet Sunday morning of December 7, 1941, in what President Roosevelt called "the day of infamy," Japan launched a surprise air attack on the U.S. Pacific Fleet anchored in Pearl Harbor, without the formality of declaring war. Damage to eight battleships anchored off Ford Island and the three main airfields on Oahu marked the beginning of war in Pacific. The AAF had 231 planes divided between Hickam Field and Wheeler Field, and the Japanese aerial attack destroyed most of them on the ground.

On December 8, Great Britain and its commonwealth nations joined the United States in declaring war on Japan. Three days later Congress extended the war declaration to include Germany and Italy. Japan's entry into the war caused changes in the ABC-1 pact. Roosevelt and Churchill agreed in ABC-2 to a "Germany first" policy in which, among other matters, the United States assumed major responsibility for conducting war in the Pacific.

## Air Readiness in the Western Hemisphere

By December 1941, after thirty months of effort, Arnold had increased the AAF to sixty-seven combat groups with eighteen deployed overseas, twenty-nine in strategic domestic reserve, and the balance still in operational training. Manpower exceeded 354,000 officers and enlisted men, more than 9,000 pilots had received their wings, and 59,000 mechanics and technicians had

**ABOVE: Developed from the Curtiss P-36A Hawk, the ubiquitous Curtiss P-40s was one of the few American fighters available at the beginning of World War II. There were many variants, including the P-40D Kittyhawks flown by the RAF.**

**BELOW: With industrial efforts at home to manufacture Lockheed P-38s on automotive-like production lines, the long-range, twin-engined Lightning entered the war in early 1942 and rapidly improved American air superiority in all theaters.**

*ABOVE: When Germany extended its combat zone to the Arctic Circle in 1941, Denmark gave the United States permission to build bases in Greenland and Iceland. Here, a Lockheed P-38 prepares for takeoff on one of the snow-covered airfields.*

northwest, Third in the southeast, and Fourth in the southwest. Each force contained a bomber command and an interceptor command for offensive and defensive operations. Because of growing concerns for the Western Hemisphere, Arnold stationed the Sixth Air Force with 300 aircraft in the islands of the Caribbean and posted the main force of B-17s and P-40s in Panama. Outlying airfields in places like Panama grew in importance as advanced training bases. This organizational structure became the nucleus for the massive air commands that soon began forming in Europe and the Pacific.

graduated from training schools. The inventory showed 2,846 first-line aircraft, but only 1,157 were actually suited for battle against enemy planes equipped with modern weapons. For several months, P-38s and P-40s shouldered pursuit duties while B-17s, B-24s, and B-25s began training for combat missions.

Arnold also created four U.S.-based air forces, stationing the First in the northeast, Second in the

Because Germany had extended its combat zone to the Arctic Circle, Denmark gave the U.S. permission to construct bases in Iceland and Greenland. The AAF built an airbase at Narsarssuak on the southern tip of Greenland and sent the 33rd Pursuit Squadron with thirty P-40s to Iceland to augment RAF units performing antisubmarine patrols. Months before Congress declared war on Germany, AAF pilots experienced their first taste of war.

## The Ubiquitous P-40s

Derived from the radial-engined P-36 Hawk, the Curtiss P-40 went through many design changes during the war. In December 1941; a few Hawks were still in service but were rapidly being replaced by P-40B and C Tomahawks with Allison V-1710 liquid-cooled inline engines. As on the P-36, machine guns were mounted on the cowling and synchronized to fire through the propeller. In 1939 the AAF issued its largest-ever contract for 524 Curtiss P-40s. At the time of Pearl Harbor, P-40 Tomahawks were the most numerous fighters in the American arsenal.

Curtiss P-40Ds flew for Great Britain, Canada, China, Australia, New Zealand, South Africa, and the Soviet Union. The D-model, which weighed 6,000 pounds

*ABOVE: Donavon R. Berlin designed the Curtiss P-40 after developing the P-36. He later claimed that had he been permitted to design the plane as he wished, the P-40 would have been superior to the North American P-51 Mustang.*

empty, came with two .50-caliber machine guns on each wing, and could carry a 500-pound bomb load. The aircraft had a rated speed of 378 mph, a service ceiling of 38,000 ft, and a range of 240 miles. The British called P-40Ds Kittyhawks and used the aircraft mainly for tactical reconnaissance.

The P-40E Warhawk debuted in 1941, all later P-40s also became Warhawks. The range improved to 360 miles and another machine gun went on each wing, but by 1944 the aircraft's speed, altitude performance, and rate of climb had become second rate, although the durability and armoring of the aircraft were exceptional. P-40Es with a shark's mouth painted under the cowling became Flying Tigers serving with General Claire Chennault's American Volunteer Group in China.

On December 7, 1941, P-40s scored their first victories against Japan. By 1945 only one AAF fighter group still flew P-40s, but the Curtiss design left an indelible mark on the aerial combat history of World War II. In all, 13,738 P-40s were produced during the war.

## Overseas Air Routes

In June 1941, with the development of airbases on Greenland and Iceland, Arnold received permission from the war department to establish the Air Corps Ferrying Command for flying American-built aircraft to British pickup points. Colonel Robert Olds took command of the service and on July 1 Lieutenant Colonel Caleb V. Haynes flew the first plane to Scotland via Montreal and Newfoundland. During the first six months of operation, the Ferrying Command delivered 1,350 aircraft. The RAF called the route the "Arnold Line."

Because of weather conditions along the northern route, Olds opened a southern route, which, with help from Pan American Airways, stretched from Miami through Trinidad, Brazil, Gambia, and Nigeria. Pilots then flew planes across Africa and landed on British bases at Cairo, Egypt. Colonel Haynes, with Major Curtis LeMay as co-pilot, first tested the route in a B-24. After landing at Cairo, Haynes and LeMay flew to Basrah, Iraq, turned around, and followed the same route back to Bolling Field, Washington, D.C., thus completing an unprecedented 26,000-mile flight.

Efforts of the Ferrying Command led to more bases and the development of Pacific air routes to Australia. The unit remained in service throughout the war and became the nucleus for the Air Transport Command in 1942.

## Women at War

In May 1942, the army authorized the Woman's Army Auxiliary Corps (WAAC), a limited service involving clerical duties and truck driving. With the door ajar for opportunity, Nancy Harkness Love pressed the army to allow women to join the air force and qualify as pilots. After a series of political battles about a woman's role in war, the USAAF finally unlocked an immense pool of talent and with Love in command formed the Women's Auxiliary Ferrying Squadron (WAFS). Soon

LEFT: These four gals from the Women's Air Force Service Pilots (WASPs) have deplaned from a Boeing B-17 Flying Fortress during advanced training at the four-engine school at Lockbourne, England.

afterwards, and following in Love's footsteps, Jacqueline Cochran persuaded General Arnold to form the Women's Air Force Service Pilots (WASPs). While the WAFs flew planes all over the world, the WASPs piloted servicemen and supplies across the United States and to far destinations.

Women proved to be tremendous assets. They took their work seriously, became exceptionally fine pilots, served their country with resolve, and relieved thousands of men for combat duty.

## The AAF Antisubmarine Command (AAFAC)

President Roosevelt's declaration of war brought immediate reaction from German U-boats, which began menacing freighters and tankers operating in U.S. coastal waters, the Gulf of Mexico, and the Caribbean. The navy did not have the resources to cope with the problem, so on December 8, 1941, the AAF began sending aircraft on antisubmarine patrols. By January 1942, the I Bomber Command operated nine B-17s, and the I Air Support Command later added more than a hundred aircraft to the effort. The navy directed most of the operations, which involved units from the recently organized Civil Air Patrol.

On October 15, 1942, Arnold formed the AAFAC around the I Bomber Command, but by then, after

ABOVE: Having long-range capabilities, Air Force Consolidated B-24 Liberators were modified to carry microwave radar and advanced search avionics for antisubmarine operations during the Battle of the North Atlantic in 1942 and 1943.

sinking forty-six merchant ships, U-boats had been driven from the American coast. Thereafter, U-boats formed wolfpacks, shifted their operations to convoy routes in the North Atlantic, and took an enormous toll on shipping. To meet the challenge, the AAFAC grew to twenty-five squadrons, which included fifteen long-range B-24 Liberator squadrons carrying microwave radar and advanced search avionics. The Liberators operated from bases in Newfoundland, Britain, and North Africa until August 31, 1943, when the navy took over the task. By mid-1943, shore-based aircraft had destroyed more submarines than the Royal Navy and the U.S. Navy combined.

## Aircraft Alpha Designations

| Alpha Designation | Such As |
| --- | --- |
| A = Attack aircraft | A-20 Boston |
| B = Bomber aircraft | B-17 Flying Fortress |
| BT = Basic trainer | BT-15 Valiant |
| C = Cargo/Military Transport | C-47 Skytrain |
| F = Fighter aircraft | P-51 (later F-51) Mustang |
| G = Glider | G-15 Hadrian |
| P = Pursuit aircraft | P-40 Warhawk |
| PT = Primary trainer | PT-13 Kaydet |
| T = Trainer | T-6 Texan |

## B-17s to England

During President Roosevelt's Washington (Arcadia) Conference in January 1942, Winston Churchill pressed hard to open a second front in North Africa to take pressure off the British Eighth Army, which was being hammered by the German *Afrika Korps*. The United States could not respond immediately, so Arnold sent Brigadier General Ira C. Eaker to London to establish a bomber command headquarters. Eaker had been a Mitchell-man, enduring all the convolutions of the air force right along with Arnold and others. On February 1, 1942, as the first AAF B-17s and C-47s arrived in England, Eaker formed them into the VIII Bomber Command, which on February 22 officially became the Eighth Air Force. He immediately began training pilots with the RAF for combat duty. Until American troops landed in North Africa in November 1942, the war would have to be fought from British air bases.

> We won't do much talking until we've done more fighting. After we've gone, we hope you'll be glad we came.
> *General Ira Eaker's brief statement to a gathering of 2,000 at High Wycombe, England.*

## The Eighth Air Force

Major General Carl Spaatz arrived, established headquarters at the Wycombe Abbey School for Girls at Buckinghamshire (outside London), and in June 1942 assumed command of the Eighth Air Force. On July 4, six Douglas A-20 Boston pilots from the 15th Bombardment Squadron, having completed training with the RAF, flew the first mission with six British aircrews in a low-altitude attack against enemy airfields in Holland. Heavy flak brought down two A-20s and disrupted bombing accuracy, but the beginning of AAF air assaults had commenced.

ABOVE: During early B-17 bombing runs by the Eighth Air Force, most escort fighters flew above the Fortresses, but there were always a few Thunderbolts or Mustangs that tagged along at lower levels to intercept enemy aircraft hidden in the clouds.

Spaatz and Eaker put their faith in the firepower of the B-17 Flying Fortress, the quality of the crews, and the accuracy of the Norden bombsight, and told the RAF that bombing precision could be vastly improved if Fortresses flew daylight missions. The RAF expressed doubts because B-17s would have to fly deep, unescorted missions into Germany, and the Eighth Air Force had no long-range fighters. Churchill agreed with the RAF and vetoed the proposal. The RAF had tried daylight bombing with disastrous results, though admitting that at night only ten percent of the bombs fell within five miles of the target and caused enormous civilian casualties. Eaker claimed B-17s could complete their missions without escorts. His entire strategy had been based on precision daylight bombing using B-17s and B-24s with Norden bombsights, but Churchill would not let Spaatz and Eaker fly without escorts.

Spaatz launched a short trial mission on August 17, 1942, and sent seventeen B-17Es from Colonel Frank A. Armstrong's 97th Bombardment Group on the first daylight heavy bomber raid against the railroad yards at Rouen Sotteville in northwestern France. Armstrong flew in *Butcher Shop*, and General Eaker rode along in *Yankee Doodle*. Escorted by Spitfires, eleven B-17s bombed the yards with exceptional accuracy, while the other six flew a diversionary sweep. All seventeen bombers returned to England untouched. Spaatz flew ten more trial missions, losing only two planes. Clear summer skies aided bombing accuracy, and Eaker, who continued to act as observer, reported that forty percent of the bombs fell within 500 yards of the target. From this modest beginning the Eighth Air Force grew to become America's aerial powerhouse in Europe.

During September 1942, Spaatz became annoyed with Arnold's constant demands for better performance while simultaneously diverting aircraft from the Eighth to Brigadier General James H. Doolittle's Twelfth Air Force, which was being organized for the invasion of

ABOVE: Daylight bombing became an issue with the RAF because heavy bombers had to fly over enemy territory without escort planes. When North American P-51s became available and teamed up with B-24s, the long-range Liberators could fly missions with fighter cover anywhere in Germany.

North Africa. Eaker complained of never having enough planes, but Spaatz had to comply with Arnold's allocation of aircraft. After the invasion of North Africa on November 8, 1942, Arnold put Spaatz in charge of the Twelfth Air Force and air operations in the Mediterranean, and Eaker took command of the Eighth Air Force in England.

As a consequence of poor flying weather and the slow infusion of aircraft, the Eighth flew only three missions in October. By then the *Luftwaffe* had found weaknesses in B-17 formations. On October 9, when 108 bombers struck targets in Lille, northern France, German fighters shot down four B-17s and threw the others into confusion. Only nine bombs struck within 500 yards of the target.

## The Case for Daylight Bombing

In January 1943, the RAF's Air Marshal Arthur "Bomber" Harris told Eaker that Churchill was becoming upset because the Eighth had flown only twenty-three short-range, RAF-escorted, bombing missions against German bases in France and none against Germany. During the same timeframe, the RAF had sent thousands of planes against targets deep in Germany. Eaker replied that he had been blocked from daylight bombing without escorts and had yet to prove his strategy. Arnold told Eaker to take his case directly to Churchill. In a short, written brief, Eaker said, "By bombing the devils around the clock, we can prevent the German defenses from getting any rest." The simple statement sent Churchill, accompanied by

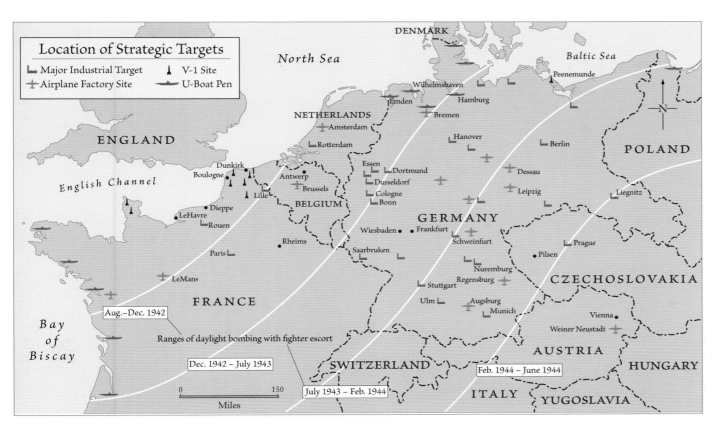

## Location of Strategic Targets

- ⌐ Major Industrial Target
- ✈ V-1 Site
- ✛ Airplane Factory Site
- ⌐ U-Boat Pen

*DENMARK*

*North Sea*

*Baltic Sea*

Peenemunde

Wilhelmshaven
Emden    Hamburg
Bremen

NETHERLANDS
Amsterdam

*ENGLAND*

Rotterdam    Hanover    Berlin

*POLAND*

*English Channel*

Dunkirk
Boulogne    Antwerp    Essen    Dortmund    Dessau
Brussels    Dusseldorf    Leipzig    Liegnitz
Lille    BELGIUM    Cologne
Dieppe    Bonn
LeHavre    *GERMANY*
Rouen
Rheims    Wiesbaden    Frankfurt
Paris    Saarbruken    Schweinfurt    Pilsen    Prague
LeMans    Nuremburg    *CZECHOSLOVAKIA*
Regensburg
Stuttgart
Ulm    Augsburg
*FRANCE*    Munich    Vienna
Weiner Neustadt

Aug.–Dec. 1942

*Bay of Biscay*

Ranges of daylight bombing with fighter escort    *AUSTRIA*

Dec. 1942 – July 1943    SWITZERLAND    *HUNGARY*

July 1943 – Feb. 1944    Feb. 1944 – June 1944

0    150
Miles    *ITALY*    *YUGOSLAVIA*

*LEFT: The first B-17 raids during the summer of 1942 flew with RAF Spitfires serving as escorts. At that time, Spitfires had an operating combat radius of 175 miles. As American fighters became available with wing and belly fuel tanks, escort ranges increased. Until then, heavy American bombers flew deep penetration daylight raids without fighter protection.*

*BELOW: This is a North American B-25G, with two .50-caliber machine guns and a 75mm M4 cannon in the nose, which was loaded manually with twenty-one rounds.*

Eaker, to the Casablanca Conference with a new point of view. Eaker made his proposal for unescorted daylight bombing and returned from Casablanca with Churchill and a "directive" listing top targets such as aircraft plants and submarine-construction facilities. Planning for daylight bombing began in earnest. With Churchill's encouragement, USAAF planners created Operation Point Blank, a combined air offensive that would ultimately destroy Germany.

On January 27, a week after Eaker's return, pilots from several airbases in eastern England knew they would be flying when at breakfast they discovered real eggs being served instead of the powdered variety. Later in the briefing room they learned this mission would be different. The chord of yarn on the big briefing map stretched across Holland and stopped at Wilhelmshaven on the North Sea, where Germany's navy built submarines. This meant a 600-mile round trip over enemy territory with partial fighter escort.

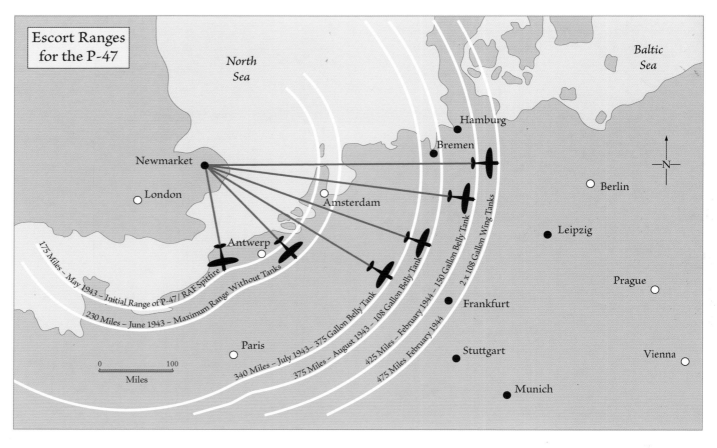

Escort Ranges for the P-47

North Sea

Baltic Sea

Hamburg

Bremen

Berlin

Newmarket

London

Amsterdam

Leipzig

Antwerp

2 x 108 Gallon Wing Tanks

150 Gallon Belly Tank

108 Gallon Belly Tank

375 Gallon Belly Tank

Maximum Range Without Tanks

Initial Range of P-47/RAF Spitfire

175 Miles – May 1943

230 Miles – June 1943

340 Miles – July 1943

375 Miles – August 1943

425 Miles – February 1944

475 Miles February 1944

Prague

Frankfurt

Paris

Stuttgart

Vienna

Munich

N

0       100
Miles

Flyers climbed into fleece-lined flight suits, which never quite kept them warm, and gathered their parachute harnesses, oxygen masks, and an escape kit containing a packet of foreign currency, which could be useful should they be shot down.

Ninety-one Fortresses and Liberators took off from several airfields and at 20,000 feet formed over the North Sea. More than a hundred *Luftwaffe* fighters met the bombers as they passed over Holland into Germany. Only fifty-one bombers reached Wilhelmshaven. Three were shot down, and the others

**LEFT: Accidents happened in the frenetic activity of a bombing run over Europe. Here, a bomb from a B-17 in an upper formation crashes through the port stabilizer of a Fortress in a lower formation.**

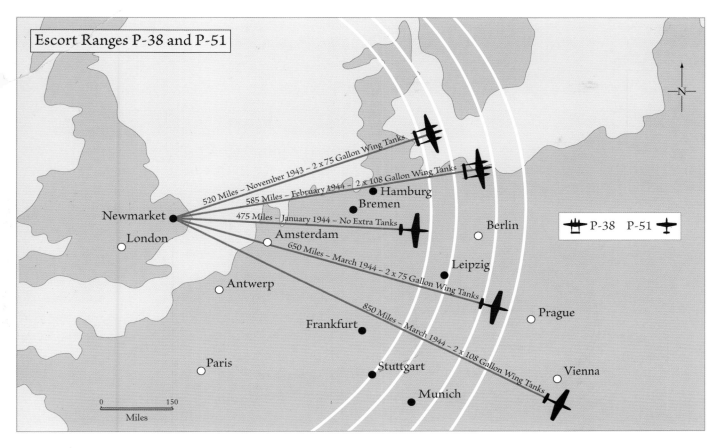

Escort Ranges P-38 and P-51

520 Miles – November 1943 – 2 x 75 Gallon Wing Tanks
585 Miles – February 1944 – 2 x 108 Gallon Wing Tanks
475 Miles – January 1944 – No Extra Tanks
650 Miles – March 1944 – 2 x 75 Gallon Wing Tanks
850 Miles – March 1944 – 2 x 108 Gallon Wing Tanks

Newmarket
London
Amsterdam
Antwerp
Paris
Frankfurt
Stuttgart
Munich
Hamburg
Bremen
Berlin
Leipzig
Prague
Vienna

P-38   P-51

0   150
Miles

LEFT: In November 1943 the Eighth Air Force began using P-38 Lightnings as escorts because of the aircraft's 520-mile operating radius, which exceeded the combat range of P-47 Thunderbolts. When P-51 Mustangs became available in January 1944, the aircraft could fly, without wing tanks, the maximum operating radius of Thunderbolts. With wing tanks, the P-51 eventually eclipsed all fighter aircraft with an 850-mile operating radius, making it possible to escort heavy bombers almost anywhere over Germany.

turned back due to damage or mechanical problems. Over Wilhelmshaven, clouds partly covered the shipyard. Despite the claims of some, most observers admitted the U-boat pens had not been hit. Gunners firing from turrets downed seven German fighters. Flyers returned in high spirits, being the first Americans in the Eighth Air Force to drop bombs on Germany. The celebration did not last. A month later Eaker sent B-17s back to Wilhelmshaven to finish the job. This time *Luftwaffe* fighters were prepared and downed seven bombers.

During April, Eaker sent 115 Fortresses to bomb an aircraft factory at Bremen. Sixteen planes failed to return. Having seldom more than a hundred bombers, Eaker could not lose aircraft at the rate of fifteen percent per mission.

What Eaker needed were long-range fighter escorts. British Spitfires and American P-47 Thunderbolts had about a 175-mile action radius, and the first North American P-51C Mustangs were just beginning to arrive in England. With souped-up Rolls-Royce Merlin V-1650-3 engines, P-51s could clock a maximum speed of 437 mph and had a 475-mile radius of operation. With two 75-gallon wing tanks, the radius increased to 650 miles. Later, when 108-gallon wing tanks became available, the radius increased to 850 miles. P-51s carried six .50-caliber machine guns and up to two 1,000-pound bombs or six 5-inch rockets. As fighter-escorts, the Mustangs outmatched Messerschmitt Bf-109s and Focke-Wulf Fw-190s, but during combat the P-51 silhouette looked strikingly similar to a Bf-109, making friendly fire a problem. Even with protective air cover, many German industrial cities lay outside the range of Mustangs, leaving bomber crews to deal with enemy fighters and survive merciless flak near the targets.

| Eighth Air Force Awards | |
| --- | --- |
| Medals of Honor | 17 |
| Distinguished Service Crosses | 220 |
| Air Medals | 442,000 |
| Fighter aces | 261 |
| Enlisted gunner aces | 305 |

## Lessons Learned

Eaker's officers became catalysts for change. Hard-driving Colonel Curtis LeMay, caustically known by his men as "Iron Ass," began studying air tactics. LeMay did not like the loose RAF night formations, so he designed the "combat box" flying formation, tightly bunching B-17s to maximize defensive firepower. With as many as twenty-one bombers staggered vertically and horizontally, machine guns from every plane could fire on attacking aircraft without being boxed-out. On large raids, three boxes formed a combat wing. One group took the lead and the other two followed, one a thousand feet higher, the other a thousand feet lower.

Another LeMay innovation improved bombing accuracy. He put the most proficient crews at the head of each combat box. When the bombardier in the lead

**ABOVE: Generals Ira Eaker (right) and Carl Spaatz were both instrumental in bringing the Eighth Air Force to England, but it was Eaker who convinced Winston Churchill and the RAF of the merits of daylight bombing.**

### General Ira Clarence Eaker (1896–1987)

Born at Field Creek, Texas, on April 13, 1896, Ira Eaker graduated from Southeastern States Teachers College, Oklahoma, in 1917 and obtained a commission in the infantry. Transferred to the Aviation Section of the Signal Corps in November, Eaker became a pilot and in 1919 began his flying career commanding a detachment from the 2nd Aero Squadron in the Philippines.

Eaker began attracting attention in the 1920s by making the longest non-stop flight in a DH.4. He earned the Distinguished Flying Cross for piloting a Pan-American amphibian plane around South America, and received an Oak Leaf Cluster for establishing a new endurance record as chief pilot of the *Question Mark*. Despite his accomplishments, Eaker did not rise rapidly in the ranks because he agreed too vociferously with Billy Mitchell's opposition to the army's position on airpower.

Promoted to major in 1935, Eaker graduated from the Air Corps Tactical School in 1936, after which he and Hap Arnold made the first transcontinental flight purely on instruments. After graduating from the Command and General Staff School in 1937, he worked in the office of chief of the Air Corps with Arnold, with whom he wrote three books, the most notable of which was *Winged Warfare*, published in 1941.

Eaker became a colonel in 1941 and commanded the 20th Pursuit Group at Mitchell Field. Promoted brigadier general in January 1942, he went to England in July to head the VIII Bomber Command. On August 17 he led the first B-17 raid on Rouen, France, rose in rank to major general, and in December assumed command of the Eighth Air Force. He directed a sustained precision bombing campaign against Germany and was the key figure at the Casablanca Conference in convincing Churchill of the merits of daylight "round-the-clock" bombing.

Arnold placed his colleague wherever organization, energy, ingenuity, and leadership were needed. In January 1944, as lieutenant general and commander of the Mediterranean Allied Air Forces, Eaker planned the first shuttle-bombing raids on Germany from Italy to Russia, and in June led the first one himself. In 1945 he became deputy commander of the Army Air Forces and chief of the Air Staff. In August 1947 he retired to become active in the aircraft industry and was still involved in aviation when he died at Andrews Air Force Base, Maryland, on August 6, 1987.

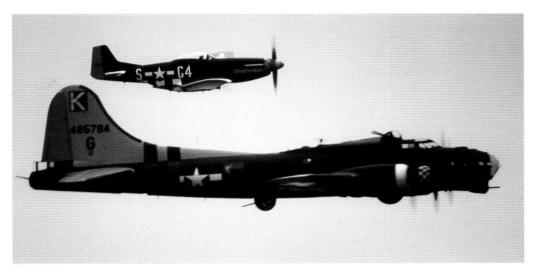

*LEFT: B-17Gs, part of a much larger formation, during daylight operations against German submarine yards at Wilhelmshaven on Jade Bay.*

*RIGHT: Boeing B-17Gs arrived in England in different color patterns, some unpainted, others in olive drab with light camouflage. Wherever Fortresses went, P-51 Mustangs followed, some wearing paint, and some not. Tail and fuselage markings designated groups and squadrons.*

plane sighted the target and released his bombs, the other planes dropped their payloads at the same time. The bombs landed in closely packed patterns and created havoc in one spot rather than falling miles away.

New instruments, such as automatic flight control equipment (AFCE), enabled the bombardier to control the plane during the bombing run by activating a switch on the Norden bombsight. When using this system over Vegesack, Germany, on March 18, 1943, ninety-seven planes dropped seventy-six per cent of their bombs within a thousand feet of the submarine base and destroyed seven U-boats and two-thirds of the shipyard.

In September 1943 the 482nd Bomb Group used the H2S, an improved, British-developed radar blind-bombing system, during the Emden raid. Because the device worked so well, the Massachusetts Institute of Technology's radiation laboratory hand-built twenty units from a sample to get the H2S in service faster. The homemade H2S fit nicely into the B-17's new "double-chin" nose geometry. Radar technology allowed the Eighth Air Force to fly in thick weather against readily readable targets because landforms and waterways could be distinguished through cloud cover.

High altitude flying impaired accuracy. At 26,000 ft flyers became so cold they could not stop shaking, so the air force began replacing leather fleece-lined clothing with electric flying suits with built-in heaters that could be plugged into aircraft receptacles. And to reduce injury from enemy fire, flyers also began wearing flak vests made of two-inch-square overlapped plates attached to heavy canvas.

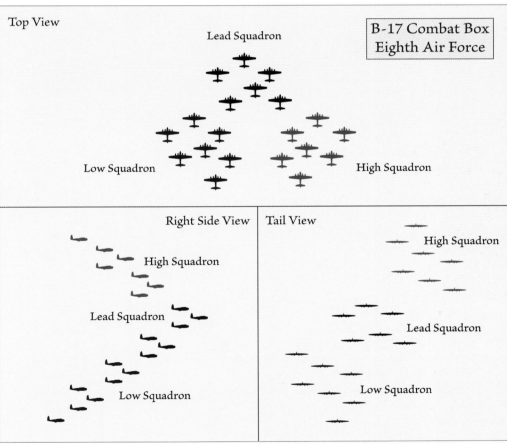

*ABOVE: During the daylight bombing campaign, General LeMay experimented with a variety of combat boxes to maximize a B-17 formation's firepower. A combat box consisted of eighteen to twenty-one planes staggered vertically and horizontally. On large raids, three such boxes formed a combat wing with one box in the lead and the other two boxes stacked, with one a thousand feet higher and the other a thousand feet lower.*

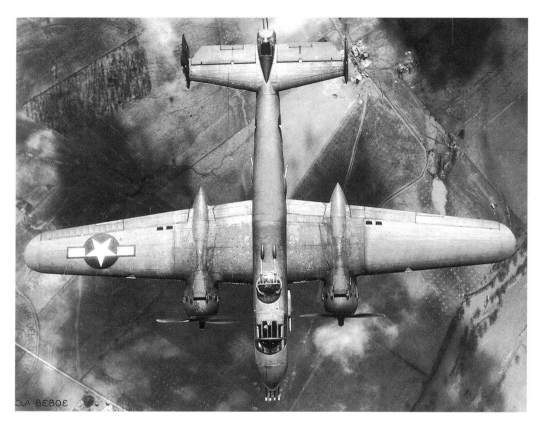

ABOVE: The B-25 Mitchell was named after the fearless and tiresome (to officialdom) "Billy," and was made by North American, which had no experience of twin-engined aircraft, bombers, or high-performance warplanes, yet it has often been described as the best aircraft in its class.

RIGHT: During a heavy raid on Berlin on April 10, 1943, a German Me-262 jet fighter shot the wing off a B-17, but the mission caught the enemy off guard and destroyed 284 Luftwaffe planes on the ground and twenty-one in the air.

## Ramping up Operations: Regensburg-Schweinfurt

When the buildup for the Allied invasion of Normandy began, General Arnold pledged to bring the Eighth Air Force to parity with the RAF. By July 1943, Eaker had received 1,000 bombers with almost an equal number of combat crews. Six months later the force would double, but Arnold wanted immediate action.

During August, Eaker developed plans for a dual sweep against Hitler's aircraft industry. The first task force would fly 300 miles into Germany and bomb the Messerschmitt works at Regensburg and Wiener Neustadt, which together built about half of the *Luftwaffe's* single-engine fighters. A second task force would fly 200 miles into Germany, well behind the Regensburg formation, and strike Schweinfurt, which produced half of the enemy's ball bearings. The plan called for the first task force, after bombing Regensburg, to fly south to bases in Algeria, thereby drawing off enemy fighters and clearing the way for the Schweinfurt raid.

On the morning of August 17, the Regensburg force of 146 bombers took off from bases in England. As soon as the escorts turned back near the Belgium-Germany border, droves of enemy fighters struck the formations and for ninety minutes never let up. German controllers brought in fighters from as far away as the Baltic, and spotters told them when, where, and how to strike. *Luftwaffe* pilots used new tactics for penetrating LeMay's combat box. They struck the upper squadron by diving and the lower squadron by approaching head-on and sweeping under the bombers. German flyers downed twenty-four B-17s but made one mistake. Not anticipating so deep a strike, the enemy planes began running out of gas and few were airborne when the B-17s struck Regensburg. The unexpected raid damaged every Messerschmitt plant in Regensburg. German pilots refueled and waited along the route back to England to attack the returning bombers, but the B-17s flew over the Alps and landed unopposed in Africa.

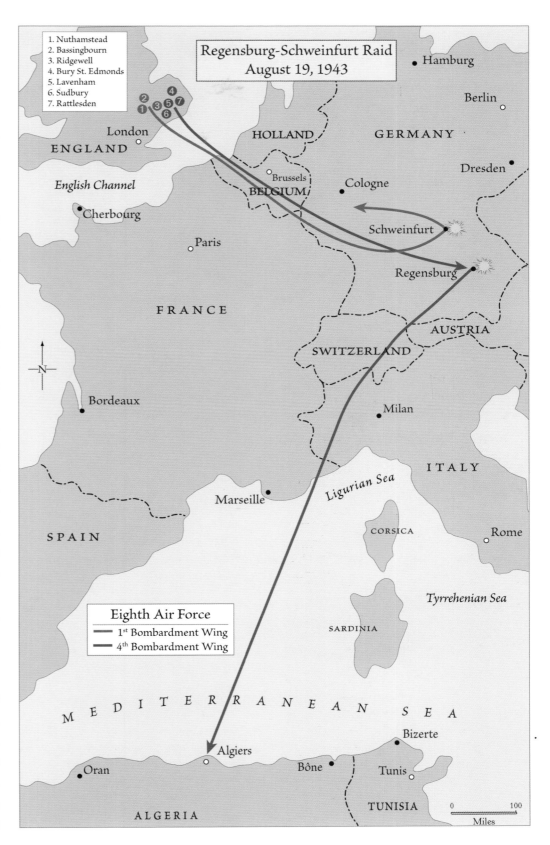

*RIGHT: Early on the morning of August 17, 1943, 146 B-17 bombers departed from England to strike Regensburg. The original plan called for another 230 B-17s to follow along the same route about thirty minutes later and strike Schweinfurt, but because of poor weather the second formation did not depart for several hours. The delay made it possible for the same German fighters that engaged the Regensburg formations to engage the Schweinfurt formations. The raid cost the Eighth Air Force ninety-four Fortresses.*

Regensburg-Schweinfurt Raid
August 19, 1943

1. Nuthamstead
2. Bassingbourn
3. Ridgewell
4. Bury St. Edmonds
5. Lavenham
6. Sudbury
7. Rattlesden

Eighth Air Force
— 1ˢᵗ Bombardment Wing
— 4ᵗʰ Bombardment Wing

Because of unfavorable weather, the Schweinfurt force lost three hours getting airborne. By the time the planes crossed the German border, enemy pilots were rested and ready to fly. Relentless attacks occurred as the bombers approached the Rhineland and continued until the task force was over the North Sea and homeward bound. Of 230 bombers, thirty-six were lost and dozens crippled. Despite broken formations and chaos in the skies, the task force scored eighty direct hits on Schweinfurt's two principal ball bearing plants.

The Regensburg-Schweinfurt raid struck a serious blow to the *Luftwaffe's* ability to keep planes in the air and marked the beginning of hundreds of raids that carried B-17s, B-24s, and RAF bombers deep into Germany, East Prussia, and Poland. Despite efforts to hit military and industrial targets and not civilian neighborhoods, accidents happened. Many cities sustained severe damage. The success of missions into Germany were best illustrated on D-Day, June 6, 1944, when Allied forces went ashore in Normandy with negligible interference from the *Luftwaffe*.

## U.S. Strategic Air Forces

In January 1944, the Eighth in England and the Fifteenth in Italy were organized under a centralized headquarters at Bushey Hall, London, as the United States Strategic Air Forces (USSTAF). The centralization occurred when General Dwight D. Eisenhower came to London to plan Operation Overlord, the invasion of Normandy. General Spaatz returned from the Mediterranean to take command of the USSTAF, Major General Jimmy Doolittle took command of the Eighth at High Wycombe, and Major General Nathan Twining took command of the Fifteenth.

By mid-1944, the Eighth reached a total strength of 200,000 officers and enlisted, and at peak strength operated forty heavy bomber groups, fifteen fighter

## General Carl A. Spaatz (1891–1974)

Born in Boyertown, Pennsylvania, on June 29, 1891, as Carl Andrew Spatz, the future general carried the original spelling of his last name when he graduated from West Point in 1914. At age forty-five he changed to Spaatz. By then he had won the Distinguished Flying Cross for shooting down two enemy planes in a single combat in 1918 and the Distinguished Service Cross when commanding the *Question Mark* during an endurance flight over Los Angeles in 1929. To friends, Spaatz was simply known as "Tooey," a nickname acquired at West Point.

Like Billy Mitchell, Spaatz became an advocate of airpower, graduating in the 1930s from the Air Corps Technical School and the Command and General Staff School. In 1940, Hap Arnold sent Spaatz to Great Britain as a special military observer and subsequently promoted him to brigadier general and chief of staff. While in London, Spaatz began planning AAF operations, after which he returned to the United States to organize the Eighth Air Force.

In 1943, after the invasion of North Africa, Arnold sent Spaatz to take command of the Twelfth Air Force in the Mediterranean. When General Eisenhower moved to London to plan Operation Overlord, he brought Spaatz along to take command of the U.S. Strategic Air Forces, which consisted of the Eighth and Fifteenth. For the remainder of the war Spaatz oversaw USAAF strategic operations, first in Europe and then in the Pacific. After the war, he succeeded Arnold as chief of staff and in September 1947 became the first chief of the independent USAF. After forty-four years of service, Spaatz retired in 1948 to serve as chairman of the Civil Air Patrol.

***ABOVE: General Carl A. Spaatz (center), commanding general of the USAAF, and deputy commander Lieutenant General Ira C. Eaker (right) witness President Harry S. Truman signing a proclamation establishing August 1, 1946, as Air Force Day.***

***ABOVE: An Air Transport Command Douglas C-47 Skytrain, operating in conjunction with the Ninth Air Force, flies in urgent supplies and materials from the United States to strategic distribution centers in Egypt.***

groups, and four specialized support groups. During the "Big Week" offensive—the assault on Germany's aircraft industry—as many as 2,000 Allied heavy bombers and more than 1,000 fighters joined in a single mission.

During operations in Europe, the Eighth Air Force suffered 47,000 casualties, including more than 26,000 killed—roughly half of all other USAAF commands combined. Germany surrendered in April 1945 and in July the Eighth began moving to Okinawa, but the war ended before the bomb wing arrived.

## The Ninth Air Force

Delays in getting the Eighth Air Force operational in England were complicated by the urgency of invading North Africa, taking control of Vichy French possessions, and defeating General Erwin Rommel's *Afrika Korps*. The Germans had been driving across the Libyan desert towards Cairo, and the only American planes in North Africa were a detachment of Colonel Harry A. Halverson's twenty-three B-24D Liberator heavy bombers at Khartoum, which were supposed to fly to China. Instead, an urgent appeal from Churchill sent the B-24s to Fayid, Egypt, where on June 12, 1942, thirteen Liberators from Halverson's detachment bombed the oil refineries at Ploesti, Romania, without causing much damage. Returning from the mission and short of fuel, B-24 pilots landed in Iraq, Syria, or Turkey. The raid earned the distinction of being the first mission flown by Americans in the European theater.

Meanwhile, Brigadier General Lewis H. Brereton arrived in the Middle East from India on June 28 with a handful of B-17s and activated the U.S. Army Middle East Air Force at Cairo, which five months later became the Ninth Air Force. By August 1942 Brereton's command consisted of the 98th (Heavy) Bombardment Group, the 12th (Medium) Bombardment Group, and the 57th Fighter Group. In September, B-17s and B-24s of the 98th began clobbering Rommel's ports and supply lines. P-40s from the 57th and B-25s from the 12th went into action alongside the RAF's Desert Air Force in support of Lieutenant General Bernard L. Montgomery's Eighth Army. During the crucial battle of El Alamein (October 24–November 5), the Ninth Air Force bombed and strafed the enemy, and helped the RAF drive the *Afrika Korps* into the desert, through Libya, and toward Allied forces occupying French North Africa.

By the end of 1942, 320 bombers and fighters had been ferried to the Ninth Air Force, along with fifty

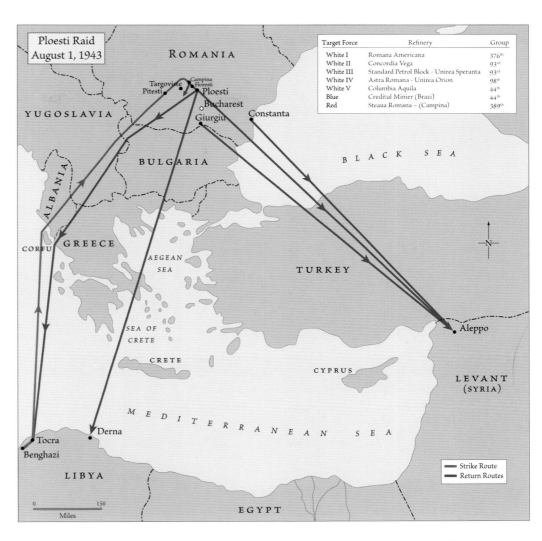

| Target Force | Refinery | Group |
|---|---|---|
| White I | Romana Americana | 376th |
| White II | Concordia Vega | 93rd |
| White III | Standard Petrol Block - Unirea Speranta | 93rd |
| White IV | Astra Romana - Unirea Orion | 98th |
| White V | Columbia Aquila | 44th |
| Blue | Creditul Minier (Brazi) | 44th |
| Red | Steaua Romana – (Campina) | 389th |

C-47 transports that Brereton used for local air service. When not attacking the *Afrika Korps*, pilots interdicted German supplies by targeting shipping and port facilities in Libya, Tunisia, Sicily, Italy, Crete, and Greece.

In February 1943, when Rommel's *Afrika Korps* mounted an offensive in Tunisia and pushed into Kasserine Pass, Brereton sent the Ninth to join the Twelfth in breaking up the offensive. With control of the air established, Allied forces began pushing the *Afrika Korps* into pockets around Bizerte and Tunis. General von Arnim, who had replaced Rommel, surrendered on May 10, enabling the Allies to use Tunisia for staging the invasion of Sicily.

*ABOVE: The raid on the oil refineries at Ploesti, Romania, began with 177 B-24 Liberators flying out of Benghazi, Libya, on August 1, 1943. Fifty-four B-24s were lost, and only fifty-five returned to Libya. Because of damage and fuel problems, the other Liberators took shorter return routes and landed in Aleppo, Syria, and other Middle East airfields.*

**LEFT: Flying barely above treetop level and in the face of intense antiaircraft fire, B-24 Liberators out of North Africa strike the strategic petroleum and gasoline refineries at Ploesti.**

**ABOVE: Despite careful pre-assignment of targets, Liberator pilots became befuddled by the terrain and dropped their bombs haphazardly, often through waves of black, sooty smoke and heavy flak.**

## The Ploesti Raid (Operation Tidal Wave)

During the war, the USAAF flew twenty-two missions against the huge Romanian oil and refinery complex at Ploesti, which had been earmarked as a strategic target at the Casablanca Conference. The Eighth Air Force, being 1,300 miles away, could not reach Ploesti. Neither could the Northwest African Air Forces (NAAF). So Brereton's Ninth Air Force drew the assignment, but all he could muster were two B-24 bomber groups. General Spaatz made up the difference by lending Brereton three bomber groups from the Eighth Air Force. Bomb group commanders were all veterans, and many of the flyers had already flown twenty-five missions

Brereton's planners opted for a low-level strike and replaced Norden bombsights with simple mechanical sights. The ground crew altered top turrets to fire straight ahead and mounted extra machine guns on the aircraft noses. Because of the distance to Ploesti, two auxiliary fuel tanks were installed in bomb bays, raising the plane's 2,480-gallon capacity to 3,100. For several weeks B-24 pilots practiced flying wingtip-to-wingtip, stirring up clouds of sand as they dropped dummy bombs a few yards above the desert's surface. Instead of studying reconnaissance photos, flyers familiarized themselves with landmarks as they would appear from treetop level.

### The Ploesti Raid Bomb Groups

| Unit | Air Force | Commander |
| --- | --- | --- |
| 44th Bomb Group | 8th | Colonel Leon Johnson |
| 93rd Bomb Group | 8th | Lt. Col. Addison Baker |
| 98th Bomb Group | 9th | Colonel John Kane |
| 376th Bomb Group | 9th | Colonel K. K. Compton |
| 389th Bomb Group | 8th | Colonel Jack Wood |

At 7:00 A.M. on August 1, 1943, a total of 177 Liberators, less one that crashed on takeoff, headed for the island of Corfu, where they would turn northeast toward Ploesti. German intelligence in Greece had cracked the Ninth's code, knew a large force from Libya was airborne, and alerted fighter squadrons.

Despite careful planning, bomb groups became separated in heavy overcast. Some turned too soon and approached Bucharest instead of Ploesti, thus putting Romania's entire defense system on alert. Fifty-four bombers became completely lost, and only six B-24s from the 376th hit their assigned targets. Other groups dropped bombs on targets of opportunity, most of which had been assigned to another group. The 44th (Johnson) and 98th (Kane) had the misfortune of running down opposite sides of a railroad and were hit hard by a German flak train. Johnson and Kane flew through exploding tanks of fuel and bombed each other's targets. The 389th arrived on the scene with its force intact and destroyed the refinery at Campina. As low-flying Liberators roared through smoke and flames, German fighters struck from above and antiaircraft blasted from below.

Forty-one bombers went down over Ploesti, and another thirteen were lost along the way. Photos showed forty-two percent of Ploesti's refinery capacity destroyed. Because of a crude oil shortage, Ploesti had been running at about sixty percent capacity. Within a few days German engineers had the refineries back in business, and Ploesti remained untouched for eight months. By the end of the war, some 7,500 Allied bombers had dropped 13,469 tons of bombs and lost 350 planes in an effort to destroy Ploesti's refineries, but neither the Ninth Air Force nor the Fifteenth Air Force ever put the facility completely out of business, though they tried.

had been P-38 Lightnings, P-40s, and P-47s, but against Germany Brereton wanted P-51s. So did the Eighth Air Force, and a new competition for Mustangs ensued between Eaker (later Twining) and Brereton.

**D-Day—Operation Overlord**

Brereton eventually received everything he wanted, and more. In England, during the buildup to the invasion of Normandy, the Ninth Air Force grew at a brisk rate. By the end of May 1944, Brereton commanded more than 200,000 men with forty-five groups operating more than 5,000 aircraft, including P-47 Thunderbolts, P-51 Mustangs, and night-fighting P-61 Black Widows.

*LEFT: The North American P-51D model with the one-piece sliding bubble canopy for better visibility began superseding earlier models in 1944, and quickly became the standard fighter for the USAAF Eighth Fighter Command.*

## End of Mediterranean Operations

After the defeat of the *Afrika Korps* in May 1943, the Ninth Air Force concentrated on bombing airfields and railroad centers in Sicily and Italy from bases in Libya. During the invasion of Sicily, C-47 transports carried paratroopers and flew supplies and reinforcements to ground units. After the Italian Armistice on September 3, Brereton began moving units from the Ninth into the Twelfth Air Force. On October 16, 1943, he deactivated command headquarters in Egypt and relocated the Ninth in Burtonwood, England, where the unit became part of Spaatz's USSTAF. Fighter strength of the Ninth

*LEFT: Northrop originally designed the P-61 Black Widow as a night fighter for the RAF. The later B-model carried four underwing hardpoints for bombs or drop tanks. The heavy aircraft first entered service over Cherbourg in 1944 but never met performance expectations.*

The Ninth's first mission out of England supported Operation Point Blank, the smashing of the *Luftwaffe* in the air and on the ground. The strikes were flown in preparation for the Ninth's major role during Overlord: direct tactical support of ground troops during the invasion of Normandy. Meanwhile, air groups used the time to sharpen their skills by striking enemy rail facilities, airfields, industrial plants, and military installations in France, Belgium, and the Netherlands.

On D-Day, June 6, 1944, the Ninth's IX Troop Carrier Command flew parachute and glider missions and carried out massive air attacks with P-47s, P-51s,

*LEFT: The Republic P-47D served with the Ninth Fighter Command in Africa and the Eighth Fighter Command in England.*

ABOVE: Still wearing invasion stripes from Operation Overlord, Martin B-26Bs from the 398th Bombardment Group overfly Allied supply ships on June 26, 1944, while on a combat mission near Caen, France.

and tactical B-25 Mitchell and B-26 Marauder medium bombers. During morning troop landings, P-38 Lightnings provided close air support over the beaches. The greatly diminished *Luftwaffe* flew only 250 sorties compared with 14,000 flown by the Allies. The Ninth eventually covered operations at Cherbourg, Caen, and General George Patton's Third Army breakout into central France.

In August, Lieutenant General Hoyt S. Vandenberg took command of the Ninth Air Force, and Brereton took over the First Allied Airborne Army. The Ninth became the operational air force for the Twelfth Army Group and was assigned to the Tactical Air Command, which supported specific ground armies. In August 1944, units from the Ninth participated in Operation Dragoon (the invasion of southern France), Operation Market Garden, (the airborne assault on the upper bridges of the Rhine), the Battle of the Bulge, and Operation Varsity (the March 1945 crossing of the Rhine).

Vandenberg continued to fly strikes over western Germany until May 7, when hostilities ended. By the time it was deactivated in December 1945, the Ninth had become the largest tactical air force in the world.

## The Twelfth Air Force

During the summer of 1942, General Arnold created the Twelfth Air Force for Operation Torch, the Allied invasion of North Africa. The unit was activated at Bolling Field on August 20, 1942, and placed under the command of Brigadier General James Harold "Jimmy" Doolittle with (then-Colonel) Vandenberg as chief of staff. Although the unit formed in the United States, more than half of the aircraft and personnel came from combat-experienced units of the Eighth Air Force in England.

experience before moving onto other battlefields. Eisenhower gave Doolittle less then three months to organize the Twelfth, put it in fighting trim, and transport the American-based portion to North Africa for combat operations.

On November 8, Allied troops went ashore in the first major amphibious operation in the European theater. The only AAF unit to get into action was the 31st Fighter Group flying Spitfires out of Gibraltar. Algiers fell on November 8; Oran on the 10th; and French forces in Morocco surrendered on the 11th after being hassled by air strikes from carrier-based aircraft. Hitler reinforced Tunisia, the Allied attack stalled, and the battle for North Africa began for Doolittle's Twelfth Air Force.

The Casablanca Conference held on January 14, 1943, between Roosevelt and Churchill produced a new command structure involving two American air units: the Twelfth Air Force as part of the Northwest African Air Forces, and the Ninth Air Force as part of the Middle East Air Forces. Both units were located in areas where combat experience could be gained before moving against the enemy's powerful air arsenal in Italy and Germany.

*LEFT: Invasion-striped P-38 Lightnings fly into France during mid-June, 1944, to attack German positions still clustered among hedgerows. The lead formation is in finger fours; the second and somewhat higher squadron is in box formation.*

*ABOVE: Douglas C-47 Skytrains from the 9th Troop Carrier Command transport paratroopers for the invasion of Holland and the opening of Operation Market Garden on September 17, 1944.*

Appointed to overall command of Operation Torch, Eisenhower went to London to plan the invasion of Algeria. In September the combined chiefs of staff decided to also invade the coast of French Morocco and capture Casablanca. Like Algeria, the Vichy army held French Morocco and nobody could be certain whether the French would fight or lay down their weapons. Doolittle hoped there would be fighting because the Moroccan cities along the Atlantic coast contained shipping, troop concentrations, supply dumps, and armored columns that could give the Twelfth combat

RIGHT: Gunner Sergeant William Watts fires his .50-caliber machine gun at a German plane passing under the B-17 during a flight over Germany. Another gunner standing behind him operates his machine gun from the side door.

ABOVE: Activated in England on February 1, 1942, "The Mighty Eighth" Air Force carried out daytime bombing operations from airfields in eastern England from July 4, 1942, until the end of the war.

BELOW: The Ninth Air Force evolved from the Middle East Air Forces in Egypt on November 12, 1942, as both a strategic and a tactical command for gaining air superiority in North Africa, Sicily, and Normandy.

## Operations in North Africa

In February 1943, Eisenhower moved all the Anglo-American air commands in North Africa into a single organization, the Northwest African Air Forces (NAAF), headed by Spaatz. Doolittle commanded the Northwest African Strategic Air Force, which consisted mainly of the Twelfth's bomb groups, and Air Vice Marshal Sir Arthur Coningham commanded the Northwest African Tactical Air Force, which included Brereton's Ninth Air Force, the RAF Desert Air Force, and other RAF units.

Most of Doolittle's Twelfth consisted of heavy bombers, which spent more time bombing targets in Sicily and Italy than flying missions over North Africa. When Doolittle discovered that his P-38 Lightning fighter groups, which had been sent to Africa for their range, endurance, and versatility, were taking a beating in the desert war, Arnold sent him all the reserve P-38s from the Eighth Air Force. When the *Afrika Korps* struck the Kasserine Pass, Doolittle ordered up anything with wings. B-17s and B-24s thundered overhead at low altitude and clobbered German positions. The air assault helped shatter the enemy attack, forcing Rommel to withdraw to Cap Bon, the only escape route available.

The Twelfth's tactical air power, augmented by A-20s, A-26s, and B-25s, chased the enemy assiduously, sank the Axis ships, and shot down enemy supply planes flying out of Italy. In one air operation over the Mediterranean, known as the "Palm Sunday Massacre" of April 18, four squadrons of 57th Fighter Group P-40s shot down more than sixty Junkers Ju-52 transports attempting to relieve enemy troops in Tunisia. In early May, after being hassled by more than 2,000 sorties a day, the Germans attempted to break out along the coastal plain. Penned against the sea on May 10, 1943, 270,000 Axis troops surrendered.

### Sicily—Operation Husky

During the last weeks of the North African campaign, the NAAF began bombing the island of Pantelleria, an Axis base that lay in the Straits of Sicily off the coast of Tunisia. Spaatz wanted the island's airfield, which could service four-engined bombers and had a 1,100-ft underground hangar capable of holding eighty fighters. On June 11, after clobbering the island for a month and dropping 6,200 tons of bombs, the 10,000-man Axis garrison surrendered. Air action alone accounted for Pantelleria's capitulation.

Prior to June, heavy bombers from the Twelfth had been making regular strikes on Sicily's airfields. By early July all but a handful of the island's thirty-one airfields had been destroyed. When on July 9–10 the Allies went ashore on Sicily, the enemy had lost 1,000 planes and flown the remaining 300 to Italy. The assault opened with large-scale airborne operations. Douglas C-47s blemished an otherwise successful assault by dropping elements from the 505th Parachute Infantry into the sea. Other paratroops were scattered about the countryside, and some were shot by friendly fire. The NAAF flew 5,000 combat sorties, maintained complete air supremacy, and concentrated mainly on enemy ground positions. Patton's Seventh Army and Montgomery's British Eighth Army fought under a

| The Twelfth Air Force | | | | | |
|---|---|---|---|---|---|
| | Bomb Wings | Fighter Wings | Bomb Groups | Fighter Groups | Recon Groups |
| The XII Bomber Command* | 4 | 0 | 25 | 12 | 1 |
| The XII Tactical Air Command† | 3 | 1 | 12 | 8 | 0 |

\* Served in combat from November 1, 1942 to March 1, 1944
† Served in combat from November 9, 1942 to May, 1945

canopy of Allied aircraft. Thirty-eight days later the Germans retreated across the Straits of Messina to Italy.

### Invasion of Italy

While Montgomery's Eighth Army pursued retreating Germans into Italy and drove northward toward Foggia, General Mark W. Clark's U.S. Fifth Army landed at Salerno on September 9, one day after Italy's surrender. The NAAF retained tactical control of the air, but German ground troops took over Italian positions and fought fiercely at Salerno. On September 14, when Clark considered withdrawing, Spaatz threw in the Twelfth Air Force and every air command at his disposal. The NAAF flew 3,400 sorties, and bombers from the Twelfth dropped the equivalent of 760 tons of munitions per square mile on enemy positions. The Fifth Army finally broke out of its beachhead and on October 1 liberated Naples.

On January 22, 1944, Clark landed another invasion force unopposed at Anzio and Nettuno, about fifty miles south of Rome. Instead of pressing inland, he dallied bringing troops and supplies ashore and gave the Germans time to reinforce the area. The Fifth Army was about to be pushed back into the sea when bomb groups from the Fifteenth Air Force, made up of units from the XII Bomber Command, put on one of the biggest air shows in the campaign and enabled the Fifth Army to secure its position for operations during the spring.

*ABOVE: Activated in mid-1942 to support Operation Torch in North Africa, the Twelfth Air Force remained in the Mediterranean theater and later served with distinction in Sicily, Italy, and southern France.*

*BELOW: Organized on November 1, 1943, as a strategic command, the Fifteenth Air Force commenced combat missions from bases in southern Italy on the very first day of its formation.*

Spaatz pulled Doolittle out of the Mediterranean in January, promoted him to lieutenant general, and put him in charge of the Eighth Air Force in England. He then sent Eaker to Italy to take command of the Mediterranean Allied Air Forces (MAAF), which consisted of the Twelfth Air Force, commanded by Major General John K. Cannon, and the recently arrived Fifteenth Air Force, commanded by Major General Nathan F. Twining.

## Operation Strangle—Liberation of Rome

Prior to Eaker's arrival in the Mediterranean, the Germans had stalled the Allied advance on the Gustav Line, a heavily fortified position that stretched across Italy from Gaeta on the Tyrrhenian Sea to Pescara on the Adriatic Sea. In the center of the line stood Monte Cassino and St. Benedict's Abbey, a sacred site that the Allies believed the Germans used for observation, communications, and sniping. On February 15, Eaker sent a force of 254 bombers from the Twelfth and Fifteenth, dropped 576 tons of bombs on Monte Cassino, and destroyed the abbey. Operation Strangle began after the air strikes failed to breach an opening through the Gustav Line.

On March 15 the entire Twelfth Air Force, together with 300 B-17s and B-24s from the Fifteenth, dropped 1,400 tons of mostly 1,000-pound bombs on Cassino. The blasts shattered every building, turned bricks and

ABOVE: During operations against the German fortified lines at Cassino, four P-51 Mustangs from the 332nd Fighter Group fly in formation above their air base at Ramitelli, Italy.

ABOVE: Flying out of air bases in Italy on March 19, 1945, a B-24 Liberator from the Fifteenth Air Force releases it bombs on railroad yards at Muhldorf, Germany, while other Liberators ascend the Alps to strike vital rail lines from Vienna to Munich.

stone to dust, and left a lunar landscape where the town stood. Allied ground forces had to clear away the debris before advancing. The delay proved costly. Rain fell, the landscape turned to mud, flying weather worsened, and Field Marshal Albert Kesselring's fifteen German divisions at the front continued to block Allied advances into central Italy.

During clear days from late-March to mid-May, fighter-bombers flew 65,000 sorties and crippled the Italian transportation system, blowing up railroads, tunnels, bridges, and supply routes. When the Allies opened the spring drive on May 11, German divisions had been reduced to daily deliveries of 4,000 tons of supplies trucked by night as opposed to 10,000 tons needed for operations. Strangling the enemy with air power worked. Resistance gradually collapsed, and though German forces in Italy continued to fight, Allied ground forces liberated Rome on June 4, two

days before the Normandy assault. After the invasion of France, Eisenhower kept enough air power in Italy to support Allied troops advancing up the peninsula and for the invasion of southern France (Operation Dragoon) on August 15, 1944.

The Twelfth Air Force remained in the Mediterranean and European theaters until the end of the war. Part of the XII Tactical Air Command was inactivated on October 4, 1945, in Pomigliano, Italy, and the other part served in Bad Kissingen, West Germany, until inactivated on November 10, 1947.

### The Fifteenth Air Force

Whenever General Arnold needed a task-oriented man for a job, he summoned Jimmy Doolittle, who had organized the Twelfth Air Force in September 1942 and led it during the North African campaign. On November 1, 1943, Arnold established the Fifteenth

RIGHT: *The year 1943 marked the beginning of daylight raids against Germany's aircraft industry, but the full thrust of America's air power occurred during the "Big Week" in February 1944 when the Eighth Air Force flew 3,800 sorties and, in a similar effort that included the RAF and the Fifteenth Air Force, virtually crippled Germany's output of aircraft.*

I could see omens of the war's end almost every day in the blue southern sky when, flying provokingly low, the bombers of the American Fifteenth Air Force crossed the Alps from their Italian bases to attack German Industrial targets.

*Albert Speer, from* Inside the Third Reich

Air Force in Tunisia and put Doolittle in charge of preparing it for combat.

Many of the aircraft and personnel were already overseas, so Doolittle took some of the strategic bomb groups from IX Bomber Command of the Ninth Air Force, which was going to England to serve as the tactical air force in the European theater. He then added a few bomb groups from the Twelfth Air Force and several bomb and fighter groups intended for the Eighth Air Force. One bomb wing flew B-17s: the other four flew B-24s. Three fighter groups flew P-38s: four flew P-51s. Each bomb group had four squadrons, and each fighter group had three to four squadrons.

In January 1944, after organizing the Fifteenth Air Force, Doolittle turned the command over to General Twining and returned to England to direct the Eighth Air Force's strategic operations against Germany.

| Fifteenth Air Force – August 1944 | | | | |
|---|---|---|---|---|
| | Bomb Wings | Fighter Wings | Bomb Groups | Fighter Groups |
| The XV Bomber Command | 5 | 1 | 21 | 7 |

The Fifteenth operated out of bases in southern Italy until the end of the war and was inactivated on September 15, 1944.

### The Big Week

The Fifteenth flew missions out of Italy at the same time that the Eighth flew missions out of England in support of Operation Argument, better known as the "Big Week." During mid-February 1944, when meteorologists predicted a break in the weather, the Eighth hurled its entire air power of more than 1,000 bombers and as many fighters against a dozen targets in central Germany and western Poland. The Fifteenth struck targets in eastern Germany, flew to air bases in the Soviet Union, refueled and rearmed, and struck enemy targets again when returning to Italy. U.S. commanders expected huge losses, but only twenty-one bombers went down.

Five more days of massive raids followed with 3,800 sorties flown by the Eighth, 3,300 by the RAF, and 500 by the Fifteenth. Ten thousand tons of bombs fell on Germany, a tonnage roughly equal to all the bombs dropped by the Eighth Air Force during its first year of operation. Losses increased with each raid, however, and by the end of "Big Week," 226 American bombers and twenty-eight fighters failed to return. The operation damaged or destroyed most of Germany's aircraft industry, demolished hundreds of planes on the ground and in factories, and crippled the Me-110 facility at Gotha and the Ju-88 factories at Aschersleben and Bernburg. The Germans, however, rounded up the machine tools and by May had production lines humming again.

## Operation Wowser

After Big Week, the Fifteenth concentrated on supporting the movements of the Fifth Army in Italy and celebrated Columbus Day, 1944, with a massive carpet-bombing strike with high explosives against the German marshalling yards and supply center at Bologna. Wretched weather closed in until mid-November, when observation planes reported the enemy moving trains, trucks, and artillery into the Balkans. Heavy bombers from the Fifteenth clobbered the Brenner Pass into Austria and German installations in the Po Valley.

By April 1945 the Germans were in full retreat when General Twining authorized Operation Wowser. Every flyable aircraft from the Fifteenth flew support for the Fifth Army to close the ring on retreating Germans. In the longest prolonged raid of the war by

the Fifteenth, 1,142 B-17s and B-24s, escorted by P-38s and P-51s, blasted bridges, German ammunition dumps, railroads, trucks, and infantry columns on the road. From then on, every air operation concentrated on plugging escape routes and thoroughly demoralizing the enemy. The Germans soon had enough and surrendered on April 29, 1945. Six days later the war ended in Europe. Hitler was dead, and the victorious Allies rested their weapons and began the celebration.

For some pilots, the war had not quite ended. The battle for Okinawa had just begun, along with plans for invading Japan.

*ABOVE: Thunderbolt pilot Lieutenant Colonel Francis S. "Gabe" Gabreski of the Eighth Air Force scored twenty-eight victories and earned the distinction of becoming America's highest scoring ace in Europe.*

# THE WAR IN THE FAR EAST 1941–1945

If we don't take the offensive soon, the Japanese will drive us out [of the Pacific]. *General Henry H. Arnold in* Global Missions.

The seeds for World War II in the Far East were sown in 1931 when Japan exposed its intention to acquire new territories by occupying Manchuria and creating the satellite state of Manchukuo. The following year, Japanese troops threatened Shanghai and in 1933 occupied two Chinese provinces north of Peking. Japanese influence spread, and an incident on the night of July 7, 1937, caused a confrontation with Chinese troops. For three weeks, while the situation festered, Japan accumulated reinforcements and on July 26 issued an ultimatum demanding control of China's northern and eastern provinces. China's military and political leader, Generalissimo Chiang Kai-shek, rejected the ultimatum and war began.

On August 1, 1941, after four years of opposition to Japan's war with China, coupled with the imperial army's occupation of Indochina, the United States halted shipments of oil and aviation fuel. The action merely pushed Japan closer to war. On August 20,

1941, Major General Frederick L. Martin, commanding the Hawaiian Air Force, forwarded a report describing how Japan might attack Pearl Harbor and requested more aircraft for defense and reconnaissance. Although aware of the deepening problems in the Far East, President Roosevelt remained more concerned about the isolation of Great Britain and the war in Europe. The situation became more serious on October 16 when General Hideki Tojo and his ministry of militants replaced Prime Minister Prince Konoye. The political situation continued to deteriorate with Japanese submarines becoming more prevalent in Hawaiian waters. On November 30, Tojo officially decided to go to war. Although U.S. cryptanalysts had broken the Japanese code and issued warnings to bases in the Pacific, the messages were neither specific nor timely. Pearl Harbor headquarters did not receive the warning until midday, December 7, five hours after the Japanese attack.

*RIGHT: A Mitsubishi A6M Reisen Model 21 fighter takes off from a Japanese carrier on the morning of December 7, 1941, to strike Pearl Harbor. Americans code-named the aircraft "Zeke," but as time went by the name "Zero" came into general use.*

RIGHT: During the Japanese attack on Pearl Harbor, the first wave of fighters strafed and bombed local airfields. When a 265-pound bomb hit Hangar No. 11 at Hickam Field, it blew away the building's roof and siding.

ABOVE: President Franklin D. Roosevelt responded to the attack on Pearl Harbor on the morning of December 8, 1941, by declaring war on Japan. Great Britain and other commonwealth and Allied nations joined by issuing similar declarations.

## Pearl Harbor

Having received vague warnings from Washington, army commander Lieutenant General Walter C. Short decided without consulting his air commander that an alert against sabotage would be sufficient. Neither Short nor Pacific Fleet commander Admiral Husband E. Kimmel believed the Japanese would strike Pearl Harbor. The December 7 attack came as a complete surprise to everyone except a radar operator at Kahuku Point who reported a massive formation of aircraft approaching from the north, 130 miles away. The only officer at the information center, a young lieutenant, decided the blips came from an expected flight of B-17 Flying Fortresses and issued no alert.

At 7:55 A.M. a force of 183 planes launched from six Japanese carriers 200 miles north of Oahu struck the battleships in Pearl Harbor, Hickam and Wheeler Fields near Honolulu, and the naval airbases at Ford Island and Kaneohe. A second wave of 170 planes followed an hour later. Out of more than a hundred combat-capable army pursuit planes in Major General Frederick L. Martin's Hawaiian Air Force, only twenty-five got airborne, and most of those came from the army airfield at Haleiwa, which Japanese pilots overlooked. Of 231 planes, the AAF lost 152 on the ground, including a number of B-17s parked in neat rows on Hickam Field. Of 169 naval aircraft, eighty-seven were shot to pieces. By chance, Pacific Fleet carriers were at sea, but the eight battleships neatly anchored off Ford Island were either sunk or damaged.

During the second attack, twelve B-17s arrived from California with no place to land and became involved in an air battle. All their guns were wrapped in cosmolene and they had no ammunition. Because Japanese planes concentrated on shipping, only one B-17 was destroyed and three damaged. Three hours passed before planes could get into the air to search for the Japanese fleet. By then, the carriers were gone.

LEFT: The wreckage of an American pursuit plane blown literally off its parking spot on Hickam Field lies in a crumpled mess in front of one of the airfield's buildings.

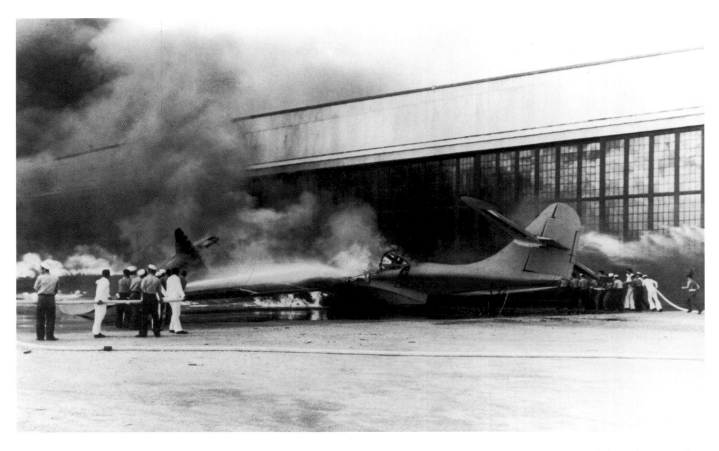

RIGHT: Following the Japanese raid on Pearl Harbor, firemen attempt to extinguish a fuel fire burning from a Consolidated Catalina PBY, which burst into flames when strafed by a Zero.

The Japanese paid an insignificant price for their insolence. Lieutenant George S. Welch lifted off at 8:15 from Haleiwa Field in a P-40 and claimed four victories. The combination of ground fire and American pilots accounted for another twenty-five enemy planes. For months to come, U.S. operations in the Pacific remained crippled.

## The AAF in the Philippines

At 4:00 A.M. on December 8 (Philippines time), General MacArthur and his air commander, Major General Lewis H. Brereton, received word of the Pearl Harbor attack. They had received warnings from Washington that the Philippines could be targeted. Brereton's Far East Air Force had two squadrons of B-17s at Clark Field, north of Manila, and two at Del Monte. Both MacArthur and Brereton had ample time to send out combat-ready, long-range bombers for reconnaissance. Instead, they waited four hours after being notified of the Pearl Harbor attack

At 8:00 A.M., Brereton sent two pursuit squadrons and two B-17 squadrons from Clark Field on patrol. Two hours later MacArthur ordered a strike on enemy airfields on Formosa, so Brereton recalled the B-17s to prepare for the mission. As the Fortresses began landing, 108 Japanese bombers and eighty-four Zero fighters were in flight from Formosa to strike Clark and Iba airfields. At 11:27 radar operators reported enemy formations seventy miles from Lingayen Gulf. At 11:30 the line went dead. At 12:33, while pilots and crews ate lunch, fifty-four Japanese bombers and fifty Zeros destroyed most of the pursuit planes on the ground at Iba. Two minutes later another formation struck Clark. Bombs ripped into buildings, hit the fuel dump, and gutted the runways. Zeros strafed the field for thirty minutes and destroyed the B-17s. Four P-40 pilots cleared the field before the air strike and shot down three planes.

Daily strikes wiped out most of the aircraft on other Philippine bases. For inexplicable reasons, the planes were always on the ground and not in the air. By nightfall on December 10, Brereton had only twelve operational B-17s, twenty-two P-40s, and eight antiquated Seversky P-35s.

While Japanese infantry landed in the Lingayen Gulf and pushed rapidly toward Manila, MacArthur waited for reinforcements and planes. None came, so Brereton sent the flyable B-17s to Australia. On December 24 MacArthur consolidated his ground troops and moved to the Bataan peninsula. Ordered to Australia on March 11 by President Roosevelt, MacArthur turned the ground forces over to Major General Jonathan M. Wainwright, who held out on the tiny island of Corregidor until May 6.

Brereton received the blame for losing so many planes on the ground, especially at Clark Field. After December 8, however, he waged a determined defensive campaign against vastly superior numbers with his remaining fighter squadrons. In March 1942, General Arnold sent Brereton to India to organize the Tenth Air Force (March–June 1942) and afterwards to the Middle East where he commanded the Ninth Air Force (June 1942–September 1943). Brereton eventually went to England to assist in the planning of the Normandy invasion and was highly regarded despite his setback in the Philippines.

## General MacArthur's Southwest Pacific Command

On March 17, 1942, MacArthur arrived in Australia to face the southward thrust of the military and naval might of Japan. For six months the Japanese overran everything blocking their way, including the Philippines, Wake Island, Guam, Singapore, Malaya, Thailand, and practically all of Burma. Farther to the south the imperial war machine had conquered the

Dutch East Indies and seized footholds on New Britain, New Guinea, and the Solomon Islands. Little stood in the way of Japan apart from MacArthur's patchwork Southwest Pacific Command and the remnants of the U.S. Navy, which on May 7–8, 1942, successfully thwarted the Japanese invasion of Port Moresby, New Guinea, during the Battle of the Coral Sea, and a month later defeated the Japanese navy at Midway. The naval victories gave MacArthur breathing space.

MacArthur's command consisted of a small number of U.S. and Australian troops, three American fighter groups, five bomb groups, two transport squadrons, and 1,602 officers and 18,116 airmen. Had Admiral Nimitz not distracted the enemy by putting marines on Guadalcanal and opening Henderson Field, MacArthur's weak force might not have held Port Moresby. Japan's campaign to recapture Guadalcanal took pressure off MacArthur, who began to strengthen his forces, and in particular, his airpower.

BELOW: When Japanese aircraft struck the Philippines on December 8, 1941, all the American planes at Nichols Field, near Manila, were neatly parked on the grass. The casualties included an obsolete Seversky P-35, which would have been quickly shot down had it gotten off the ground.

## Thirty Seconds over Tokyo—The Doolittle Raid

Though 500 years had passed since a typhoon demolished an invading Mongol armada, the Japanese still believed a kamikaze, or Divine Wind, protected their home islands from foreign intervention. With their war machine running rampant and their navy master of the seas, the Japanese public felt safe from harm.

In early 1942, Captain Francis S. Low, a member of Admiral Ernest J. King's navy staff, conceived the idea of surprising the Japanese with a carrier air strike on Tokyo. Navy planes did not have sufficient range, so King's air operations officer, Captain Donald Duncan, took the idea to the air force. General Arnold said he had the perfect man for the task, and Lieutenant Colonel James "Jimmy" Doolittle began training North American B-25B Mitchell pilots for short takeoffs at Eglin Field, Alabama. Unaware of the mission, the flyers finished training, flew to the naval air station at Alameda, California, and watched as cranes hoisted their sixteen Mitchells onto the aircraft carrier *Hornet*. When Doolittle informed the men of the mission, every flyer volunteered. Each plane would be armed with three 500-pound demolition bombs and one 500-pound incendiary cluster. Their targets would be Tokyo, Yokohama, Nagoya, Osaka, and Kobe. After bombing Japan, they would fly to China and join the Tenth Air Force.

Admiral William F. Halsey intended to launch the strike about 400 miles from Japan, but enemy picket ships spotted the force 600 miles out at sea. The greater distance created fuel problems, but every man agreed to fly. At 8:24 A.M. on April 18, with Doolittle at the controls, the first B-25 followed white lines painted on the carrier

deck and lurched into the air. The last bomber cleared the flight deck one hour later and joined the formation.

In a spectacular, low-level bombing run, Mitchells roared over Tokyo just as civilians returned to work after a mid-day air raid exercise. The explosions caused a great deal of commotion without doing much damage to targets. Because of the premature launch, none of the planes landed safely in China, and some flyers lost their lives. Viewed from the psychological impact on the Japanese, the mission was a tremendous success, but Doolittle expressed grief over the losses. When the Japanese began searching for Doolittle's airfield of departure, President Roosevelt suggested they look in "Shangri-la," the Tibetan hideaway in James Hilton's novel *Lost Horizon*.

The raid forced Japan to expand their defensive perimeter by making adjustments in how they deployed their navy. One citizen admitted, "We started to doubt that we were invincible."

**TOP LEFT: Colonel James "Jimmie" Doolittle (left) and Rear Admiral Marc A. Mitscher confer on board the USS Hornet the day before the launching of the April 18, 1942, raid on Tokyo.**

**TOP RIGHT: Officers and crew from the USS Hornet watch pensively as one of sixteen specially modified North American B-25B Mitchell bombers, named after the venerable Billy Mitchell, stagger aloft from the carrier's heaving deck.**

**ABOVE: From the nose of one of Doolittle's B-25s, a photograph is taken of Japan's Yokohama naval base. The raid caused only minor damage but inflicted a massive psychological blow to Japan's security claims.**

LEFT: Every flyer in the Pacific, along with ground crews, received a quick course in aircraft identification. From a table full of models, an instructor holds up a B-17 replica, which happens to be an aircraft unlike any plane produced by the Japanese.

## The Fifth Air Force

The Fifth originated in the Philippines as the Far East Air Force (FEAF). After being severely mauled, surviving planes relocated southward to bases in the Dutch East Indies and Australia. Those same planes played a minor role in the Battle of the Coral Sea by helping to repulse Japan's Port Moresby invasion fleet.

On July 29, 1942, Major General George C. Kenney arrived with more squadrons, toured the airbases, and summarily fired the entire command air staff. "No matter what I accomplished," Kenney concluded, "it would be an improvement." He reorganized the demoralized FEAF, named Brigadier General Ennis C. Whitehead as his deputy at Port Moresby's advanced base, and put Brigadier General Ken Walker in charge of the V Bomber Command and Brigadier General Paul B. Wurtsmith in charge of the V Fighter Command. Whitehead would remain Kenney's No. 1 combat commander throughout the war, eventually rising to the rank of lieutenant general and commander of the Fifth Air Force. On September 3, the two commands became the nucleus of the Fifth Air Force with headquarters in Brisbane, Australia. The Fifth became one of the few air forces organized outside the United States.

ABOVE: The Far East Air Force was first organized in the Philippines in September 1941. The remnants moved to Australia and in August 1942 became the Fifth Air Force, commanded by Major General George Kenney.

| Fifth Air Force—September 3, 1942 | |
| --- | --- |
| V Fighter Command | V Bomber Command |
| 8th Fighter Group (P-39s) | 3rd Bomb Group (B-25s, A-20s, A-24s) |
| 49th Fighter Group (P-40s) | 19th Bomb Group (B-17 FEAF survivors) |
| 35th Fighter Group (P-40s)* | 22nd Bomb Group (B-26s)<br>38th Bomb Group (B-25s)<br>43rd Bomb Group (No planes) |
| *Located at Port Moresby | |

ABOVE: A formation of basic training planes, piloted by instructors and closely observed by aviation cadets, soar over the Stars and Stripes fluttering at the entry to the 170-foot tower at Randolph Field, Texas.

LEFT: During an advanced training session at Carlsbad, New Mexico, pilots use Beech AT-11s for firing, formation flying, and synchronized bomb release.

## Early Operations on New Guinea—Buna

Kenney made his objective clear: "To take out the Jap air strength until we owned the air over New Guinea." He encountered major problems. Japanese bombers flew above the ceiling of Port Moresby's P-39s, and only four of the thirty-two battered B-17 survivors from the Philippines could fly. Hence, Kenney concentrated on low-level attacks on Japanese airfields on Buna and Lae, which were located over the Owen Stanley Mountains and on the northeastern tip of New Guinea.

Kenney's planes were not suited for operations against Buna, so he modified air tactics. First he used B-17s and B-25s to perforate enemy airfields the conventional way. Then he used low-level attacks with A-20s and B-25s armed with a new weapon designed by mechanical genius Major Paul Gunn, instantaneous-fused 23-pound fragmentation bombs attached to mini-parachutes. Parafrag bombs actually traced back to experiments conducted in 1928. They exploded on contact, sending a shower of steel splinters scything through planes on the ground. To give A-20s and B-25s extra strafing firepower, Gunn removed the glazing from the aircraft noses and installed four .50-caliber guns. The tactic involved flying low over the enemy's airfield, disabling planes with parafrag bombs, then circling back to strafe. By mid-September the Fifth Air Force owned the skies over Buna and opened the way for MacArthur to begin pushing the enemy off New Guinea.

After Allied ground troops operating out of Port Moresby drove the Japanese back across the Owen Stanley Mountains, Kenney airlifted 4,500 fresh troops from Australia, flew two regiments over the mountains, and deposited them on an Allied-occupied airstrip near Buna. In November, when ground forces could no longer be supplied by sea, Kenney's air transport group filled the void by delivering 2,450 tons of supplies. After P-38 Lightnings joined Kenney's command in December, American forces gained air superiority, and on January 2, 1943, the Japanese deserted Buna.

## Salamaua and Lae

After Buna fell, air reconnaissance reported the enemy falling back to Salamaua and Lae, located 150 and 175 miles, respectively, to the west. With both sites being reinforced, Gunn packed eight machine guns into the noses of B-25s where one had been before and created the war's first gunship. He had already added ship-killing 75mm cannon to several of the bombers.

### General George C. Kenney (1889–1977)

Born in Yarmouth, Nova Scotia, on August 6, 1889, Kenny graduated from the Massachusetts Institute of Technology in 1911 and worked as an engineer until 1917, when he enlisted as a private in the Aviation Section of the Signal Corps. After pilot training, he shipped to France and served for sixteen months with the 91st Aero Squadron. He flew seventy-five combat missions, shot down four German planes, and earned the Distinguished Service Cross and the Silver Star for bravery.

Kenney continued to advance his education, eventually graduating from every school the army offered, including the Army Command and General Staff School (1927) and the Army War College (1933).

After commanding the Fourth Air Force in April 1942, Kenney went to Australia to organize the Fifth Air Force and prepare the unit for combat. He modified B-25s for low-level attacks, developed skip-bombing techniques, and used airpower to wreck Japanese efforts to reinforce Lae during the Battle of the Bismarck Sea. His Fifth supported all of General MacArthur's Southwest Pacific campaigns in New Guinea and during the liberation of the Philippines.

Promoted to general in March 1945, Kenney commanded all Allied air forces in the Pacific. After the war he served as senior U.S. representative to the military staff committee of the United Nations and in 1946–1947 as head of Strategic Air Command. An immensely energetic, aggressive, and far-sighted air commander, and

regarded by MacArthur and the Joint Chiefs of Staff as a brilliant air strategist, Kenney retired in 1951 and died near Miami, Florida, on August 9, 1977.

**ABOVE: Commissioned as a pilot during World War I, George C. Kenney rose rapidly during the transformation of the Air Service to become one of the few true architects of air victory in the Pacific.**

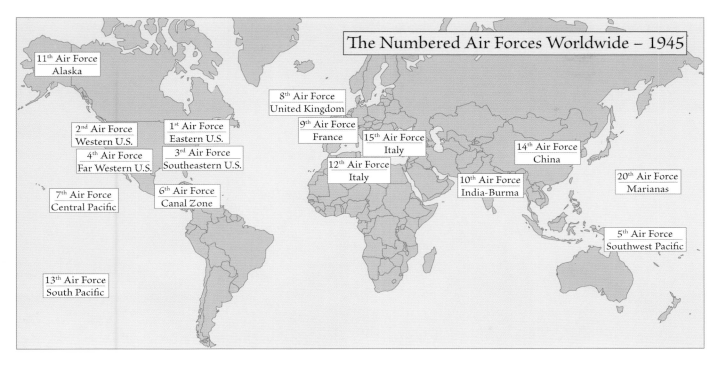

The Numbered Air Forces Worldwide – 1945

11th Air Force
Alaska

2nd Air Force
Western U.S.

4th Air Force
Far Western U.S.

7th Air Force
Central Pacific

6th Air Force
Canal Zone

13th Air Force
South Pacific

1st Air Force
Eastern U.S.

3rd Air Force
Southeastern U.S.

8th Air Force
United Kingdom

9th Air Force
France

12th Air Force
Italy

15th Air Force
Italy

10th Air Force
India-Burma

14th Air Force
China

20th Air Force
Marianas

5th Air Force
Southwest Pacific

*Sixteen numbered U.S. air forces were created during World War II. Many of them moved about as the war began closing on Germany and Japan. As an example, headquarters for the Twentieth Air Force never moved from Washington, D.C., because General Hap Arnold formed it and never relinquished complete control of how it operated. After serving briefly in India and China, the Twentieth moved to the Marianas. Likewise, the Ninth Air Force began operations in North Africa and moved to England, the Twelfth Air Force began operations in North Africa but moved to Italy, and the Fifteenth Air Force began operations in the Mediterranean and settled in Italy.*

On March 1, 1943, a roaming B-24 reported a sixteen-ship enemy convoy steaming through the Bismarck Sea off Cape Gloucester, New Britain, bound for Lae with a fresh division of Japanese troops. Kenney went after the convoy with every flyable plane, including Bristol Beaufighters piloted by the Royal Australian Air Force (RAAF). For three days during the Battle of the Bismarck Sea, B-25s and A-20s skip-bombed and blasted the convoy while P-38s provided air cover. The air attack sank eight transports, four destroyers, wiped out twenty-five enemy planes, and took the lives of more than 3,500 Japanese infantry, thus ending enemy efforts to reinforce Lae.

Kenney urged MacArthur to delay the assault on Salamaua and Lae until the Fifth neutralized the Japanese airbase at Wewak, 300 miles farther west. On August 17, eighteen B-25s and A-20s hit Wewak at low altitude and destroyed 175 planes on the ground. On September 4, supported by cover from the Fifth, the 9th Australian Division bypassed Salamaua and landed near Lae. Operations against Salamaua followed several days later. In one of the classic airborne operations of the war, transports

dropped the 503rd Parachute Regiment and artillery about nineteen miles west of Lae. By mid-September, pressure from all sides and continuous air attacks brought an end to resistance on Salamaua and Lae.

## Expanding Air Operations

MacArthur continued to press up the northern coast of New Guinea, and in early October the Fifth Air Force began moving onto bases captured at Finschafen. This enabled the Fifth to support advances into New Britain and westward toward Wewak. On November 1, 1943, when the 3rd Marine Division assaulted Bougainville, Kenney began a campaign to gain air control over New Ireland and New Britain to neutralize the Japanese air base at Rabaul. He now commanded the Thirteenth Air Force, which covered the Solomons, as well as the Fifth Air Force, and he used both commands to establish air supremacy. By mid-December, Japanese air strength on New Ireland and New Britain had been destroyed. By February 1944 the powerful base at Rabaul lay in shambles. There remained about 70,000 enemy troops on New Guinea

with considerable air strength at Wewak and Hollandia.

While the Fifth Air Force demolished the airbase at Wewak, MacArthur planned to leapfrog to Hollandia, which lay about 450 miles northwest of Finschafen. He could not risk the landing without first destroying the enemy's aircraft. The Fifth now had B-24s, along with A-20s and B-25s, and had extended the operating radius of P-38s to 650 miles by adding wing tanks. During the first few days of April, bombers from the Fifth escorted by P-38s completely demolished the airfields at Hollandia. During operations, Captain Richard I. Bong surpassed Eddie Rickenbacker's World War I record by shooting down his twenty-seventh plane. In quick succession, Allied forces leapfrogged to Aitape and Hollandia on April 22, Wadke Island on May 17, Biak on May 27, Sansapore on July 31, and Morotai in the Moluccas on September 15. Mindanao in the Philippines now lay but 250 miles away.

**ABOVE: Flying Fortresses were not as prevalent in the Pacific as in Europe, but the Fifth Air Force used them in the Solomons. During a sortie on October 5, 1942, this Fortress flew over Gizo Island in the Solomons during operations aimed at curbing Japanese attempts to reinforce Guadalcanal.**

**LEFT: Douglas Aircraft developed the fast, hard-hitting A-20 attack bomber at their flight line plant at Long Beach, California. The gunship-like aircraft carried nine .50-caliber machine guns and 6,000 pounds of bombs.**

**RIGHT: General Arnold (left) brought high-scoring Major Richard I. Bong back to the United States to receive the Medal of Honor and to promote recruitment. Bong disliked inaction, returned to the Pacific, and shot down another fifteen planes.**

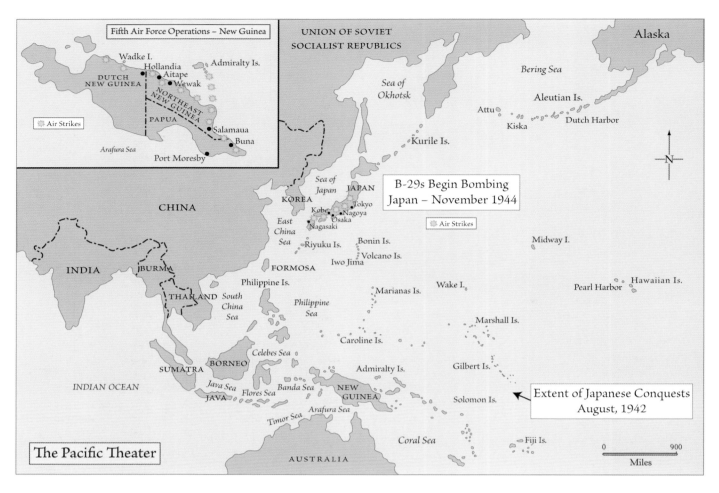

*USAF air operations were scattered all over the Pacific and southeastern Asia. Although every campaign was important, there were none more so than Fifth Air Force operations on New Guinea and Twentieth Air Force B-29 operations against Japan from islands in the Marianas.*

## Operations in the Philippines

In August 1944 the Fifth flew the first air strikes against bases on Mindanao. Kenney's air strikes, combined with those flown by Admiral Halsey's Third Fleet, quickly destroyed Japan's air strength on the islands with very little loss. After Halsey reported the island of Leyte virtually undefended, MacArthur decided to bypass Mindanao. Halsey's report was not quite accurate. When on October 20, 1944, MacArthur's Sixth Army went ashore on Leyte there were 20,000 enemy troops on the island and two powerful Japanese fleets on their way. MacArthur expected the Third Fleet to provide air coverage, but the Japanese decoyed Halsey away by sacrificing a squadron of battle-scarred carriers and cruisers. MacArthur still had protection from Vice Admiral Thomas C. Kinkaid's Seventh Fleet, which

contained battleships and escort carriers, but the Fifth Air Force had not arrived, having no place to land.

While Halsey's fleet returned to Leyte, the first Japanese *kamikaze* attacks struck Kinkaid's Seventh Fleet and sank two escort carriers. The problem became more complicated because Halsey had to stagger his carrier forces back to Ulithi to refuel. Army engineers hurriedly built a single fighter strip at Tacloban, and on October 27 Fifth Air Force P-38s flew in to defend against kamikaze attacks and provide air defense for the beachhead. As ground forces moved inland, engineers built more airfields. By the end of the year, Kenney's pilots had shot down 314 enemy planes over Leyte while losing only sixteen. On December 15, when ground forces invaded Mindoro, there were no Japanese planes in the air.

On January 7, 1945, two days before the first American troops went ashore in the Lingayen Gulf on Luzon, forty B-25s and ninety-seven A-20s from the Fifth struck Clark Field with 8,000 parafrags, circled back to strafe, and destroyed sixty Japanese aircraft. The enemy still had a few planes on other fields, and on January 9, 1945, when the first troops went ashore on Luzon, flights of *kamikazes* reappeared. Young, inexperienced Japanese pilots flew the planes, and they were easy targets. During air operations on the Philippines, more than 1,500 enemy planes were destroyed. Japan recalled its remaining aircraft to save

LEFT: Flying Fortress "Goonie" shows seven Japanese aircraft to her credit during fifteen missions in the South Pacific. Although aces did not normally come from bombers, some B-17 crews racked up amazing records.

## Aces of the Fifth

Some of the greatest fighter pilots in World War II became aces while flying for the Fifth Air Force. They attacked even when their planes had been damaged and odds against them were six to one. Pilots kept their radios on Japanese frequencies to trade insults. When dogfighting, they became cocky, brave, determined, iron-nerved, and half-crazed warriors.

Richard I. "Bing" Bong became America's ace of aces by shooting down forty Japanese planes. He flew P-38s with the 35th Fighter Group and by November 1943 had racked up twenty-one combat victories. Transferred to the Fifth's operations staff, Bong said he would rather fly. He joined the 49th Fighter Group and scored another seven victories. Bong had never been a good shot. He scored victories by diving on the enemy, coming dangerously close before firing, then pulling up at the last second. Thinking that Bong might kill himself, the Fifth sent him back to the United States for gunnery training. Bong returned and shot down another twelve planes, bringing his total to forty. Awarded the Medal of Honor in December 1944, Bong stayed stateside and became a test pilot.

ABOVE: Flying a P-38 Lightning, Major Richard I. "Bing" Bong established a new record of forty kills for American pilots, and he also became the top ace for the Allies in World War II.

He was safer dogfighting. Bong lost his life in August 1945 while testing an F-80 near Burbank, California.

Major Thomas B. McGuire, Jr., of the 431st Fighter Squadron came within two victories of tying Bong's record. He and Bong were rivals. They took risks trying to outdo each other. In an incident over Wewak, McGuire closed head on with an equally determined Japanese fighter pilot,

ABOVE: Captain Thomas P. Lynch, from the 35th Fighter Group, Fifth Air Force, scored twenty victories while flying a P-38 Lightning in the same operational theater as Richard Bong.

grazing in midair. In 1945, after scoring his thirty-eighth victory and winning the Medal of Honor, McGuire disappeared during a mission over the Philippines.

Other fighter pilots from the Fifth also became aces. Unlike Bong, most of them were superb shots. Next to McGuire, Colonel Charles H. MacDonald of the 475th Fighter Group scored twenty-seven kills, and Captain Thomas J.

Lynch, flying a P-38 for the 35th Fighter Group, downed twenty enemy planes. Lieutenant Colonel Gerald Johnson, perhaps the best shot of all, knocked down three Japanese fighters in forty-five seconds with three gun-bursts, and tallied twenty-two kills.

Mustang pilot Captain William A. Shomo of the 82nd Tactical Reconnaissance Squadron became an ace during his first aerial combat. Shomo shot down six fighters and a bomber and established a record that has never been surpassed. Kenney needled him, asking why two fighters got away. Shomo tersely replied, "I ran out of bullets." His pals nicknamed him "The Flying Undertaker," and the army awarded him the Medal of Honor.

Colonel Neel E. Kearby, commanding 384th Fighter Group, came close to matching Shomo's record. On October 11, 1943, while leading four P-47s on a routine reconnaissance, he attacked a formation of twelve bombers escorted by thirty-six fighters, and in an action involving 10:1 odds, shot down six planes. Kearby posted twenty kills and was awarded the Medal of Honor.

Dogfighting was not a game for the weak-hearted. Those who survived were lucky as well as brave.

them for the defense of the home islands, and the Fifth Air Force spent the remainder of the Philippines campaign flying close air support for ground troops.

With the liberation of Manila in early February and the recapture of Corregidor on the 27th, the mopping-up of the Philippines became a matter of time. On April 1, operations moved to Okinawa, 325 miles from the shores of Kyushu. MacArthur's forces remained in the Philippines, but in June General Whitehead sent the Fifth Air Force to join the Seventh Air Force on Okinawa as part of the larger Far East Air Force. Both units were still there on August 15 when Japan surrendered.

## The Seventh Air Force

The Seventh Air Force evolved from the Hawaiian Air Force, often called the "Pineapple Air Force" because of its easy-going, idyllic environment. The unit was established on October 19, 1940, to control the growing number of air squadrons arriving on the islands. In July 1941, Hawaiian Air Force headquarters moved to Hickam Field at Honolulu. Redesignated the Seventh Air Force on February 5, 1942, the unit became part of U.S. Army Forces, Central Pacific. Major General Willis H. Hale had few places to send his flyers until 1943, when Admiral Nimitz launched the first island-hopping campaign in the Pacific. Meanwhile, Hale switched from B-17s to B-24s and sent his pilots on long-range reconnaissance missions over far-distant islands in the central Pacific. To everyone's surprise, the flyers discovered dozens of islands containing previously unknown enemy installations and air bases.

Though thoroughly decimated by the Japanese attack on Pearl Harbor, the reorganized Seventh slowly revived. Its first major action occurred on June 3, 1942, when B-24s, B-25s, and torpedo-carrying B-26s staging through Midway sortied against the Japanese invasion fleet, but with unimpressive results. The action demonstrated that, while bombers could hit stationary

ABOVE: The Hawaiian Air Force, formed on the islands on October 19, 1940, became re-designated as the Seventh Air Force on September 18, 1942, and headquartered at Hickam Field. The unit operated in the central Pacific, including Saipan in December 1944 and Okinawa in July 1945.

targets on the ground with some degree of accuracy, they could not hit maneuvering targets on water.

Hale probably commanded the most widely spread air force in the Pacific. He distributed squadrons from a single bomb group over bases 600 miles apart. Part of the 11th Bomb Group flew down to Henderson Field

## The Island-hopping Campaign

Prior to the navy's amphibious assault of Tarawa Atoll in the Gilbert Islands, Hale moved bomb groups and two fighter squadrons to Funafuti in the Ellice Islands, 2,600 miles from Hickam Field. When marines went ashore on Tarawa on November 20, 1943, and moved up the atoll, the Seventh Air Force opened the way.

From January 31 to February 5, 1944, during operations in the Marshall Islands, heavy and medium bombers from the VII Bomber Command flew 2,000-mile round trips to soften Japanese airfields on Wotje, Mili, and Maloelap during the invasion of Kwajalein Atoll. Crews spent ten to fifteen hours in the air, averaging a mission every three days. Prior to the assault, Major Gunn's innovations from the Fifth Air Force made their first appearance in the Seventh when new B-25Gs arrived with a 75mm cannon mounted in the nose.

To keep his widespread detachments supplied, Hale formed Air Service Support Squadrons, or ASSRONS, which were small and compact units for moving supplies to tiny atolls already congested by ground units. ASSRONS set up overnight as planes moved in, and then instantly pulled out as fighting units and planes jumped to another island airbase. The island-hopping campaign became an exercise in misery. As one flyer recalled, "Flies in the day, mosquitoes at night, and dysentery all the time."

## The Seventh in the Marianas

What General Arnold wanted were bases for B-29 Superfortresses, so the VII Bomber Command became intensely involved in the Marianas campaign, where massive amphibious assaults were planned against the heavily fortified islands of Saipan, Tinian, and Guam. During pre-invasion planning, the Seventh flew photoreconnaissance missions and thoroughly plotted Saipan's and Tinian's military installations and defensive positions. In April 1944, B-24 shuttle-bombing missions from bases on Eniwetok in the Marshalls

on Guadalcanal and participated in the Solomons campaign. During the contest for Guadalcanal, the detachment lost twenty-one bombers but destroyed or damaged 181 Japanese planes on the ground. "The thrust into the Solomons," Hale wrote, "directly diminished the threat to Hawaii."

*LEFT: During the island-hopping campaign in the Pacific, B-24 Liberators began using the airbase at Eniwetok while construction workers were still spreading coral to develop the runways.*

After the first shock of the Jap attack, the immediate reaction was to throw everything into the defense of Hawaii. *Major General Willis H. Hale.*

ABOVE: As longer-range North American P-51D Mustangs became available for escort duty in Europe, earlier P-51B/C models of the aircraft were moved to the Pacific, where deep penetration bombing missions had not begun.

struck Guam, Saipan, and Tinian, swinging south through the Carolines to American bases in the Admiralties. After refueling, the Liberators bombed Ponape on the flight back to Eniwetok. The mission covered 4,300 miles over open water.

To prepare for the Marianas assault, heavy bombers from the Seventh and Thirteenth Air Forces flew great distances to strike the island of Truk, from which Japanese forces in the Marianas drew their aircraft, supplies, and naval support. Left untouched, Truk could have menaced the flank of the invasion fleet. By D-day on Saipan, Truk was a wreck.

The huge Marianas operation required a naval task force larger than the entire Japanese navy. On June 15, when marines went ashore on Saipan, P-47s of the Seventh flew close support alongside planes from the navy and the Marine Corps. To penetrate the enemy's extensive network of caves and pillboxes, Thunderbolts from the 318th Fighter Group dropped napalm, the first use of the fiery, jelled gasoline in battle. Defended by 29,662 stubborn Japanese troops, the enemy held out for a month. All but 1,780 survivors committed *hara-kiri* before the fighting ended on July 12. By then, Hale's fighter and bomber commands were already operating from Saipan air bases and flying sorties against Tinian and Guam. When the 3rd Marine Division assaulted Guam on July 21, and the 2nd Marine Division went ashore on Tinian three days later, Seventh Air Force pilots teamed up with navy and marine flyers to provide air support.

The first B-29s began arriving on Saipan in mid-October, 1944. They were the property of the Twentieth Air Force, personally commanded by General Arnold. Lieutenant General Millard F. Harmon, commanding general of the AAF in the Pacific, pushed the construction of bomber bases and eventually built one on Saipan, two on Guam, and two on Tinian. General Hale never received an allotment of B-29s and the Seventh Air Force fought the balance of the war, much of it from bases in the Marianas, with B-24s and B-25s of the VII Bomber Command and P-51s and P-47s of the VII Fighter Command.

## Iwo Jima and Okinawa

During late fall, 1944, the VII Bomber Command, flying out of the Marianas, struck the Volcano and Bonin Islands because General Arnold wanted an emergency air base for B-29s established on Iwo Jima, the halfway point between Saipan and Tokyo. After pulverizing the eight-square-mile island for seventy-four consecutive days without seriously depleting the 21,000-man Japanese garrison, the 4th and 5th Marine Divisions waded ashore on February 19, 1945, and stumbled into a meat-grinding machine. The contest for control of the island lasted thirty-four days and cost the marines 5,981 killed and 19,920 wounded. The payback came during the next five months when 2,251 B-29s carrying 24,761 crewmen made emergency stops at Iwo Jima.

With Iwo declared secure on March 16, the VII Fighter Command's P-51 Mustangs moved onto airbases to escort B-29 missions to Japan. When the B-29s switched to night incendiary raids, fighter escorts became unnecessary. So between April 7 and August 14, the fighter command flew thirty-eight of its own 1,200-mile missions to bomb and strafe airbases at Tokyo, Nagoya, and Osaka.

Though the Seventh was one of the smaller air forces in the Pacific, it got around. During operations on Okinawa, it became part of General Kenney's Far East Air Force, which also included the Fifth and the Thirteenth. While bomb groups blasted Kyushu, the 507th Fighter Group moved its P-47Ns to a base on Ie Shima and flew a 1,600-mile mission to strike the large Japanese airfield at Keijo, Korea. When attacked by fifty enemy aircraft, the fighter group downed twenty, losing one of its own. The group won a Distinguished Unit Citation, the only one awarded to a P-47 unit in the Pacific.

ABOVE: A P-51D Mustang takes off from an airbase on Iwo Jima in the Volcano Islands. The improved P-51Ds began arriving in the Pacific in 1944 with Boeing B-29 Superfortresses for the long-range bombing of Japan.

General Hale contrasted bombing in the Pacific to Europe when he wrote: "There was no such thing as area bombing in this theater. We had to pinpoint our targets for the simple reason they were small and hard to hit squarely. The difference of 40 feet one way or the other meant that the bomb would either hit the target or land in the water. And we didn't fly 2,000 miles to kill fish."

The Seventh was still flying bombing missions against Japan when in mid-August the first atomic bomb exploded over Hiroshima.

ABOVE: Millions of Americans helped to finance the war by responding to thousands of posters nailed to telephone poles across the country urging the public to "BUY WAR BONDS."

**ABOVE: Activated at New Caledonia in the Coral Sea on January 13, 1943, the Thirteenth Air Force went wherever ground forces went. Under General Kenney the unit staged most missions out of tropical jungles and remote islands.**

## The Thirteenth Air Force

Like the Fifth Air Force, General Kenney's Thirteenth Air Force had never been stationed in the United States. Even today, it is also one of the oldest, continuously active, numbered air forces. Established on December 14, 1942, and activated in the lush landscape of New Caledonia in the Coral Sea on January 13, 1943, the Thirteenth moved two weeks later to Espiritu Santo Island, New Hebrides, as part of the U.S. Army Forces, Far East.

The organization became known as the "Jungle Air Force" because it served as widely scattered independent units posted in jungles and on remote islands wherever marines went. Originally charged with fighting enemy forces in the South Pacific, the Thirteenth went on the offensive in the Solomons before joining with the Fifth Air Force for operations in the Admiralties, New Guinea, Morotai, and the Philippines. The Jungle Air Force served

**ABOVE: Mechanics in a South Pacific war zone kept this B-17 in the air. For every member of a flying crew, ten men on the ground worked long hours to keep the plane operational.**

in five different areas of operation and participated in thirteen campaigns. The XIII Bomber Command flew B-17 Flying Fortresses, B-24 Liberators, B-25 Mitchells, and B-26 Marauders: the XIII Fighter Command flew P-38 Lightnings, P-39 Airacobras, P-40 Warhawks, and P-61 Black Widows: the Air Transport Command flew C-46 Commandos, C-47 Skytrains, and L-5 Sentinels.

On January 13, 1943, General Kenney put Major General Twining in charge of the Thirteenth Air Force and instructed him to cooperate with the navy, gain air superiority in the central Solomons, and destroy enemy supply lines in the northern Solomons. Twining encountered a welter of command problems and inter-service rivalries trying to fit his organization into a theater run by Admiral Halsey. The navy wanted B-17s used for reconnaissance, and Twining wanted them

**LEFT: After returning from a bombing mission in the Solomons, the gun-crew from a Flying Fortress clean the aircraft's thirteen .50-caliber machine guns at the unit's home base in New Hebrides.**

used for bombing. Determining the use of fighters never became a problem. Several combat units moved onto Guadalcanal's Henderson Field and flew missions side-by-side with pilots from the Marine Corps, navy, and the Royal New Zealand Air Force. On June 14, 1943, when 120 Japanese planes approached Guadalcanal, Thirteenth Air Force pilots lifted off Henderson Field and together with Allied flyers shot down ninety-four enemy planes.

The Seventh had the only big bombers in the Solomons, and they mercilessly pounded Japanese airfields and enemy shipping from New Georgia to New Britain and Rabaul. As the navy and Marine Corps forces began amphibious assaults up the Solomons chain in June 1943, the Thirteenth followed, flying off jungle airbases on tiny islands as fast as Seabees could put fields in operating order. Munda, Vella Lavella, New Georgia, Choiseul, Kolobangara, and Bougainville became principal targets. As soon as captured airfields could be restored, fighter squadrons from the Thirteenth moved in with the marines.

*ABOVE: During operations on New Guinea, Douglas C-47 Skytrains from Ward's Drome, Port Moresby, line up on a landing strip at Wau, near Lae and Salamaua, to offload supplies for MacArthur's rapidly moving army.*

In January 1944 Major General Hubert R. Harmon took command of the Thirteenth Air Force and moved headquarters to Guadalcanal. When Kenney concentrated the Fifth Air Force on pushing the Japanese off New Guinea, Harmon took the task of neutralizing Rabaul. By the time the Allies gained control of the Bismarck Sea, the XIII Bomber Command had rendered Rabaul strategically impotent.

**ABOVE: As preparations are made to move up the Solomon Islands in 1943, Major General Nathan F. Twining (right), commanding USAAF forces in the South Pacific, meets with army commanders Lieutenant General Millard F. Harmon, (center), and Major General Alexander D. Patch.**

Operating out of Guadalcanal, the 868th Bomber Squadron (B-24s) pioneered low-altitude radar night bombing of enemy shipping and inflicted so much damage that Japanese attempts to supply troops by water, especially during operations at Bougainville, were abandoned.

Months before the navy could establish airbases in the central Pacific, Liberators from the XIII Bomber Command began flying fourteen-hour, 1,800-mile unescorted missions against Truk, Yap, and Palau in the Caroline Islands. When hammering targets, they

## The Death of Yamamoto

In April 1943, Pearl Harbor cryptanalysts decoded the itinerary of Admiral Isoroku Yamamoto's inspection of Japanese forces in the Solomons and notified Admiral Halsey. Halsey had no long-range fighters, so he passed the message to Rear Admiral Marc A. Mitscher, Commander Air Solomons. On April 18 Captain Thomas H. Lamphier, Jr., led eighteen P-38s from three XIII Fighter Command squadrons on

Guadalcanal and shot down Yamamoto's plane near Kahili airfield, Buin, exactly where indicated by navy intelligence. The death of Yamamoto, commander-in-chief of the Imperial Japanese Navy, struck a serious blow to Japan. Lamphier of the Seventh Air Force received the Navy Cross, a rare bestowal by the navy to an army pilot.

**TOP: The remains of Admiral Isoroku Yamamoto's downed G4M "Betty" lay crumpled in the jungle near Buin. Japanese searchers removed the admiral's body from the site and shipped it to Japan for a state funeral.**

**ABOVE: A squadron of P-38F Lightnings out of Guadalcanal intercepted Yamamoto's flight after receiving the admiral's itinerary from navy code-breakers stationed at Pearl Harbor.**

fought off enemy fighters and dodged antiaircraft concentrations. Later, when the Seventh Air Force took over the job, several squadrons of B-24s moved to the Admiralty Islands to support MacArthur's landings, and struck Hollandia, Aitape, and Woleai.

## The Thirteenth Merges With the Fifth

In May 1944 the Thirteenth Air Force came under the command of Major General St. Clair Streett, who replaced General Harmon, and began softening up the island of Biak in the Schouten group. When Australian troops invaded Balikpapan in the East Indies on July 1, 1944, the Thirteenth provided the air coverage. Meanwhile, the Thirteenth joined with the Fifth Air Force as part of the newly created Far East Air Forces (FEAF), which Streett commanded for the remainder of the war. Until the summer of 1945, the Thirteenth operated out of Palawan, striking the final blows of the Jungle Air Force.

## The Twentieth Air Force

General Arnold formed the Twentieth Air Force on June 20, 1941, and headquartered it in the United States as his personal strategic bombing command. Before the war, Arnold had personally masterminded the specifications for the B-29 Superfortress, and he expected to see the heavy bombers used as he intended. Arnold also decided where to deploy them. B-29s that formed the Twentieth Air Force went to the China-Burma-India theater and to the Pacific, not to Europe.

## China-Burma-India

Although Arnold's original plan had been to deploy B-29s on Pacific islands in range of Japan, the bombers became available months before the capture of the Marianas. Instead of waiting, Arnold organized the XX Bomber Command under Major General Kenneth B. Wolfe and in April 1944 sent the first B-29s to India. Since June 1942, when Japanese infantry closed off the

## The B-29 Superfortress

When developing the B-29 Superfortress, General Arnold told his engineers to "make them the biggest, gun them the heaviest, and fly them the farthest." At times, engineers doubted that everything Arnold wanted could be achieved, but the general insisted. The Boeing B-29 would become the most complex aircraft conceived up to that point, with sixty-five tons of fighting machinery, four 2,200 horsepower Wright R-3350 engines, 50,000 separate parts, and thousands of miles of wiring traveling through a ninety-nine-foot body and a 142-foot wing span. Arnold expected his B-29s to fly sixteen-hour missions at top speeds of 350 mph with a 20,000-pound bomb load. With a range of 4,100 miles, a 32,000-foot service ceiling, and thirteen machine guns, the B-29 became one of the most destructive weapons of the war.

The B-29 had a crew of eleven, the first pressurized fuselage and turrets, and long, narrow wings. The smaller gun turrets were remotely controlled, reducing air drag caused by large, protruding turrets. The B-29 also carried the most accurate AN/APQ-13 bombing radar, which was located between the two bomb bays. The long, cylindrical body was topped by a huge tail, which became the B-29s recognition feature.

The AAF placed 1,600 B-29s on order before the first one had ever flown. Boeing built four new factories to fill the order. The 58th Bombardment Wing received the first aircraft on July 1943 for test and evaluation. Three months later, Boeing went into full production. Had the B-29 failed as a weapon, the war with Japan could have continued for another year or two.

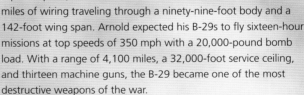

*TOP: American air power came of age in the Pacific when Boeing B-29 Superfortresses began operations in 1944. An empty B-29 weighed 2,000 pounds more than a fully loaded B-17.*

*ABOVE: Boeing turned the B-29 into an awesome weapon well beyond the scope of any aircraft produced by any other nation. The bomber carried twice the fuel and enjoyed twice the combat range of a B-17.*

RIGHT: During a break in monsoon rains in February 1943, a B-25 Mitchell pounds Japanese positions in support of British Chindit ground operations behind enemy lines in the mountainous Burmese jungle. Chindits fought in support of General Joseph Stilwell's Chinese divisions commanded by Brigadier General Frank D. Merrill.

ABOVE: Activated by General Arnold on June 20, 1941, headquarters for the Twentieth Air Force remained based in Washington, D.C. The B-29s and other aircraft that comprised the unit served in India, China, and the Pacific under Curtis LeMay and Nathan Twining.

Burma Road, the Tenth Air Force in India had been trying to keep the Fourteenth Air Force in China supplied with gasoline, ammunition, and spare parts by flying over the Himalayas, known as "The Hump." Six months prior to the availability of the bombers,

| Components of the Twentieth Air Force | |
| --- | --- |
| Unit | Formed |
| XX Bomber Command | 1944–1945 |
| XXI Bomber Command | 1944–1945 |
| VII Fighter Command | 1945 |

Arnold had American engineers and more than 35,000 Chinese coolies building four bases in western China and four in eastern India. Wolfe could not rely on the Tenth for supplies, so the XX Bomber Command took control of its own logistics and began flying gasoline and ordnance from India to Chengtu, China. B-29s had to make six round trips over the Hump to supply a single combat mission.

On June 5, 1944, the XX Bomber Command flew its first mission against Japanese installations in Bangkok, Thailand. Ten days later forty-seven B-29s flew the first night mission out of China and struck Japan's steel industry at Yawata on Kyushu. Damage was slight, but the B-29 blitz had begun.

**ABOVE: During operations in Burma, General Curtis LeMay (right) confers with General Joseph "Vinegar Joe" Stilwell regarding the movement of B-29s from the XX Bomber Command to China for operations against Japan and Formosa.**

**RIGHT: Steady and regular aerial supply drops kept the fierce Chindits fighting against strongly held Japanese positions in Burmese jungles, and greatly aided in the complete devastation and rout of the enemy during 1944.**

During September, thirty-eight-year-old Major General Curtis E. LeMay arrived from the Eighth Air Force in England. An outspoken and brilliant tactician, LeMay disapproved of night bombing and changed to high-level, tight-formation day bombing at altitudes above the range of antiaircraft fire and beyond the capabilities of Japanese interceptors. Damage inflicted by the bombers immediately increased. October air strikes virtually wiped out Formosa's Okayama Aircraft Assembly Plant and crippled the island's two most important airfields at Heito and Einansho, thus supporting MacArthur's invasion of the Philippines. LeMay continued to stage raids out of China, despite miserable ground and weather conditions.

### B-29s in the Marianas

In early September 1944, Brigadier General Haywood S. Hansell, commanding the XXI Bomber Command, personally landed the first B-29 on the Marianas. As the 73rd Wing arrived, Hansell stepped up training and in late October flew the first combat mission over Truk. On November 1 *Tokyo Rose* became the first B-29 over Tokyo, flying an important reconnaissance mission to locate targets. Japan had a powerful jet stream with winds up to 180 mph and a well-dispersed industry that made high-level targeting difficult. During twenty-two missions involving 2,148 sorties, B-29s dropped 5,398 tons of bombs on Japan. Only half struck the primary target. Each mission cost the

ABOVE: Carpet bombing by B-29s, referred to as "inferno from the skies," plastered Tokyo's scattered industrial shops. Despite acres of massive destruction, the strikes failed to bring the Japanese to the peace table.

command about six percent of its planes, which meant that Hansell had to replace the equivalent of his entire force every seventeen missions.

At Arnold's bidding, Hansell tried different tactics, including incendiary bomb strikes on Japan's principal cities, but during the first attack on Nagoya, bombs passed through clouds and missed the target area. Hansell tried bombing at altitudes between 20,000 and 35,000 ft, with little improvement. Arnold was not getting the results he expected from his B-29s, so in January 1945 he replaced Hansell, one personal friend with another, LeMay.

LeMay had developed a reputation for being a first-class pilot and navigator. After World War II began, he had received command of the 305th Bombardment Group and taken it to England as part of General Eaker's Eighth Air Force. Because of LeMay's talent for tactics, Arnold promoted him to major general and put him in charge of the XX Bomber Command in China. When LeMay replaced Hansell, he was ordered to get B-29s operating at tactical expectations.

LeMay wasted little time, but he first ran some tests. He sent the bombers out in hundred-plane formations and struck Kobe on February 4, Nagoya on February 15, and Tokyo on February 19. On February 25 he increased the strike force to 200 planes and dropped 600 tons of bombs on urban Tokyo. Still dissatisfied, LeMay began scorching Japan's principal cities with jellied gasoline-magnesium bombs. He tried and analyzed different bomb loads, formations, altitude effectiveness, weather conditions, and concluded, after

industrial sectors. Although area bombing ran contrary to the accepted tenets of air doctrine, LeMay considered it necessary because much of Japan's military industry was performed in thousands of wooden mini-shops embedded inside industrial cities.

### Inferno from the Skies

In early March, LeMay gave the order to burn out the industrial centers of Tokyo, Kobe, Nagoya, and Osaka. After midnight on March 10, 1945, some 285 B-29s roared over Tokyo at 5,000 to 6,000 ft and torched 15.8 square miles of area containing 11,000 mini-factories. On March 12, another 286 Superforts dropped 1,950 tons of incendiaries on Nagoya's aircraft center. Five days later B-29s blasted the city's untouched mini-factories, wiping out five square miles of the city. On March 14 a force of 280 B-29s scattered 2,240 tons of incendiaries over Osaka's industrial center

*LEFT: The first atomic bomb, dropped over Hiroshima on August 6, 1945, virtually leveled one of Japan's largest and most populous cities, leaving only a few buildings standing along the outskirts.*

*ABOVE: After completing its mission over Hiroshima, the B-29 named Enola Gay touches down at its Marianas airbase. The crew did not learn until later of the horrendous damage inflicted by the bomb they dropped.*

evaluating all the reports and compiling his own statistics, that a lot of effort had been "thrown away."

Because Japanese fighter strength had been sharply reduced, LeMay increased formations up to 629 bombers. He also reduced the total 135,000-pound takeoff load and increased the operating radius by replacing tons of concussion bombs with lighter loads of new, powerful, incendiaries. He then ordered pilots to fly at 5,000 to 8,000 ft instead of 30,000 ft because Japanese antiaircraft weapons were less effective at lower altitudes. He also removed machine guns to lighten the load and switched to visual area bombing, using flares when necessary, to burn out entire urban-

ABOVE: Colonel Paul W. Tibbets (center), pilot of the Enola Gay, stands with the rest of the crew beside the aircraft that dropped the first atomic bomb, on Hiroshima.

and incinerated 8.3 square miles. Three days later 309 bombers spread 2,328 tons of incendiaries on Kobe's shipping and munitions plants and destroyed three square miles of the city. The mid-March bombing blitz destroyed thirty-two square miles of Japan's four most important cities, and it was only the beginning.

The Twentieth also flew 1,500 sorties along strategic maritime routes, dropping more than 12,000 mines and sinking 800,000 tons of Japanese shipping, more than navy submarines sank during the same period.

LeMay could not understand why Japan refused to surrender, nor was he inclined to ease the pressure. Incendiary raids continued for another four and a half months and by August had completely destroyed Japan's industry. By then, LeMay had enlarged his command to five wings—the 58th, 73rd, 313th,

314th, and 315th—and 1,000 Superforts. The last incendiary strike occurred on August 2 when 855 B-29s dropped 6,632 tons on industrial cities.

The next two raids were single-plane missions. On August 6 the *Enola Gay*, piloted by Colonel Paul Tibbets, Jr., dropped the first atomic bomb on Hiroshima and flattened the city. Three days later the *Bock's Car*, flown by Major Charles W. Sweeney, dropped another fission bomb over Nagasaki. Six days later the Japanese surrendered.

ABOVE: Smoke and debris billow skyward seconds after Major Charles W. Sweeney, flying the B-29 Bock's Car from the 509th Composite Group, flattened Nagasaki with a second atomic bomb on August 9, 1945.

General Arnold's B-29s had done their work, and so had LeMay and the men of the Twentieth Air Force. Strategic air power—dreadful, holocaustic, and decisive—had come of age.

## The Tenth and Fourteenth Air Forces

Activated on February 12, 1942, the Tenth Air Force established headquarters at New Delhi, India. Commanded by Major General Louis H. Brereton, who had led the Far East Air Force in the Philippines, the Tenth inherited Brigadier General Claire L. Chennault's American Volunteer Group of "Flying Tigers," which operated in China at the pleasure of Generalissimo Chiang Kai-shek. In July 1942, Brereton inducted Chennault's organization into the Tenth as the China Air Task Force. For several months, most of the Tenth's planes were those that had escaped from the Philippines and the Dutch East Indies, and those units became the India Air Task Force. The Tenth Air Force served as the only American air establishment in the India-Burma-China theater until March 1943, when General Arnold activated the Fourteenth Air Force in China and placed Chennault in command. The Tenth then operated in India and Burma until it moved to China in July 1945.

ABOVE: During the early fighting in western China, pilots from General Claire Chennault's Flying Tigers scramble to their P-40s on receiving word from far-distant Chinese spotters of the approach of Japanese bombers.

ABOVE: Formed on February 12, 1942, the Tenth Air Force served in India, Burma, and China and became heir to General Chennault's American Volunteer Group of Flying Tigers, the China Air Task Force, and the India Air task Force.

## General Claire L. Chennault (1893–1958)

Born in Commerce, Texas, Chennault entered the infantry as a first lieutenant in 1917, decided to become a pilot, and that year earned his wings. Assigned to command a pursuit squadron, Chennault studied fighter tactics, and after graduating from the Air Corps Tactical School in 1931, he spent the next five years serving as an instructor. He believed too vociferously in the future of fighters and irritated the "bomber club," so he resigned his commission as captain. Chennault wanted to fight somebody, and on July 7, 1937, Japan provided the opportunity by invading China. At the invitation of Chiang Kai-shek, Chennault became special adviser to the Chinese Air Force.

Some months later, Chennault obtained permission from the generalissimo to return to Washington and ask President Roosevelt's permission to strengthen the Chinese Air Force with a group of American volunteers, thus emulating the Lafayette Escadrille. Roosevelt consented because he wanted to defend the Burma Road and keep China in the war.

Chennault returned to China with 100 pilots and 200 ground personnel, and formed the American Volunteer Group (AVG), or Flying Tigers. To fight technologically superior Japanese aircraft, the air force provided Chennault with 100 obsolescent P-40B Tomahawks

*ABOVE: General Chennault, wearing a leather jacket, did not believe in commanding from an armchair. Very much involved with his unit at all times, the general directs a group of mechanics servicing a P-40.*

intended for Sweden. Chennault chose his men carefully and trained them so thoroughly that, after operations began in December 1941, the Flying Tigers shot down 299 Japanese aircraft during the first seven months, losing only thirty-two planes and nineteen pilots. In July 1942, the Flying Tigers officially became the 23rd Fighter Squadron in the Tenth Air Force.

In April 1942, Chennault rejoined the USAAF as a colonel, took command of the China Air Task Force, and rose to major general. Eight months later the organization became the Fourteenth Air Force and supported General Joseph Stilwell's army operations in the China-Burma-India theater. Even while commanding the Fourteenth Air Force, Chennault continued to remain an irascible maverick. He confounded his superiors by ignoring the chain of command and dealt directly with Chiang. President Roosevelt did not want to disturb relations with Chiang and kept Chennault in China.

Chennault retired after the war but remained in China, ever loyal to Chiang. He organized the Chinese National Relief and the Civil Air Transport to fight communists. The USAF promoted Chennault to honorary lieutenant general nine days before he died of cancer in 1958.

## Flying the Hump

The Flying Tigers and AAF squadrons in China could not survive without supplies. They became completely dependent on the Tenth Air Force's Air Transport Command (ATC). When in June 1942 General Brereton took all the bombers and a dozen transports to the Middle East, he left his successors with broken squadrons of old aircraft. By December 1942, Major General Clayton Bissell had only twenty-two operational heavy bombers, forty-three medium bombers, and 160 combat-capable fighters. The ATC, which had a number of two-engined Douglas C-46A Commandos and C-47 Skytrains, took over the job of supplying the Tenth Air Force in China after the Japanese captured the Burma Road.

The only route from Assam, in northeastern India, to the Chinese cities of Kunming and Chungking, was a 500-mile flight over some of the worst terrain and

**LEFT: A pair of P-40N Warhawks taxi across an airfield carved out of the jungle in Burma. The P-40N, the last production model produced by Curtiss, clocked 375 mph but by 1944 had become a second-rate fighter.**

**ABOVE: A pair of Curtiss C-46 Commandos begin the long, arduous flight over the wind-swept Himalayas, "Flying the Hump" to deliver gasoline and supplies to the Tenth Air Force operating out of Kunming, China.**

weather in the world. The Santsung Ridge, an extension of the Himalayas known to pilots as "the Hump," lay between Assam and China's two terminals. Santsung's peaks topped 16,000 ft with the lower passes at 14,000 ft. Thunderstorms, icing, 100 mph winds, and violent turbulence made the route a pilot's nightmare.

In early 1943, tonnage over "the Hump" began to steadily increase. Deliveries of gasoline and supplies were small because the transports had to consume almost as much fuel as they delivered. The ATC had an added responsibility because Allied forces fighting in Burma also needed regular airdrops. General LeMay also drew on ATC capabilities when he moved B-29s into China to stage strikes against Formosa and Japan.

By war's end, the ATC had ferried 650,000 tons of supplies over a treacherous stretch of mountains that consumed men and planes, damaged health and careers, and wasted money and material, but war could not have been sustained in China without the effort.

### The Eleventh Air Force

The Alaskan Air Force, activated on January 15, 1942, at Elmendorf Field, lost its name three weeks later and became the Eleventh Air Force. The first arrivals consisted of Major Everett S. Davis, two enlisted men, and a six-year-old Martin B-10. Davis's job was to train personnel for reconnaissance operations in the Alaskan climate. More planes arrived, and by spring 1942 the Eleventh Air Force operated two 5,000-ft airstrips at Dutch Harbor in the Aleutians. Brigadier General William O. Butler took over operations on March 8, 1942, and established headquarters at Kodiak.

| The Eleventh Air Force in Alaska |
| --- |
| 11th Fighter Command |
| 11th Bomber Command |
| 11th Air Force Service Command |

LEFT: Activated as the Alaskan Air Force, January 15, 1942, at Elmendorf Field, the unit became the Eleventh Air Force on September 18, 1942, and expanded operations into the Aleutians.

Japan also knew the value of the Aleutians. The wind-swept atoll provided potential sites for waging air strikes against Canada and the northwest coast of the United States. During the Battle of Midway the Japanese, unaware of U.S. airbases at Dutch Harbor, attempted to seize the port but were surprised by the unexpected appearance of American fighter-bombers. A follow-up attack by B-17s and B-26s on the Japanese fleet resulted in damage that was unknown because of thick weather. The Japanese transports withdrew from the area and put infantry ashore on two remote islands, Attu and Kiska, at the far western end of the Aleutians.

During 1942-1943, while the army built bases so that the Air Transport Command could ferry aircraft and supplies to the Soviet Union, the Eleventh, which was tactically under the jurisdiction of the navy, staged regular bombing sorties against Attu and Kiska whenever weather permitted. The enemy's presence was mainly a nuisance, but the JCS wanted the Aleutians cleared. American troops landed on Attu and on May 29, 1943, wiped out the Japanese garrison. Two months later Japanese troops withdrew troops from Kiska. The Eleventh moved onto the airfield at Attu and in July 1943 B-24s began staging 1,600-mile raids against Japan's Kurile Islands. Strikes continued until the end of the war, destroying nearly all of the sixty-five Japanese canneries that processed fish for military consumption.

Unlike many of the other air forces, the Eleventh remained active as the Alaskan Air Command to manage America's emerging air defense system.

### Big Ticket Aircraft (1944)

| Bombers | Fighters | Transports | Trainers |
|---|---|---|---|
| B-29 $605,500 | P-38 $97,100 | C-54 $260,000 | AT-7, AT-11 $68,000 |
| B-24 $215,500 | P-47 $85,600 | C-46 $222,000 | |
| B-26 $192,500 | P-51 $51,500 | | |
| B-17 $204,400 | P-39 $51,000 | | |
| A-26 $176,000 | P-40 $45,000 | | |

### Combat Losses in Aircraft

| | |
|---|---|
| Against Germany and Italy | 22,948 |
| Against Japan | 4,530 |
| Combat Losses in USAAF Personnel | |
| Killed in combat | 40,000 |
| Captured | 41,500 |
| Missing and believed dead | 12,000 |
| Wounded | 18,000 |
| Other (disease, etc.) | 10,500 |
| Total | 122,000 |

## Mobilization in America

In early 1940, the AAF had few planes and not many that could perform at the level of European and Japanese aircraft. During the war, the United States spent $45 billion for aircraft, which was more than the entire munitions program. Up to V-J Day, the AAF accepted delivery of 158,000 planes, including 51,221 bombers and 47,050 fighters.

In 1943 Congress authorized an air force of 2,734,000 men, but the AAF never quite reached that figure. Having grown from 354,000 personnel in December 1941, the air force peaked at 2,411,294 in March 1944, and dropped to 2,282,000 as war ended in August 1945.

In five years the United States had leaped from being the sixth airpower in the world to becoming the first.

*ABOVE: During World War II, every component going into an aircraft came off mass production lines, including the rows of Plexiglass nose fixtures for A-20 attack bombers photographed under the glow of overhead factory lights. American assembly plants delivered 158,000 aircraft between July 1, 1940, and August 31, 1945, all from parts manufactured in thousands of factories.*

### Planes Produced July 1, 1940, to August 31, 1945

| | |
|---|---|
| North American | 41,188 |
| Consolidated Vultee | 30,903 |
| Douglas | 30,696 |
| Curtiss | 26,154 |
| Lockheed | 18,926 |
| Boeing | 18,381 |
| Grumman | 17,428 |
| Republic | 15,603 |
| Bell | 13,575 |
| Martin | 8,810 |
| Chance Vought | 7.890 |

# CHAPTER 6

# COLD WAR: FROM BERLIN TO KOREA 1945–1955

**RIGHT: After being sworn in as first chief of staff of the United States Air Force, General Carl Spaatz (right) confers with W. Stuart Symington, who on September 18, 1947, became the first secretary of the air force.**

At the end of World War II, General Arnold created the United States Strategic Bombing Survey to evaluate the impact of aerial bombing. He concluded that success in modern warfare hinged on air superiority for both offense and defense. He also implied that the price of liberty is eternal vigilance, and believed that " … the first essential of the airpower necessary for our national security is pre-eminence in research." President Harry S. Truman had witnessed enough war and set another world record for demobilization. By December 1945, America's airpower existed only in memory. General Eaker, former commander of the Eighth Air Force, admitted that by 1946 the AAF did not have one operational group ready to defend the United States. Almost overnight the most magnificent air force in the world wilted from 2,300,000 men and women and 72,000 planes in 1945 to 300,000 men and 10,000 planes in May 1947. Yet, when Arnold retired in March 1946, there was still one important, unaccomplished mission that he redirected to his successor, General Spaatz.

**Creation of the United States Air Force (USAF)**

In 1946, the battle shifted to the Pentagon and Congress. The debate involved the importance of coordinated unity of command of all three services in modern war. During World War II a few near-disasters might have been avoided had army, navy, and air units fought together and not independently. The army and the AAF strongly believed in the creation of a department of defense with three separate but equal and coordinated services under its control. The admirals objected, accusing the AAF of attempting to diminish the importance of seapower in exchange for airpower. To some degree this was true, because men like Spaatz and LeMay believed all future wars would be nuclear with victory hinging on strategic bombing.

> We were required to lose the [Korean] war. We weren't allowed to win it…
>
> *Lieutenant General George E. Stratemeyer, USAF, to Senate Subcommittee on Internal Security, 1954.*

LEFT: The enormous Convair B-36 intercontinental bomber was activated by the 5th Bombardment Wing in 1951. It had six radial piston engines and four turbojets, and was designed with a 10,000-mile range. This version is a GRB-36F in flight with a Republic YRF-84F Thunderstreak "parasite" fighter intended to protect the mother aircraft.

After months of debate, compromises were reached, including the continuation of navy and Marine Corps aviation. Congress passed the National Security Act of 1947 establishing the Department of Defense and a separate air force. President Truman issued Executive Order No. 9877 defining the roles and missions of the armed services, and nominated former Secretary of the Navy James V. Forrestal first defense secretary, with Stuart Symington first secretary of the U.S. Air Force.

USAF air generals were mistaken in their assumption that all future wars would be nuclear. Nevertheless, the program for the huge, ten-engined Convair B-36, which later became the RB-36E intercontinental bomber, finally got off the ground in 1951 as part of the 5th Bombardment Wing. Primary responsibilities of the USAF remained essentially the same, but with secondary duties such as interdicting enemy seapower, antisubmarine warfare, and aerial mine-laying operations. What the air generals did not anticipate was a new international crisis occurring in Germany.

LEFT: General Hoyt S. Vandenberg succeeded Spaatz in 1948 as air force chief of staff and served in that position for five years. He led the air force through the Berlin airlift and the Korean War, and before retiring in 1953 tried to convince a parsimonious Congress to not cut back a 143-wing program for the air force.

| The First Air Force Chiefs of Staff | |
| --- | --- |
| Carl A. Spaatz | 1947–1948 |
| Hoyt S. Vandenberg | 1948–1953 |
| Nathan F. Twining | 1953–1957 |

## The Air Force Academy

With the creation of the USAF in 1947, Generals Spaatz and Vandenberg began lobbying for an Air Force Academy, thus pulling instruction away from West Point and building a new institution with a curriculum focused on airpower. Seven years passed and in 1954, after the Korean War ended, President Eisenhower approved the funds. A year later the first classes convened at Lowry Air Force Base near Denver, Colorado.

Lieutenant General Hubert R. Harmon, former commander of the Seventh Air Force, emerged from retirement to become the academy's first superintendent. On assuming the post, Harmon said, "The mission of the academy will be to train generals, not second lieutenants." He probably also had a hand in the academy's motto: "Man is sustained in his flight through life by the power of his knowledge."

In August 1958, cadets moved to the magnificent new campus at Colorado Springs. The first class graduated the following year. Six years later those young officers would be among the flyers serving in combat in Southeast Asia.

*ABOVE: A row of Douglas C-47 Skytrains, many of which had entered the service in 1942, line up to discharge their cargoes at Templehof Air Base. C-47s carried everything from engine crates to milk bottles, coal, food, and passengers.*

### The Berlin Airlift

Alliances forged between western nations and the Soviet Union rapidly disintegrated after World War II with the military partitioning of Germany. In March 1948, Soviet infantry began detaining U.S., French, and British troop trains bound for their respective sectors in Berlin. On June 7, western nations announced their intention to create the capitalist state of West Germany. Two weeks later Soviets blockaded West Berlin and declared that, by virtue of its location, the city could never serve as West Germany's capital. To lose Berlin posed a threat to all of Germany, so President Truman called upon the now-independent USAF to organize a massive emergency airlift to keep West Berlin supplied.

On June 25, 1948, Lieutenant General Curtis LeMay, commanding U.S. Air Forces in Europe, received a telephone call from army General Lucius D. Clay, who asked: "Curt, can you transport coal by air?" LeMay replied: "Sir, the air force can deliver anything." On June 26 LeMay began marshaling Douglas C-47 Skytrains and C-54 Skymasters from Alaska, the Caribbean, Hawaii, Europe, and elsewhere, ordering them to Weisbaden and other West German airbases.

A day later LeMay appointed Brigadier General Joseph Smith to lead Operation Vittles, the Berlin Airlift Task Force. Each plane made three round trips to Berlin daily. Smith's Air Traffic Control Center at Frankfurt handled the schedules and coordinated flights. On July 23 Smith passed the baton to Major General William H. Tunner's Military Air Transport Service, which set a goal of landing a plane every minute of day and night. Tunner rounded up a few Fairchild C-82 Packets and C-74 Globemasters, replaced all the C-47s with four-engined C-54s, and kept about 225 planes in the air while the other seventy-five underwent maintenance.

| Daily Shipments to Berlin, October 20, 1948 | |
| --- | --- |
| Item | Tons |
| Food | 1,435 |
| Coal | 3,084 |
| Commercial/industrial items | 255 |
| Newsprint | 35 |
| Liquid fuel | 16 |
| Medical supplies | 2 |
| **Total for German populace** | **4,827** |
| For U.S., British, and French military | 763 |
| For three daily passenger flights | 30 |
| **Total** | **5,620** |
| (Source: Alfred Goldberg, History of the United States Air Force, 240) | |

**ABOVE: Military Air Transport Service Douglas C-54s, which could carry and enormous variety of cargo, eventually replaced C-47 Skytrains, and as the Berlin airlift came to a close, one enterprising crew took credit for being "The last vittles flight . . . to Berlin."**

RIGHT: During the Korean crisis following the invasion by Chinese troops from Manchuria, General Douglas MacArthur, Supreme Commander Allied Forces, greets Air Force Chief of Staff General Vandenberg at Haneda Air Base in Tokyo for a strategy session on military options.

From June 26, 1948, to September 30, 1949, the USAF made 189,963 flights over East Germany and into West Berlin, transporting 1,783,573 tons of food, coal, and other cargo while carrying 25,263 inbound passengers and 37,486 outbound passengers. On May 12, 1949, the Soviets officially lifted the blockade, after which the states of West and East Germany were formally established. The Soviets made a serious miscalculation: blockading Berlin became the rationale for forming the North Atlantic Treaty Organization (NATO).

## The Korean Surprise

Demobilization put the aircraft industry deep into the red. General Vandenberg, USAF chief of staff, warned that Russia was building "twelve military planes for every one built in America." In 1948 Secretary of the Air Force Thomas K. Finletter headed the President's Air Policy Committee and in his report, titled "Survival in the Air Age," called for a seventy-group air force to be equipped and ready by January 1, 1950, with a reserve of 8,100 modern planes and 401,000 uniformed personnel. In 1948 Congress appropriated the money Finletter requested, but Truman overrode Congress and the recommendations of his own committee and impounded funds allocated for new aircraft. Despite the vast buildup in Russia, aircraft contracts were cancelled. Everyone became shocked when in August 1949 the Soviets exploded an atomic bomb and wiped out America's monopoly on nuclear power.

On March 28, 1949, Louis A. Johnson, an influential fund-raiser during Truman's 1948 presidential campaign, replaced Forrestal as secretary of defense. He vowed to cut the fat out of the military establishment and in July 1949 pulled the last American postwar security troops out of South Korea. He also assured concerned Americans that no enemy could surprise the United States by a sudden "4-o'clock-in-the-morning attack" without suffering "a successful counterattack by the Air Force."

At roughly 4:00 A.M. on Sunday, June 25, 1950, the communist-led North Korean People's Army (NKPA) crossed the thirty-eighth parallel and attacked the weak internal security forces of the Republic of Korea (ROK). Six hours later the news reached Japan. At midnight, John J. Muccio, U.S. ambassador at Seoul, arranged for American dependents to be evacuated from Inchon by ship. A full day passed before Major General Earle E. Partridge, commanding the Fifth Air Force in Japan, received permission from Lieutenant General George E. Stratemeyer, commander of the Far East Air Forces (FEAF), to accelerate the evacuation. Partridge dispatched the 374th Troop Carrier Wing with C-54s

| FEAF Commanders | |
|---|---|
| Lieutenant General George E. Stratemeyer | June 25, 1950 |
| Lieutenant General Earle E. Partridge | May 21, 1951 |
| General Otto P. Weyland | July 10, 1951 |

escorted by F-82 Twin Mustang fighters. The precaution paid off. On June 27, when five Soviet Yak fighters appeared over Kimpo Airfield, Lieutenant William G. Hudson of the 68th Fighter Squadron scored the first air victory of the Korean War. Major James W. Little and Lieutenant Charles B. Moran shot down two more. The other Yaks fled. At 4:00 P.M., eight North Korean Ilyushin Il-10s attempted to strafe Kimpo Airfield. Lockheed F-80 Shooting Stars downed four, and the others turned back. C-54s evacuated 851 civilians with no further interference from Soviet-built planes.

On June 26, backed by U.N. Security Council resolutions, President Truman authorized General

| Fifth Air Force Commanders | |
| --- | --- |
| Lieutenant General Earle E. Partridge | June 25, 1950 |
| Major General Edward Timberlake | May 21, 1951 |
| Lieutenant General Frank F. Everest | June 1, 1951 |
| Lieutenant General Glenn O. Barcus | May 30, 1952 |
| Lieutenant General Samuel E. Anderson | May 31, 1953 |

*ABOVE: Four Lockheed F-80 Shooting Stars from the 8th Fighter-Bomber Wing demonstrate precision flying while returning to a forward airstrip in South Korea after performing close air support strikes on two strategic hills held by Chinese divisions near the front.*

MacArthur, head of Far East Command, to employ air and naval forces to support the South Korean (ROK) army, but not to attack above the thirty-eighth parallel except in an emergency.

## The USAF Goes to War

ABOVE: Armed with para-demolition bombs, a Douglas B-26 (also A-26) Invader of the 3rd Bomb Wing prepares to attack the marshaling yards at Iri, near the strategic port of Kunsan on Korea's west coast. Invaders were the last propeller-driven light bombers to serve in the USAF.

RIGHT: B-26 Invaders from the 3rd Bomb Wing also carried percussion and fragmentary bombs on their missions over Red Chinese targets in North Korea. The light bombers flew night and day, attacking key military targets, communication centers, railroads, and bridges.

On June 27, 1950, General Partridge mustered his severely reduced combat teams and moved the 35th Fighter-Interceptor and 49th Fighter-Bomber Groups, each with two squadrons of F-80s, to Kyushu. That night twelve Douglas B-26 Invaders from the 3rd Bombardment Group flew the first combat mission. On June 28 B-26s teamed up with F-80s and struck enemy positions on the Han River. During the afternoon four B-29s, having moved from Guam to Okinawa, struck NKPA columns on roads leading to Seoul. The following day a larger formation bombed Kimpo Airfield. When air attacks failed to slow down the NKPA and prevent Soviet-built aircraft from flying out of North Korea, MacArthur authorized raids against the enemy's main airfield at Pyongyang. Two squadrons of B-26s plastered the airfield, marking the beginning of the end of the North Korean air force.

Air superiority became the FEAF's first objective. By August 10, American pilots had destroyed 110 North Korean planes, leaving the enemy with about twenty. With the threat of air assault removed, Partridge's Fifth Air Force concentrated on harassing the movement of enemy troops, clobbering their sources of supply. Confusion occurred in early July when General Vandenberg detached the 22nd and 92nd B-29 bomb groups from the Strategic Air

Command (SAC) and sent them to Japan as the FEAF Bomber Command (Provisional). He put Major General Emmett O'Donnell, Jr., in charge of bomber operations and instructed him to destroy North Korea's war-production industries. MacArthur changed Vandenberg's orders and told Stratemeyer he wanted B-29s to concentrate on targets closer to the battlefield.

All the lessons learned during World War II still applied to the Korean War. High-flying B-29s were not ideal aircraft for providing close air support. During most of July, and in obedience to MacArthur's orders,

O'Donnell's B-29s bombed enemy positions behind the front lines, with little effect, while Partridge deployed his Fifth Air Force fighter-bombers for close air support missions. To eliminate confusion, B-29s and B-26s began flying missions on one side of the Han River and into North Korea, striking bridges and rail centers, while Partridge's command concentrated on striking enemy dispositions on the opposite side of the Han. The combined air strikes, particularly those of the Fifth Air Force, gave Lieutenant General Walton H. Walker time to move the Eighth Army into South Korea and maintain a flimsy perimeter around Pusan.

## General Earle Everard Partridge (1900–1990)

General Partridge ws commander of the Fifth Air Force in Japan and Korea (1948-1951), and no one faced a more difficult task than his in responding to the suddenness of the Korean War. Unlike General Stratemeyer's headquarters in Tokyo, from which B-29 missions were launched, Partridge operated near the battlefield with his headquarters tent next to General Walker's. Partridge's Fifth Air Force was Stratemeyer's FEAF tactical unit. Charged with the responsibility of obtaining and maintaining air superiority, Partridge's pilots flew missions of close air support, interdiction, and reconnaissance.

During the first months of the war, Soviet-built MiGs outclassed all of Partridge's available aircraft. In order to bring high performance jets to Korea, Partridge had to convert primitive fields in Korea to useable airbases. By July 1950, the Fifth Air Force had established air superiority over all of Korea, flying mostly propeller-driven aircraft.

After the capture of Inchon, Partridge opened the way for the invasion of North Korea by using F-51 Mustangs and F-80 Shooting Stars to clear roads and bridges for the Eighth Army. By November 1, North Korean resistance had virtually stopped when MiG-15s operating out of Manchuria began appearing in greater numbers. A month later the first F-84s and F-86s arrived from the United States, just in time to keep MiGs from interfering with General MacArthur's withdrawal from North Korea.

When General Stratemeyer suffered a heart attack in May 1951, Partridge assumed temporary control of the FEAF and turned the Fifth Air Force over to Major General Edward Timberlake. On June 10, 1951, General Otto P. Weyland arrived in Japan, relieved Partridge, and took command of the FEAF. Assigned to a new command in the United States, Partridge returned to Japan in April 1954 as a four-star general and replaced Weyland as commander of the FEAF.

**TOP LEFT: After General Partridge took command of the Fifth Air Force in Korea, he demonstrated the flexibility of air power by changing targets of missions already en route in response to requests by ground commanders.**

**TOP CENTER: For close-support missions in the rugged and forested hills of Korea, the slower and more adaptable air speeds of F-51 Mustangs often proved more effective when engaging enemy troops on the ground.**

**TOP RIGHT: A row of North American F-86C Sabres served as penetration fighters in Korea. Technically advanced, but still small enough to be delightful to fly, the Sabre was favored by pilots for its handling and maneuverability.**

**ABOVE: The pilot of the Republic F-84 Thunderstreak with PS-515 painted on its fuselage carried a hard hat, a parachute, G-suits, survival kits, side arms, first-aid supplies, navigation kits, and other impedimenta every time he stepped into the cockpit.**

## The Pusan Perimeter

Holding Pusan's perimeter became critically important to MacArthur's strategy for liberating South Korea. During August, Partridge's F-82Gs, F-51Ds, and F-80Cs flew an average of 340 fighter-bomber and 239 close-support sorties per day. Coordinating strikes worked effectively because Walker and Partridge occupied adjacent headquarters at Taegu. On August 16, when the enemy gathered for a thrust across the Naktong River at Taegu, O'Donnell led ninety-eight B-29s on a carpet-bombing strike that disorganized the enemy assault. Wherever Walker needed help, Partridge and O'Donnell provided it.

In late August, NKPA generals decided they must win quickly or lose everything and hurled six divisions at the U.S. 2nd and 25th Infantry Divisions defending the southwestern perimeter. The FEAF and the Fifth Air Force marshaled every plane and stopped the enemy at the Naktong River. By the second week of September the NKPA had exhausted its reserves, lost most of its tanks and artillery, and no longer resembled a cohesive fighting force.

## Strategic Bombing Campaign

Although most of the NKPA's weapons and aircraft came from Chinese or Soviet bases off limits to American bombers, there were armament industries in North Korea. On July 29 the JCS offered to send two more B-29 groups, provided that MacArthur agreed to target industries in North Korea and not Manchuria. The general agreed, an in early August the 98th and 307th Bombardment Groups joined the 22nd and 92nd in Japan. The only industrial targets in North Korea were located at Pyongyang, Chongjin, Wonsan, Hungnam, and Rashin. General O'Donnell proposed using area bombing tactics and incendiaries. Truman hesitated because of communist propaganda concerns. Stratemeyer authorized two-group attacks every third day with high-explosive bombs. The decision meant

more sorties, but B-29 pilots used their all-weather radar-sighting equipment and by September 15 had wiped out every military target in North Korea except for Rashin, which Truman struck from the bomb-list because it lay near the Siberian border.

On October 27, 1950, the 22nd and 92nd Bombardment Groups returned to the United States, and the FEAF stood down. Although the strategic bombing of North Korea met every expectation, it marked the beginning of political micromanagement of airpower that fifteen years later grievously frustrated another generation of flyers.

**ABOVE: With pinpoint accuracy, Boeing B-29s rapidly destroyed the industrial base of North Korea. When U.N. forces moved north of the 38th parallel into Pyongyang and Wonsan, they found buildings gutted, mounds of twisted steel, scorched oil refineries, but surrounding civilian homes and business districts unharmed.**

**LEFT: Major Harry B. Bailey, former 98th Bomb Wing intelligence officer, briefs a mission group on Sinuiji targets. One of the most frequently hit cities along the Yalu River, Sinuiji was bombed repeatedly by B-29 crews stationed in Japan and Okinawa.**

ABOVE: In order to tool up for the Korean War, the Combat Cargo Command hurried Fairchild C-119 Flying Boxcars into the area to haul troops into the Pusan perimeter, transport evacuees out, and carry tons of cargo to where there were no roads.

## Invasion of Inchon

In August, while the Fifth Air Force worked the Pusan perimeter with Walker's Eighth Army, General MacArthur began planning the assault of Inchon, which lay about thirty miles south of the thirty-eighth parallel on the northwest coast of South Korea. For the Inchon operation, MacArthur planned to use Major General Edward M. Almond's X Corps and Major General Oliver P. Smith's 1st Marine Division for ground operations, and General Stratemeyer's FEAF

for air operations. In addition to combat aircraft, Stratemeyer would provide the FEAF Combat Cargo Command's (Provisional) C-54s under Major General William H. Tunner, and the 314th Troop Carrier Group's C-119s after Kimpo Airfield became available. After securing Inchon, MacArthur planned to have Walker's Eighth Army break out of Pusan and close the pincers by driving the NKPA into Almond's X Corps.

When typhoon *Kezia* threatened to delay the assault of Inchon, Stratemeyer moved F-51s from the 8th and the 18th Fighter-Bomber Groups onto small airfields inside the Pusan perimeter. On September 15, 1950, however, the Inchon assault began on schedule with the 1st Marine Division spearheading the way for the X Corps. During seven days the FEAF flew 3,257 sorties of all types, and B-29s pulverized the enemy's marshaling yards and rail lines running into South Korea from Pyongyang and Wonsan. Four days after the assault, C-54s from Tunner's Combat Cargo Command flew into Kimpo with supplies and commenced airlifting operations.

With strong support from the Fifth Air Force, Walker's Eighth Army broke out of the Pusan perimeter. Fighters removed obstacles in the way of Walker's advance and set fire to the walled, fortified city of Yongchon. The following day, forty-two B-29s removed another obstacle by blasting enemy positions near Waegwan. By September 22 the Eighth Army was attacking straight ahead in column, a tactic impossible without the Fifth Air Force clearing the roads ahead.

FAR LEFT: A paratrooper, dropped from a C-46 of the 437th Troop Carrier Wing, clings to a cross beam after becoming entangled, while a comrade from the 187th Regimental Combat Team glides by in an open parachute.

LEFT: In close formation with other Flying Boxcars, a C-119 from the Combat Cargo Command para-drops rations and gasoline to U.N. troops clustered in the snow-covered battlefield near Chungju.

| USAF Units Based in South Korea | |
|---|---|
| Yalu Offensive | |
| 8th Fighter-Bomber Wing | F-51s |
| 18th Fighter-Bomber Wing | F-51s |
| 35th Fighter-Interceptor Wing | F-51s |
| 49th Fighter-Bomber Wing | F-80s |
| 51st Fighter-Interceptor Wing | F-80s |
| 502nd Tactical Control Group | C-47s/C-119s |

By September 28, the NKPA no longer existed as a unified fighting force. Sandwiched between the X Corps and the Eighth Army, and mercilessly bombed and strafed, NKPA soldiers either dissolved into the countryside or surrendered.

On September 29, President Syngman Rhee returned to Seoul and reestablished the government of the Republic of Korea. MacArthur had fulfilled the United Nations objective and driven the NKPA out of South Korea.

## The Yalu River Campaign

MacArthur informed the U.N. and President Truman that removing the enemy from South Korea did not guarantee an end to trouble, and recommended that steps be taken to insure peace throughout the peninsula. Because of the easy victory and MacArthur's announcement that the men would be home by Christmas, the U.N. agreed, and so did Truman. MacArthur immediately initiated the Yalu offensive with General Partridge's fighters and bombers and sent the Eighth Army up the western side of North Korea while General Almond shipped the X Corps to Wonsan on the east coast.

Despite capturing Pyongyang and Wonsan with very little effort, MacArthur underestimated the repercussions of pushing to the Yalu. Within three weeks complete victory seemed assured. Bombers found nothing to bomb, and fighters encountered no

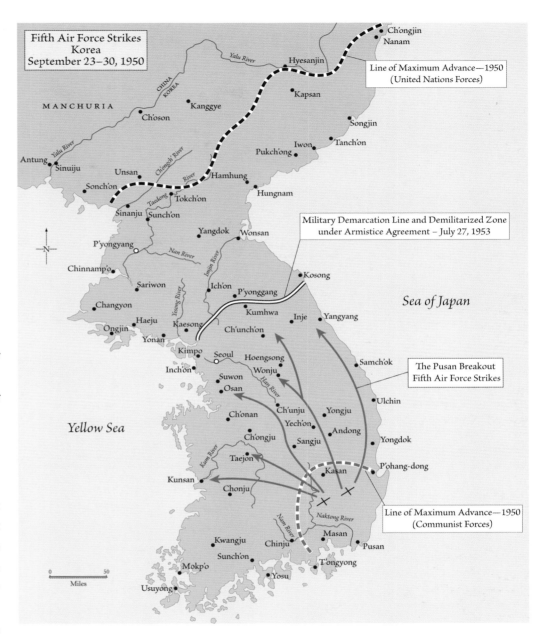

**ABOVE: After the Inchon assault, the Eighth Army broke out of the Pusan perimeter and attacked the North Korean army. Those spearheads received support from USAF F-51 Mustangs, F-82 Twin Mustangs, and USMC F-4U Corsairs, which ranged in advance of ground troops and wiped out enemy tanks, artillery, and motorized vehicles, and created considerable chaos. Propeller-driven aircraft were used because the few airfields built inside the Pusan perimeter were too small to accommodate jets.**

ABOVE: Under constant guard by air police at an airbase on Okinawa, a reassembled Soviet-built MiG-15 fighter is taxied to the flight line to be flown by five USAF pilots during a week of extensive testing.

TOP RIGHT: A photograph printed from actual gun camera film from an F-86 Sabre shows smoke pouring from a swept-wing Soviet-built MiG-15, shot down in an area in northwestern Korea known as "MiG Alley."

RIGHT: Turning into the skies over "MiG Alley," a squadron of F-86 Sabre jets from the 51st Fighter Interceptor Wing maneuver in search of a dogfight. Sabre pilots scored a 15:1 advantage when dueling with MiG-15s.

enemy combat planes. Though rumors circulated that Chinese "volunteers" might join their North Korean brethren, none did until November 1 when six MiG-15 jet fighters unsuccessfully jumped a flight of F-51s near the Yalu River, which formed the border between China's Manchuria and North Korea. Eight days later the first all-jet dogfights in history took place high above the Yalu when MiGs attacked F-80C Shooting Stars. Although F-80s were already obsolete and no match for speedy, swept-wing MiG-15s, Lieutenant Russell J. Brown of the 51st Fighter-Interceptor Wing scored the first victory and became the first pilot to win the honor in jet-to-jet combat.

The appearance of MiGs foreshadowed more trouble for MacArthur. The following day Chinese forces encircled forward elements of the U.S. 8th Cavalry Regiment near Unsan. To meet the threat, Partridge moved three F-51 groups into North Korea with transports to airdrop supplies to the Eighth Army. While Walker pulled back to the south bank of the Chongchon River to reform, MacArthur asked for help from Stratemeyer, who had pulled the FEAF back to Japan. In an effort to discourage the Chinese from

meddling in North Korea, Stratemeyer sent B-29s to clobber the international bridges over the Yalu and "to destroy every means of communication and every factory, city, and village." B-29s could not destroy the Yalu bridges without over-flying Manchurian territory, which was off limits. Early in December the Yalu froze solid, and bridge attacks became less meaningful.

LEFT: Flying at about 500 knots over Korea's northern mountains, three F-86E Sabres from the 51st Fighter-Interceptor Wing streak towards a reported approaching squadron of MiGs after lifting off the K-14 airbase at Kimpo, about twenty-five miles northwest of Seoul.

## Red China Intervenes

On November 18, MacArthur believed the ten-day air assault had suppressed the enemy, and gave Walker, Almond, and Partridge six days to prepare for a new offensive. On November 24, Walker's Eighth Army and Almond's X Corps, supported by the Fifth Air Force and navy planes, moved forward on schedule. One day later 300,000 Chinese crossed into Korea with more on the way. Confronted by a war with China, Walker and Almond immediately pulled back. By early December the Eighth Army and the X Corps were in full retreat, saved only by airpower.

The appearance of MiGs concerned Partridge because Fifth Air Force aircraft lacked equal capabilities. During the retreat of U.N. forces, however, the enemy lost an opportunity to compete for air control by not acting aggressively. In mid-December American jets arrived, the 4th Fighter-Interceptor Wing with North American F-86 Sabres and the 27th Fighter-Escort Wing with Republic F-84 Thunderjets. Given the task of covering northwestern Korea, F-86A pilots recorded their first victories on December 17 by shooting down four MiGs. MiG-15s were superior aircraft in

performance, but Americans were better-trained pilots. During December, Sabre pilots shot down four more MiGs and temporarily cleared the skies.

During the Eighth Army retreat, Chinese forces entrapped the 2nd Infantry Division, which was forced to break through a five-mile cordon of enemy artillery, mortar, and machine gun fire. Though taking heavy casualties, the division escaped the ambuscade because low-flying fighter-bombers from the Fifth Air Force strafed and pounded enemy positions with rockets and napalm.

ABOVE: A low-flying F-86 provides close air support by firing rockets at Red Chinese positions during the Eighth Army's withdrawal from North Korea in December 1950.

After retreating to the outskirts of Seoul, the Eighth Army began massing along the Imjin River. Stratemeyer and Partridge collaborated on restraining immense columns of Chinese troops jamming the roads to Seoul. FEAF B-29s disrupted troop movements and shut down railroad routes, while the Fifth's fighter-bombers flew daylight strikes against entire divisions of Chinese troops strung out on roads. Stratemeyer estimated that 33,000 Chinese troops—the equivalent of four divisions—had been either killed or wounded by FEAF air strikes. Despite heavy casualties, the Chinese continued to advance and on January 5, 1951, recaptured Kimpo Airfield and pushed the Eighth Army out of Seoul.

### A Change in Strategy

During December 1950, President Truman feared that any further effort to unify Korea could result in another world war. The U.N. General Assembly agreed and opted for a settlement by peaceful means. The Chinese, however, sought to capitalize on their military momentum and drive the U.N. out of Korea. Unsettled by a change of course, MacArthur intended to inflict the maximum amount of damage on the enemy and perhaps regain the initiative. During the retreat, General Walker had been killed in an accident, and in late December Lieutenant General Matthew B. Ridgway arrived to take command of the Eighth Army. Ridgway understood his instructions were to contain the Chinese around the original thirty-eighth parallel but make them pay a huge price in manpower and material.

Though MacArthur admitted that "we face an entirely new war," Washington advised him to forget unification, that "Korea is not the place to fight a major war." The general presented new demands, including the lifting of bombing restrictions along the Yalu, while at the same time Ridgway performed a remarkable task

*FAR LEFT: U.S. medics gently carry a wounded soldier from a Bell H-13 helicopter used as an aerial ambulance. With helicopters, a wounded soldier could be transported from the battlefield to a modern hospital within a few hours.*

### Helicopters in Korea

During the Korean War, the USAF activated several helicopter-equipped air rescue squadrons with Sikorsky H-5s, and on September 4, 1950, a unit performed the first rescue of a downed pilot behind enemy lines. The rescue marked the beginning of helicopters on the battlefield.

Army officers recognized that severely wounded soldiers would not survive a long overland haul by ambulance to field hospitals and demanded more helicopters. On November 22, 1950, Bell H-13s arrived in Korea and were attached to the 8055th Mobile Army Surgical Hospital (MASH) during the 1950-1951 winter campaigns. Helicopters were not exclusively attached to the air force, but were used by all the services. Specifically designed as air ambulances, H-13Es came equipped with two external litters. The death rate in Korea fell to half the ratio recorded during World War II.

When in 1952 Sikorsky H-19 and Hiller H-23 Ravens arrived in Korea, the army deployed them in combat operations. Although early rotary-wing aircraft manifested many drawbacks, including excessive noise and fragility, helicopters saved lives and proved their value in the Korean War.

*ABOVE LEFT: When Sikorsky H-19 Chickasaw helicopters began arriving in Korea in 1952 to replace the obsolete H-5 Dragon Flys, the air force and the army used the larger H-19s for combat operations as well as for search and rescue.*

of stabilizing lines around the thirty-eighth parallel. MacArthur could not accept defeat or stalemate, and openly defied President Truman over efforts to negotiate peace. On April 11 the president recalled the recalcitrant general and replaced him with Ridgway. A month later Lieutenant General Mark Clark, who had led the U.S. Fifth Army during World War II, assumed command of the Eighth Army.

## The Air War

In January the Fifth Air Force lost its advanced airfields at Kimpo and Suwon, and the FEAF withdrew the F-86 Sabre jets to Japan and nearly lost air superiority over northwestern Korea. MiGs enjoyed greater freedom in an area between the Yalu and Chongchon rivers known as "MiG Alley." The FEAF attempted to interdict MiG activity by sending B-29s escorted by long-range F-84 Thunderjets to bomb enemy airfields. On January 23, the largest all-jet air battle occurred when thirty-three F-84s tackled twenty-five MiGs near the Yalu and shot down three. Soon afterwards, the Eighth Army recaptured Seoul and Kimpo Airfield, and the Fifth Air Force's Sabres returned to Korea.

Political restrictions worked both ways. While U.N. forces could not bomb MiG airbases in Manchuria, MiG pilots were barred from attacking U.N. ground

positions except when operating from airbases in North Korea. MiGs, however, were short-range jets and unable to operate effectively from Manchuria to the thirty-eighth parallel. The Chinese desperately needed air support, but during the winter of 1951 B-29s pummeled North Korean airbases and rendered them unserviceable. In March, when Chinese laborers attempted to repair the bases, Fifth Air Force reconnaissance pilots reported the activity. Brigadier General James E. Briggs, who succeeded O'Donnell, waited until construction was nearly completed before ordering B-29 strikes. In mid-April FEAF bombers clobbered two large airfields at Pyongyang, another at

*TOP LEFT: Watching the take off of F-86 Sabre jets are, left to right, Colonel George J. Ola, 4th Fighter Interceptor Wing; Major General Bryan L. Milburn, assistant chief of staff; General Matthew B. Ridgway; and Lieutenant General Frank F. Everest, Fifth Air Force.*

*ABOVE: During operations over North Korea, Douglas B-26 Invaders from the 3rd Bomb Wing, Fifth Air Force, use para-demolition bombs to pulverize supply warehouses and dock facilities at Wonsan.*

*ABOVE LEFT: Lieutenant General George E. Stratemeyer, commanding the Far East Air Force, pins a Distinguished Flying Cross on Major General Emmett O'Donnell, Jr., who commanded the FEAF's bomber group during the Korean War.*

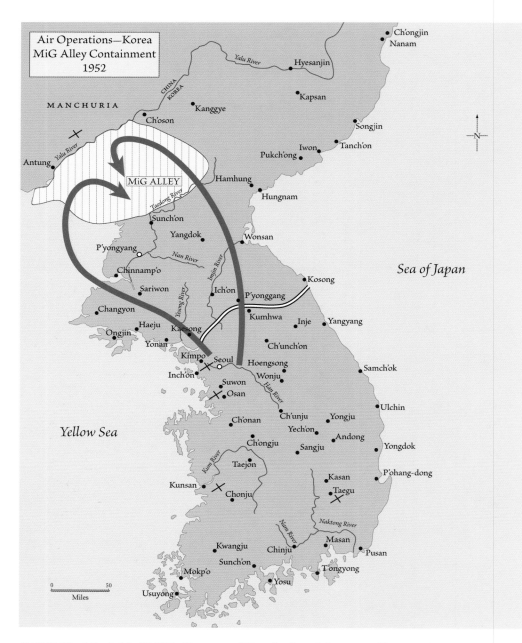

Air Operations—Korea
MiG Alley Containment
1952

| USAF Air Operations in Korea | |
| --- | --- |
| Enemy deaths | 145,000 |
| MiGs destroyed | 838 |
| Total aircraft destroyed | 1,018 |
| Vehicles destroyed | 75,000 |
| Locomotives destroyed | 1,000 |
| Rail cars destroyed | 16,000 |
| Tanks destroyed | 1,000 |
| Bridges destroyed | 2,000 |

With occasional interference from MiGs, the FEAF and the Fifth Air Force began relentless attacks on railway bridges, marshaling yards, and supply depots. B-29s using radar-directed bombing operated deep in North Korea and eventually destroyed most of the bridges over the Yalu, while the Fifth Air Force concentrated on driving Chinese ground forces back beyond the thirty-eighth parallel. Chinese prisoners admitted that U.N. airpower had not only interdicted their supplies but had inflicted about half of their casualties.

As the ground campaign see-sawed at the thirty-eighth parallel, in May 1952 Lieutenant General Glenn O. Barcus took command of the Fifth Air Force and devised new stratagems for luring MiGs into dogfights with his swifter, higher-altitude-flying F-86Fs. The air war rapidly escalated when Sabres began concentrating in "MiG Alley" and along the Yalu. During September 1952, F-86 interceptors destroyed sixty-three MiGs while losing only six. For several months MiG pilots

*ABOVE: Most Soviet-built MiGs flew out of Manchurian air bases. Unlike American jets, MiGs had a shorter combat radius. Most air battles occurred in the northwestern reaches of North Korea, which also happened to be the entry point for most MiGs en route to the combat zone. In 1952 the USAF developed a strategy to contain MiGs within a designated airspace, and the area became known as MiG Alley.*

Siuniju, and nine newer and smaller airbases about seventy miles south of the Yalu. The campaign destroyed scores of the communist planes on the ground and eventually ended the enemy's effort to establish airbases in North Korea.

| Far East Air Forces Operations in Korea | |
| --- | --- |
| Sorties flown | 720,980 |
| Counter-air ops | 66,997 |
| Interdictions | 192,581 |
| Close air support | 57,665 |
| Air cargo ops | 181,659 |
| Other* | 222,078 |
| *Reconnaissance, air control, rescue, etc.* | |

refused to fight, but in May 1953, as MiG-17s became available, air battles temporarily resumed. Sabres destroyed fifty-six MiGs against the loss of one. In June, Chinese pilots made one more effort, this time losing seventy-five MiGs without scoring a single victory. Sabres shot down another thirty-two MiGs before the war ended in July 1953.

Thirty-eight USAF jet-versus-jet aces emerged from the Korean War. Six of them had also aced in World War II. On May 20, 1951, Major James Jabara, a World War II veteran, became the first ace. Captain Joseph McConnell, Jr., topped all jet aces with sixteen victories. U.S. aces accounted for 305.5 kills out of the 810 air-to-air combat victories credited to flyers during the war.

### An Indecisive Finale

After three years, one month, and two days of fighting, the war ended on July 27, 1953, with a ceasefire agreement. Captain Ralph S. Parr, flying an F-86, shot down the last enemy plane. A B-26 dropped the last bombs exactly twenty-four minutes before the official signing. The Korean War ended indecisively, with no

| Korean War USAF Statistics | | | |
|---|---|---|---|
| Served | KIA/MIA and died of wounds | Other deaths | Wounded in action |
| 1,285,000 | 1,198 | 298 | 368 |

winner and no loser. The thirty-eighth parallel continued to be the dividing line between the two Koreas.

The war did provide an important benefit for the USAF. It proved the value of the strategic bomber in Cold War battles, and it compelled the U.S. government to upgrade its jet-powered aircraft.

Without airpower, the numerically inferior U.N. ground force could not have survived against the massive Chinese People's Volunteer Army. As Lieutenant General Nam Il, chief North Korean delegate to the peace talks observed, "Without the support of the … bombardment by your air and naval forces, your ground forces would have long ago been driven out of the Korean peninsula by our powerful and battle-skilled ground forces."

The Cold War, however, had just begun.

*ABOVE LEFT: Fellow comrades hoist James "Jabby" Jabara after he returns from a dogfight during which he became America's first jet ace. Jabara went on to score fifteen victories and become the second highest scoring ace in Korea.*

*ABOVE: Captain Joseph McConnell, Jr., a pilot with the 51st Fighter Interceptor Wing, chats with his crew chief before exiting from the cockpit of his F-86 Sabre jet, "Beauteous Butch." McConnell became the top jet ace in Korea with sixteen victories.*

# THE VIETNAM WAR 1955–1975

RIGHT: During a sweep through Viet Minh areas in the Red River delta between Haiphong and Hanoi, a French Foreign Legionnaire treks across the dry rib of a rice paddy followed by a surplus U.S. tank donated to France.

[I can foresee] no greater tragedy than for the United States to become involved in an all-out war in Indochina.
*General Dwight D. Eisenhower*

The Vietnamese nationalist effort to end French colonial rule began during World War I. France resisted until overrun by Germany in 1940. Japan promptly replaced France, extending its empire to include Indochina. In the wake of the seizure, Viet Minh formed a nationalistic front. Although many Vietnamese welcomed the Japanese as liberators, Ho Chi Minh's communists were as wary of the Japanese as they were of the French. Ho's followers went underground and became the principal organ of Vietnamese resistance and nationalism. During the last months of World War II, AAF parachutists dropped into central Indochina, joined insurgent Viet Minh forces led by Ho, and provided them with weapons and tactical advice to fight the Japanese. When Japan surrendered in August 1945, the Viet Minh disarmed the enemy and seized their weapons. Ho's communists now had an organized and well-armed military force.

On September 9, 1945, 200,000 Chinese troops arrived in Hanoi and discovered that Ho had replaced all French street signs with Vietnamese signs and taken control of the city. In March 1946, after French troops arrived at Saigon to reclaim the colony, the Chinese withdrew. French General Jacques-Philippe Leclerc struck an agreement with Ho to divide Vietnam, but the pact soon collapsed. Ho's supporters initiated guerrilla warfare, and Viet Minh General Vo Nguyen Giap began launching attacks on French posts and truck convoys.

As Vietnam gradually turned into a tinderbox, President Truman became preoccupied with the Soviet effort to control Germany. On February 16, 1950, France officially requested assistance from the United States. With the outbreak of the Korean War in June 1950, combined with Communist expansion in Southeast Asia, Truman supported French interests by sending the Military Assistance Advisory Group (MAAG) to Vietnam. The unit included USAF

personnel, military advisors, maintenance and supply experts, and combat crews to keep U.S.-loaned aircraft in flying condition.

When in 1953 Eisenhower became president, he cautiously followed Truman's policies of containment, believing that a Viet Minh victory in Vietnam would bring communists to power throughout Southeast Asia, and in 1954 he supported the division of Vietnam at the seventeenth parallel. Although Eisenhower increased support through the MAAG, he turned away overtures of military intervention even when Brigadier General Joseph D. Caldara, commanding FEAF, claimed that a B-29 strike might save the surrounded and doomed French garrison at Dienbienphu. The defeat at Dienbienphu marked the beginning of the

end of French involvement in Vietnam, but not the end of U.S. involvement.

Eisenhower left office in 1961, having told incoming President John F. Kennedy to stand firm in Southeast Asia but avoid military entanglements. Kennedy adopted his own counter-insurgency plan. He increased military assistance, provided helicopters and North American T-28 trainers, escalated USAF involvement by sending the 507th Tactical Control Group to Saigon with Fairchild C-123 transports, and destabilized the situation further by authorizing the overthrow of South Vietnamese President Ngo Dinh Diem. Three weeks later an assassin shot Kennedy, and on November 22, 1963, Vice President Lyndon B. Johnson assumed control of the U.S. government.

**ABOVE: During the early months of the Vietnam War, President Lyndon Johnson greets U.S. troops at an air base near Saigon. Not until later do those same men come to understand how the president intended to micromanage the war.**

ABOVE: A Martin B-57G Canberra Night Intruder, based at Ubon, Thailand, uses its package of low-light TV, infrared, and detection gear tied to laser ranging devices to drop its payload on Viet Cong units near the Ho Chi Minh Trail.

## President Johnson's War

Lyndon Johnson may have warranted a more distinguished legacy had he heeded Ho's words and not used the trivial 1964 Tonkin Gulf incident—a poorly executed and unsuccessful attack by North Vietnam torpedo-boats on the destroyer USS *Maddox*—as an opportunity to escalate American military involvement in Vietnam. On August 4, after a second alleged torpedo-boat attack that likely never occurred, Johnson authorized a retaliatory strike by USAF and navy planes against North Vietnam ports. After the attack, General Giap imported thirty MiG-17 fighters from China.

From his office in Saigon, Ambassador Maxwell Taylor called for more bombing, and the JCS agreed. With a minimum of debate, Congress passed the Tonkin Gulf resolution on August 7, 1964, giving President Johnson the option of taking America to war. Johnson also had the authority to step away from a costly war and concentrate the nation's resources on building his "Great Society," but the JCS convinced the president and Robert S. McNamara, secretary of defense, that military efforts should be escalated in Vietnam.

Air units began immediate deployments. Two Martin B-57 squadrons also equipped with McDonnell RF-101s moved into Bien Hoa Air Base from the Philippines, and North American F-100 fighters and Convair F-102 interceptors flew into Danang. Other air units landed in Thailand. With jets in place, Johnson approved operations against the Viet Cong's supply line—the long, winding Ho Chi Minh jungle trail stretching through North Vietnam, Laos, and Cambodia. Fighter-bombers struck the route with little effect on the transit of VC materiel. On November 1

It took us eight years of bitter fighting to defeat you French… The Americans are much stronger than the French, though they know us less well. It may perhaps take ten years to do it, but our heroic compatriots [Viet Cong terrorists] in the South will defeat them in the end."
*Ho Chi Minh to Bernard B. Fall in* Last Reflections on a War.

the VC retaliated with mortars, destroying five and damaging fifteen B-57s at Bien Hoa airbase. VC also struck the Pleiku barracks and Tuy Hoa, destroying five helicopters and inflicting 132 American casualties.

Constantly at odds with the Kennedy and Johnson administrations over the retaliatory concept of flexible response, air force chief of staff General Curtis LeMay retired in disgust on January 31, 1965, later declaring, "Instead of swatting flies, we should be going after the manure pile." On February 7, 1965, having won reelection, President Johnson authorized Operation Flaming Dart to swat more flies, and dragged America deeper into a controversial war.

## Flaming Dart—Rolling Thunder

Of the many mistakes made during America's involvement in Southeast Asia, the most unpardonable was McNamara's fabrication, on which he based American strategy, that the conflict in South Vietnam was not a war but a civil insurrection. He knew North Vietnam was causing all the trouble in South Vietnam, but by denying this publicly he could promote his experimental military strategy of gradual response. After the VC attack on Pleiku barracks, McNamara urged a war of "tit-for-tat." Johnson approved Operation Flaming Dart and retaliatory strikes began against enemy troop concentrations in southern areas of North Vietnam. Forty-nine navy planes struck Donghoi, while USAF A-1 Skyraiders and F-100 Super Sabres struck a North Vietnamese barracks at Chap Le.

During Flaming Dart, General John P. McConnell, who replaced LeMay as chief of staff, moved Boeing B-52s from the 7th and 320th Bomb Wings to Guam. He produced a list of ninety-four strategic targets in North Vietnam and proposed a massive air offensive to destroy the enemy's ability to wage war. The targets could have been eliminated quickly and with little loss of life, but McNamara did not want the United States to appear to be at war with North Vietnam. Instead, Johnson

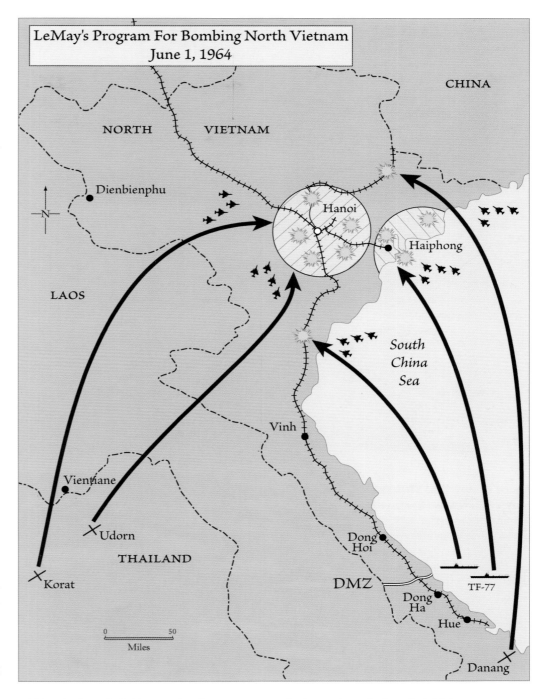

ABOVE: On June 1, 1964, a top-level strategy conference took place in Honolulu to discuss how best to address war with North Vietnam. General Curtis LeMay recommended a heavy and sustained bombing of ninety-four strategic sites in North Vietnam, in particular Hanoi and Haiphong. Had President Johnson approved the strikes instead of adopting gradual response, the longest war in America's history might have ended in a few weeks. LeMay's recommendations were tabled until December 1972, when President Nixon authorized Linebacker II, blasting the North Vietnamese to the peace table. By then, the number of strategic targets had increased from ninety-four to 265.

ABOVE: A Douglas EB-66C from 355th Tactical Fighter Wing at Takhi, Thailand, leads a squadron of four aircraft, of which two would be F-105Gs or F-4Cs, to a bomb drop over North Vietnam. F-4s carried "Paveway" laser-guided bombs among their weaponry.

*ABOVE: North Vietnamese SA-2 missile crews rush to their launchers as USAF B-52s carry out air strikes during Linebacker II. SAMs accounted for all fifteen B-52s shot down during the raids in December 18-29, 1972.*

*RIGHT: A North American F-100D Super Sabre operating out of Tuy Hoa Air Base fires a salvo of 2.75-inch rockets at an enemy concentration in South Vietnam.*

*FAR RIGHT: Among the USAF's inventory during the Vietnam War was the Lockheed F-104A Starfighter, developed in 1951. Obsolete by the time of the war, the Starfighter went through many modifications, eventually becoming F-104G strike-reconnaissance aircraft and F-104S interceptors, although they saw very little action during the war.*

Countermeasures executed by Douglas EB-66s loaded with chaff and jamming equipment disrupted SAM targeting and NVA ground-control communications. In July, the USAF finally obtained permission to strike SAM sites after a McDonnell F-4C became the first victim. A flight of F-105s destroyed the site.

Restrictions against striking SAM sites enraged pilots. Already overloaded with cockpit data, flyers were not permitted to strike SAM sites operating radar in search mode. They could only attack if the site switched to track mode seconds before launching.

During 1965, the Republic F-105 Thunderchief became the primary USAF fighter-bomber because of its supersonic speed and range. Other aircraft included the F-100 Super Sabre, the Lockheed F-104 Starfighter, and the Martin B-57 Canberra. Boeing KC-135A tankers orbited between northern Laos and the Gulf of Tonkin to keep fighters, bombers, reconnaissance, and observation planes refueled. When the first Rolling Thunder strike began on March 2, 1965, twenty-five F-105s and twenty B-57s wiped out a small ammunition dump at Xan Bong, a few miles north of the DMZ.

## The Wild Weasels

To parry SAM threats, Major General Garry Willard organized a team of air and ground personnel into the first Wild Weasel unit. On November 21, 1965, seven specially instrumented, two-man F-100F Super Sabres arrived in Thailand as a detachment from the 6234th Tactical Fighter Wing (TFW). The planes had been fitted with APR-25 Radar Homing and Warning systems along with IR-133 panoramic receivers for analyzing radar signals to determine whether they came from an antiaircraft battery, ground control intercept radar, or a SAM site. A third instrument, an APR-26 Launch Warning Receiver, detected increased power from SAM guidance systems on launch mode. All of the instruments were packed into aging F-100F fighters armed with 20mm cannon, 2.75-inch rockets, and eventually AGM-45 Shrike missiles.

Wild Weasel missions, called Iron Hand strikes, could not attack SAM sites within ten miles of Hanoi or Haiphong, and sites within thirty miles of Hanoi could be struck only if operating on track mode. The restrictions put Wild Weasel pilots at an enormous disadvantage, and when sorties began on December 20, Captains John Pitchford and Robert Trier were shot down exactly thirty miles northeast of Hanoi. Both men ejected. Pitchford spent seven years as a prisoner of war. Trier was killed. A few days later Captains Al Lamb and Jack Donovan destroyed a site seventy-five miles northwest of Hanoi, after which SAM-hunting began in earnest.

Only the very best flyers performed Wild Weasel missions. While the pilot flew the plane, an equally skilled electronic warfare officer had to operate new radar warning systems during high G-force maneuvers. In addition to managing electronics, the warfare officer spotted SAMs in the air and sites on the ground and guided the pilot into position to launch ordnance. The first Iron Hand flights destroyed seven SAM sites but lost two planes from antiaircraft fire.

Because Iron Hand missions often required F-105 escorts, the air force began replacing the older F-100Fs with a pair of two-man F-105Gs, each with a single-seat F-105D on its wing. The F-105Ds took care of SAMs in the air while the F-105Gs blasted sites and intercepted MiGs.

ABOVE: Flying through low clouds under radar control with an EB-66 Destroyer, four F-105D Thunderchiefs release 3,000-pound bombs on a military target over the southern panhandle of North Vietnam, June 14, 1966. Electronic systems enabled U.S. bombing forces to counter the North Vietnamese SAMs by warning that SAM guidance radars were transmitting.

SAMs could not be ignored. They had to be suppressed.

Wild Weasels also paved the way for fighter-bombers during Rolling Thunder. The basic package consisted of sixteen F-105s in four flights of four with two flights of F-4s positioned ahead and behind for fighter cover. Wild Weasels preceded F-105s to the target and followed them out after the strike. McNamara's staff specified the targets, what ordnance to use, and the time of the strike, but ignored weather conditions. Pilots regularly jettisoned bomb loads because they could not see the target.

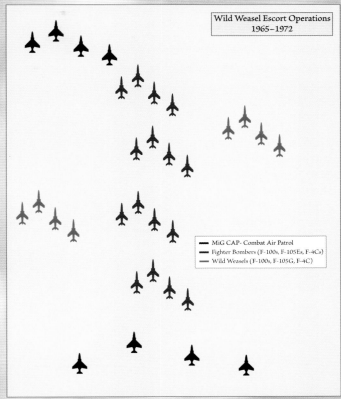

Wild Weasel Escort Operations 1965–1972

— MiG CAP- Combat Air Patrol
— Fighter Bombers (F-100s, F-105Es, F-4Cs)
— Wild Weasels (F-100s, F-105G, F-4C)

ABOVE: Wild Weasel flights, code-named Iron Hand, consisted of four aircraft, typically F-100Fs in the early days and later F-105Gs, and then F-4Cs; two fighter-bombers carrying four Shrike or nine Standard Arm missiles would be accompanied by two wingmen carrying conventional bombs. As MiGs became prevalent, a typical USAF bombing formation consisted of sixteen strike bombers arranged in a center column flanked by two Wild Weasel squadrons to attack SAM sites. Two fighter escorts, flying at higher altitudes, provided a Combat Air Patrol against MiG attacks. Wild Weasels performed the most difficult tasks by being the first to go into the target area and the last to come out.

| USAF Loss Rates to SAMS | | | |
|---|---|---|---|
| Year | SAMs Fired | Planes Lost | Percent |
| 1965 | 194 | 11 | 5.7 |
| 1967 | 3,202 | 56 | 1.75 |
| 1972 | 4,244 | 49 | 1.15 |

RIGHT: A Mikoyan-Gurevich MiG-17 Fresco, flying at about 915 mph over North Vietnam, is about to be struck by a USAF Sidewinder air-to-air missile. MiG-17s were soon phased out in favor of supersonic MiG-19s.

BELOW: A North Vietnamese pilot climbs into a Soviet-built MiG-21 Fishbed interceptor. He did not suffer the complex and restrictive rules of engagement that were forced upon his USAF opponent.

## The Price of Frustration

In 1971, General John D. Lavelle, commanding the Seventh Air Force, became concerned about the safety of pilots, who were barred from striking unauthorized targets unless attacked. Lavelle deplored the policy because it wasted flyers' lives, so he quietly authorized his own personalized strikes against certain North Vietnam targets in violation of Washington's rules of engagement. He also enabled returning flyers to concoct reports to make it appear that they had been provoked. After investigating the affair, air force chief of staff John D. Ryan had the unpleasant duty of relieving Lavelle of command, stripping him of two stars, and forcing him into retirement. In Vietnam, no good deed went unpunished.

## The MiG War

Anxious to establish air superiority and perhaps join the ranks of aces, American fighter pilots soon discovered that North Vietnamese flyers, despite having very capable and often superior Soviet planes, preferred sneak attacks to dogfights. The MiG-19 Farmer (Chinese designation Shenyang J-6) was actually the first supersonic jet when it appeared in early 1953. Armed with cannon and missiles, it was a rugged fighter during the early stages of the Vietnam War. But the pride of the North Vietnam Air Force were delta-winged MiG-21 Fishbeds, which in 1965 outclassed most American planes appearing over North Vietnam.

| Vietnam-era Air Force Chiefs of Staff | |
|---|---|
| Thomas D. White | 1957-1961 |
| Curtis E. LeMay | 1961-1965 |
| John P. McConnell | 1965-1969 |
| John D. Ryan | 1969-1973 |
| George S. Brown | 1973-1974 |
| David C. Jones | 1974-1978 |

## Fighter Aircraft 1965–1972

| Type | Crew | Top Speed (mph) | Ceiling (feet) | Armament |
|---|---|---|---|---|
| MiG-17 | 1 | 711 | 54,560 | cannon |
| MiG-19 | 1 | 920 | 58,725 | cannon/missiles |
| MiG-21 | 1 | 1,384 | 50,000 | cannon/missiles |
| MiG-25 | 1 | 1,848 | 80,000 | missiles |
| A-4 | 1 | 661 | 45,000 | cannon/missiles |
| F-4B/E | 2 | 1,485 | 58,000 | cannon/missiles |
| F-8E | 1 | 1,120 | 17,983 | cannon/missiles |
| F-100 | 1 or 2 | 864 | 46,000 | cannon/bombs |
| F-101 | 2 | 1,221 | 54,800 | AIM missiles |
| F-102 | 1 | 825 | 54,000 | rockets/AIM-4 missiles |
| F-104 | 1 | 1,453 | 58,000 | cannon/AIM-9 missiles |
| F-105 | 1 or 2 | 1,480 | 52,000 | cannon/bombs |

*LEFT: Colonel Robin Olds, commanding the 8th Tactical Fighter Wing in Southeast Asia, preflights his McDonnell Douglas F-4C Phantom. Olds shot down four MiGs in aerial combat during his service in Vietnam.*

North Vietnam pilots vectored MiG-21s in pairs behind an incoming American air strike, accelerated to supersonic speed behind the formation, fired heat-seeking Atoll missiles, and swooped away to avoid air battle. The tactic was performed to force American fighter-bomber pilots to jettison ordnance, which they often did. MiGs took a toll on American planes until AWACs-type early warning aircraft with airborne radar warning and control systems became available,. Until 1968, when McDonnell F-4Es became available, F-4B pilots carried only Sparrow and Sidewinder missiles, which were inadequate because they were designed for use against bombers. Locking onto a MiG flying at Mach-2 was nearly impossible. The American pilot's task was further muddled by Washington's insistence that positive visual identification must first be made before firing. During 1966, USAF fighters lost six crews shooting down nineteen MiGs.

In December 1966, Seventh Air Force commander General William W. Momyer authorized veteran ace Colonel Robin Olds of the 8th TFW to organize Operation Bolo, a plan to decoy the enemy into a trap. On January 2, 1967, Olds launched a fighter sweep that resembled a typical F-105 mission, but he used F-4

*ABOVE: Convair F-102A Delta Daggers were designed for air defense of the continental United States, but the USAF sent several squadrons to Thailand to defend air bases, escort B-52s, and perform limited operations requiring air-to-air missiles and rockets.*

*ABOVE: The North Vietnamese newspaper Nhan Dan published this photo of USAF Captain Edwin L. Atterberry on August 14, 1967, two days after his capture. Though his name never appeared on a PoW list, he was later listed as "died in captivity, negotiated remains returned."*

Phantoms armed for air-to-air combat and equipped with the same electronic countermeasure (ECM) pods used by Wild Weasels. The MiGs attacked as before, but this time encountered F-4s with tanks jettisoned and waiting to fight. In short order, American pilots shot down seven MiGs, including two by Olds. Four days later North Vietnamese pilots lost two more MiG-21s in another skirmish, and dropped out of sight for several months.

## The Son Tay Raid: November 20–21, 1970

Concerned at reports of brutality inflicted upon American PoWs by their North Vietnamese captors, in June 1970 Brigadier General Donald D. Blackburn, USAF, organized an effort to study the feasibility of rescuing some fifty PoWs held in Son Tay prison north of Hanoi. On August 8 he assigned the rescue mission to Brigadier General Leroy J. Manor (USAF) and army Colonel Arthur "Bull" Simons. Blackburn did not know that, because of putrid water, the PoWs had been relocated to another compound in July. Over the next three weeks the two officers assembled a planning team to launch a rescue attempt code-named Operation Ivory Coast.

The plan involved Army rangers, who would be flown to Son Tay in one HH-3 and four HH-53 Aerospace Rescue and Recovery Service helicopters supported by five A-1E Skyraiders and two C-130E Combat Talons provided by Special Operations Forces. The HH-3 would crash-land inside the compound, after which rangers would pour from the helicopters and neutralize opposition inside while other rangers landed outside the walls and broke through the entry to complete the rescue.

Training for the raid finished in mid-November at Takhi Royal Thai Air Force Base. With a typhoon developing in the Gulf of Tonkin, General Manor launched the mission late on November 20. To add to the confusion, a massive joint navy/air force strike also clobbered North Vietnam and completely bewildered the enemy's defenses. The severity of the bombing of Hanoi gave rise to rumors that the city had suffered a nuclear attack.

Meanwhile, two C-130s dropped napalm over Son Tay to serve as reference points, but during the confusion three rescue helicopters attacked a nearby North Vietnamese sapper school instead of the prison compound. Fifty rangers burst into the sapper school, engaged in a brief firefight, withdrew to collect their bearings, and soon began descending on the prison.

During the muddled affair, the assigned HH-3E crash-landed inside the compound. Rangers killed the guards, but found no prisoners. Thirty minutes later the mission headed back to Thailand with only one casualty, an air force flight mechanic with a broken ankle.

Although the mission succeeded tactically, and American PoWS would have been rescued had they been at Soy Tay, Hanoi responded by closing all small compounds and moving prisoners to large, central prisons where such raids could not be conducted. Centralizing more PoWs, however, inadvertently boosted prisoner morale.

*TOP: Raiders in helicopters from the Aerospace Rescue and Recovery Service follow a Special Forces C-130E Combat Talon as the assault force approaches the Son Tay prison compound north of Hanoi.*

*ABOVE: Colonel Arthur D. "Bull" Simons, who led the Son Tay raid, answers questions at a Pentagon briefing conducted by (left to right) Secretary of Defense Melvin R. Laird; JCS chairman Admiral Thomas Moorer; and USAF Brigadier General Leroy J. Manor, who planned the operation.*

*RIGHT: EC-47s were among the first surveillance aircraft introduced in Vietnam and dated back to 1961. The 360th Tactical Electronic Warfare Squadron still used the aircraft for monitoring the Ho Chi Minh and Sihanouk Trails in 1970.*

### The Hidden War

From 1960 to 1968, Presidents Kennedy and Johnson attempted to downplay CIA involvement in Laos and Cambodia, where communists were industriously destabilizing both governments while using the Ho Chi Minh Trail to transport supplies to the Viet Cong. For several years the CIA tied up the assets of the Seventh Air Force at a time when pilots and planes were needed in Vietnam. During the early 1960s, prop planes did the work. By 1968, when the North Vietnamese response increased, the CIA began fighting an unpublicized war with jets and B-52s.

Because the fighting occurred on jungle roads weaving through mountains, the USAF used AC-130s with low-light-level television, infrared, radar, and 20mm side-firing Gatling guns to locate and pummel the enemy. Some AC-130s used 40mm Gatlings with laser designators. Phantoms also operated at night, often flying at dangerously low levels to deliver bombs costing more than the trucks they destroyed. At one point, McNamara's "whiz kids" considered building a high wall with sensors and air surveillance along the Laotian border as an alternative to wasting munitions, but the JCS called the idea ridiculous. General Momyer, Seventh Air Force commander, claimed the Ho Chi Minh Trail could be rendered useless by bombing Hanoi, Haiphong, and rail centers near the Chinese border, thereby disrupting the flow of all supplies. Instead, sorties continued, millions of mines were dropped by air, and the operation became a world-class fiasco. In February 1968 McNamara left the Pentagon to head another dysfunctional organization, the World Bank.

## Republic F-105 Thunderchief

Although the F-105 became the workhorse of the war, it earned the mordant nickname "Thud" because of the noise it made when crashing. Originally built to carry nuclear bombs, Republic readapted the sleek F-105 for conventional war. The Mach-2-capable aircraft carried up to 10,000 pounds of bombs, a heavier bomb-load than B-17s had carried during World War II.

The first F-105 squadron deployed to Thailand in 1965 and racked up 2,231 sorties during a five-month tour. Seven more squadrons belonging to the 355th and 388th TFW followed, also flying from airbases in Thailand. F-105s bore the brunt of Rolling Thunder. Out of 833 planes produced by Republic, more than 350 were lost in Vietnam. Despite their lack of maneuverability, F-105 pilots were credited with shooting down more than twenty-seven MiGs, usually by picking off an enemy attacking another F-105.

*RIGHT: The Republic F-105 Thunderchief became the USAF's workhorse in Vietnam. Six hundred and ten F-105Ds and 143 F-105F two-seaters served multi-purpose missions. Fighter wing squadrons contained some of each, the F-105Fs becoming Wild Weasels.*

## McDonnell Douglas F-4E Phantom II

First developed as a navy fighter in 1953, the F-4 was readapted in 1962 for USAF operations. The huge aircraft, weighing 62,000 pounds on takeoff and powered by twin General Electric J79 turbojets, routinely clocked Mach 2.27 speeds. Early models were armed with missiles, which rendered pilots helpless during close-in fighting. E models in Vietnam carried an internally fitted M61A1 Vulcan 20mm multi-barrel Gatling gun in the nose and four Sparrow missiles.

The Phantom's in-flight-fueling capability from KC-135 tankers gave the aircraft range and the ability to takeoff with less fuel and up to seven tons of bombs. While MiGs had greater maneuverability, quicker acceleration, and a faster turn rate, the speed and power of the Phantom gave it greater rolling up and down mobility. During Rolling Thunder, F-4s served as escorts and had to cruise at the same speed as F-105s. If attacked, F-4 pilots jettisoned their bombs to build the speed necessary to gain altitude and fight off MiGs attacking from the rear. F-4Es eventually became part of Wild Weasel operations, replacing F-105s during the SAM war.

**ABOVE: A flight of McDonnell Douglas F-4C Phantoms armed with general purpose bombs and rockets refuel from a Boeing KC-135 tanker prior to striking targets in North Vietnam during November 1971.**

## Boeing B-52G Stratofortress

In the mid-1950s, work began on the Boeing B-52D or "Buff," short for Big Ugly Fat Fellow. Built originally for nuclear operations, the 300,000-pound, eight-engined behemoth had to be modified for conventional warfare in Vietnam when strikes began on June 18, 1965. Armed with four 12.7mm Browning M3 machine guns in the tail turret, the Buff carried up to 54,000 pounds of bombs. Over time, AGM-28 Hound Dog missiles and AGM-69A short-range attack missiles (SRAM) enhanced the B-52's firepower.

The 7th and 320th Bombardment Wings flew the first mission out of Anderson Air Force Base, Guam, against Viet Cong positions near Saigon. The mission resulted in two B-52s colliding midair while refueling from KC-135 tankers. Bomber groups eventually relocated to a naval air base in Thailand, which reduced refueling to once per mission and missions to a few hours compared with twelve from Guam. Two years passed before B-52 pilots became adept at hitting difficult targets. The two most important missions involved Operation Niagara, which plastered some 30,000 NVA regulars besieging the marine base at Khe Sanh, and President Nixon's authorization of Operation Linebacker II. During Linebacker, B-52s flew 461 missions composed of 2,701 sorties, and dropped 75,631 tons of munitions on Hanoi, Haiphong, and other cities, which ultimately led to peace talks.

**ABOVE: The B-52 Stratofortress was designed to deliver nuclear weapons to distant enemies, but during the Vietnam War its only combat function was to rain down conventional high explosive iron bombs on the Viet Cong.**

ABOVE: After completing combat operations against Viet Cong in the Mekong Delta, a Bell UH-1 Iroquois helicopter hovers above Vietnamese air force personnel at the 211th Helicopter Squadron base near Saigon.

### .USAF Helicopters in Vietnam

| Model | Introduction | Purpose |
|---|---|---|
| Hiller H-23 Raven | 1954 | Observation |
| Bell H-13 Sioux | 1954 | Observation |
| Kaman H-43 Husky | 1958 | Search and rescue |
| Sikorsky H-19 Chickasaw | 1960 | Troop movement/supply |
| Piasecki CH-21C Shawnee | 1961 | Search and rescue |
| Sikorsky H-34 Choctaw | 1961 | Troop movement/supply |
| Sikorsky CH-37 Mojave | 1962 | Heavy lift |
| Bell UH-1H Iroquois | 1962 | Multi-mission |
| Boeing CH-47 Chinook | 1965 | Medium lift/multi-mission |
| Sikorsky CH-54 Tarhe | 1965 | Heavy lift to 12.5 tons |
| Bell AH-1 HueyCobra | 1967 | Fire support |
| Sikorsky HH-3 Sea King | 1968 | Search and rescue |
| Sikorsky HH-53 Sea Stallion | 1969 | Search and rescue |
| Hughes OH-6A Cayuse | 1969 | Observation |
| Bell OH-6A Kiowa | 1969 | Observation |

## Helicopters and Airmobility

More helicopters of different types were used for more purposes in Vietnam than in any previous war. Because of poor roads, dense jungles, and guerrilla activity, few operations could be conducted without using helicopters for reconnaissance, insertion and extraction missions, evacuation of wounded, command and control, heavy lift capability, base security, and psychological warfare. Vietnam provided the laboratory for the USAF to experiment with the concept of airmobility, which involved flying troops into battle and providing them with fire support and supply.

Airmobility would not have been possible without vast improvements in the durability of helicopters in combat situations. Rotor blades were changed from wood to composite material, and power plants were changed from piston drives to turboshaft engines. Many helicopters were heavily armed with combinations of machine guns, Gatling guns, and rockets.

Helicopter weapons also increased. Bell Iroquois "Hueys," the most ubiquitous helicopter in Vietnam, were modified in 1962 to carry 2.75-inch folding-fin aerial rockets and 7.62mm forward-firing machine guns. Several models carried a pair of machine guns located at side doors. The Bell AH-1 Cobra carried a mix of weapons, including 7.62mm miniguns, a 40mm grenade launcher, 20mm cannon, antitank missiles, and a variety of rockets.

LEFT: Sikorsky HH-3E "Jolly Green Giant" helicopters, named for the green-and-brown camouflage scheme, made their debut in Vietnam in 1965 and served throughout the war, rescuing pilots downed inland or in the South China Sea.

BELOW: A helicopter from the 40th Aerospace Rescue and Recovery Squadron plucked Captain Robert S. Dotson from the Laotian jungle after he bailed out from his aircraft, which had been damaged by antiaircraft fire.

## Military Air Transport Service

The Military Air Transport Service (MATS) entered the Vietnam War with an obsolete fleet of transports, which included the durable Douglas C-47 Skytrains, dating back to 1942, and Douglas C-124 Globemasters, dating back to the 1948 Berlin Airlift.

In 1956 the Douglas C-133A Cargomaster became the first USAF turboprop transport capable of carrying 52,000 pounds of cargo at a cruising speed of 323 mph over a 4,000-mile route, but by 1966 the planes were worn out and retired. For a while, Lockheed C-130s and Boeing C-135s picked up the slack.

The Lockheed C-130 Hercules, which flew for the first time in August 1954, required updates to serve in Vietnam. New C-130Es could carry a maximum of ninety-two troops, sixty-four paratroops, seventy stretchers with six attendants, or a total payload of 42,000 pounds. C-130s were also converted into AC-130E transports, AC-130H gunships, and WC-130E weather reconnaissance aircraft C-130 variants

ABOVE: Using the Low Altitude Parachute Extraction System (LAPES), a C-130 Hercules crew delivers a load of supplies to the 1st Cavalry Division at An Khe in the II Corps sector. Platform-mounted loads were often discharged at an altitude of five feet.

would set records for longevity, utility, versatility, and dependability. In terms of efficiency, 100 C-130Es could do the work of 1,500 C-47s.

The Boeing C-135 Stratofreighter, which Lockheed eventually modified and redesignated C-141, became operational in April 1965 and arrived just in time to assimilate the workload of Douglas Globemasters and Cargomasters. By 1968, some 284 C-141 StarLifters had entered the fleet and brought MATS airlift capabilities to new levels. New material handling equipment allowed a C-141 to off-load 68,500 pounds of cargo, refuel, and reload in less than an hour.

The tactical airlift in Southeast Asia grew from 30,000 tons a month in 1965 and in March 1968 peaked at 209,000 tons a month. In January 1966 MATS was succeeded my Military Airlift Command—MAC. As C-135s and C-141s became available, the USAF began converting more C-130s to gunships and search-and-rescue missions. Between 1964 and 1973, gunships and helicopters rescued 3,883 flyers, military personnel, and civilians.

ABOVE: MK-84 2,000-pound bombs with laser-guided or electro-optical guidance systems became the ordnance of choice during Linebacker operations in 1972. Here a munitions specialist prepares a MK-84 for delivery to a B-52.

RIGHT: During Linebacker, a Strategic Air Command Boeing B-52 Stratofortress ejects a plume of smoke in the sky as it takes off from Guam, while another "Buff" waits on the tarmac for instructions.

USAF, army, navy, and marine helicopters in Vietnam flew more than 36,000,000 sorties. Tasks included 21,000,000 for observation, reconnaissance, and search-and-rescue; 7,500,000 for troop assaults; 4,000,000 for attack; and 3,500,000 for cargo and supply. More than 4,500 helicopters were lost during operations in Vietnam.

## Linebacker

President Nixon took office in January 1969 after running on a platform to end the war, though he had no clear plan other than "Vietnamization," which meant training the South Vietnamese to defend themselves. During the four-year bombing halt that began in 1968, North Vietnam strengthened its forces and in March 1972 violated negotiations and crossed the DMZ into South Vietnam with mechanized divisions. Nixon halted peace talks and on April 17 ordered Linebacker I, a B-52 strike above the twentieth parallel that clobbered several cities, mined the strategic port of Haiphong, and drove the North Vietnamese back to the peace table. When Nixon halted the bombing, General Giap interpreted the suspension as a sign of weakness and increased military pressure.

When in late 1972 it appeared that North Vietnam was clearly mobilizing to gain a total military victory rather than a negotiated peace, Nixon ordered Linebacker II. During December 19–30, B-52s flew 729 sorties against the Hanoi-Haiphong area where air defenses were the strongest in the world, and dropped 15,000 tons of bombs. The USAF devastated the two principal cites of

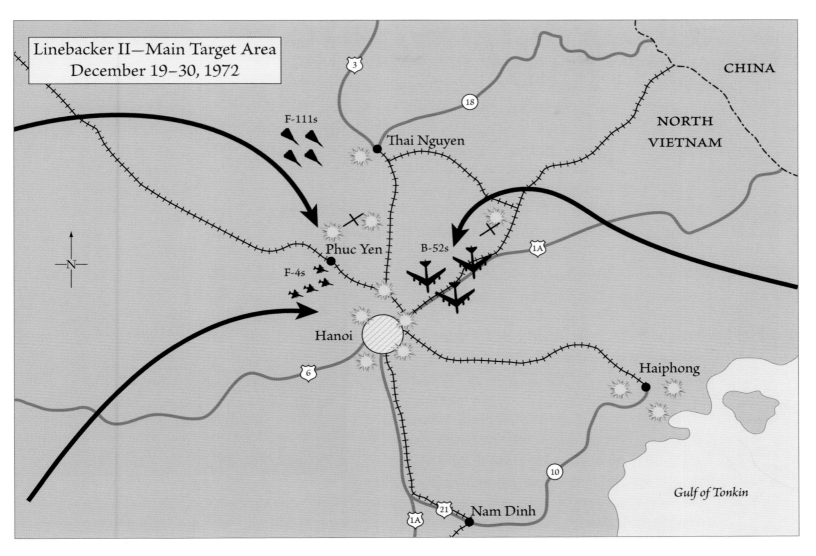

**Linebacker II—Main Target Area December 19–30, 1972**

North Vietnam but lost fifteen bombers over a period of twelve days to SAMs. USAF commanders tried to suppress their irritation, knowing what might have been accomplished in 1965 without loss.

On January 3, 1973, the North Vietnamese hurried back to the Paris peace table. Against the advice of the JCS, Nixon suspended Linebacker. Had the bombing raids continued, the North Vietnamese would have been forced to accept military defeat. Instead, they secured a non-military victory at the peace table and three years later conquered South Vietnam.

Retired General Curtis LeMay observed that the air force had dropped 502,000 tons of bombs on Japan to win World War II in the Pacific, and 6,162,000 tons of bombs on Southeast Asia to lose the war. "The difference," LeMay lamented, "was that I was calling the shots in Japan, and Lyndon Johnson was calling the shots in Vietnam."

One simple fact became clear to every flyer: the proper application of total air power in 1965 could have dominated North Vietnam and curtailed America's longest war, saving millions of lives and hundreds of billions of dollars. Communists would not have ravaged South Vietnam and Cambodia, and media coverage would not have turned millions of Americans against their government.

*ABOVE: Linebacker II began on December 19, 1972, with 2,123 sorties against Hanoi, Haiphong, and other North Vietnamese targets. During an eleven-day period, B-52s out of Guam and Thailand flew 729 sorties. By December 26, F-4s accompanied by F-111s had completely wiped out North Vietnam's air defenses. The operation finally brought North Vietnam to the peace table.*

# FROM COLD WAR TO DESERT WAR 1977–2007

**ABOVE: General David C. Jones, Chairman of the Joint Chiefs of Staff, gives a briefing. Known for his fiery temperament, Jones made a great number of friends and enemies as he approached his task with energy and intellect.**

**ABOVE RIGHT: Left to right are former U.S. secretaries of defense Casper Weinberger, Frank Carlucci, William Perry, James Schlesinger, Vice President Richard Cheney, Donald Rumsfeld, William S. Cohen, and Robert McNamara.**

| Air Force Chiefs of Staff—1980s | |
|---|---|
| Lew Allen, Jr. | 1978–1982 |
| Charles A. Gabriel | 1982–1986 |
| Larry D. Welch | 1986–1990 |

Following the fiasco in Vietnam, the USAF tried to reorganize in a turbulent political environment marked by the resignation of President Nixon in August 1974, the lame-duck presidency of Gerald R. Ford, and the election of James Earl "Jimmy" Carter, Jr., in 1976. Combined with culture change and national nausea over the Vietnam War, such political chaos gave great encouragement to Red China and Soviet Russia. General David C. Jones, who had commanded an F-4 wing in Vietnam, inherited enormous challenges from his predecessor when in 1974 he became air force chief of staff. Despite a national contempt for war, Jones had to contrive a way to keep the air force competitive with the U.S.S.R. at a time when Jimmy Carter vowed to cut the military budget by $7 billion and congressional Democrats held the purse strings.

**The Carter Years (1977–1981)**

Being an astute politician and a respected USAF general, Jones cultivated a close relationship with Jimmy Carter's secretary of defense, James Schlesinger. Carter had already halted the B-1 bomber program, expressed his disdain for the JCS, vowed to gut the Pentagon, and threatened to get rid of all but 200 nuclear weapons on a misguided premise that the Soviets could be coaxed to do the same. At the time, Warsaw Pact forces consisted of 1.8 million men, 50,000 tanks, 20,000 pieces of artillery, and 5,000 tactical aircraft poised to strike NATO forces, which depended on America's nuclear shield in Western Europe.

Jones used his relationship with Schlesinger to appease Carter by graciously accepting the B-1 bomber halt, something he could do nothing about, but obtained the secretary's help in getting four wings of General Dynamics F-16 Fighting Falcons approved during a time when McDonnell Douglas's F-15E Strike Eagle and Northrop's XF-17 were also in limbo. The F-16 quickly became the standard international "swing-force" fighter of the free world because it could perform air-to-ground missions as efficiently as air-to-air missions. The novel lightweight fighter served in NATO countries as well as in Turkey, India, South Korea, Thailand, Singapore, Venezuela, Egypt, and Israel. In June 1981 eight Israeli F-16s, with six F-15s as escorts, destroyed the Iraqi nuclear reactor under construction at Osirak, near Baghdad. A year later,

**ABOVE: The supersonic Rockwell International B-1B, wearing desert camouflage, endured a controversial development program, one which President Jimmy Carter cancelled in 1977 and President Ronald Reagan resurrected in 1981.**

**ABOVE LEFT: Armed with AIM-9 Sidewinder missiles, a pair of General Dynamics F-16 Fighting Falcons from the 120th Fighter Interceptor Group, Montana Air National Guard, perform ninety-degree aerial maneuvers as they streak skyward.**

**RIGHT: Filled with simulated solid fuel, an assembled MX missile is stress tested in all four stages to ensure each section fits properly and that the missile is structurally sound should a retaliatory launch become necessary.**

during the Lebanon War, F-15s and F-16s shot down eighty Syrian fighters and five helicopters without loss.

In 1978 General Lew Allen, Jr., one of the air force's top missile scientists, replaced Jones as chief of staff. While Carter pressed for a second round of Strategic Arms Limitation Talks (SALT II) with the Soviets, Allen pressed for the advanced MX intercontinental ballistic missile (the Peacekeeper) as a bargaining chip. On June 18, 1979, Carter and Soviet President Leonid Brezhnev signed SALT II, but the U.S. Senate felt that Carter had bargained away national security and rejected the agreement. By the end of his administration, Carter had cut the air force to 9,263 planes (including those in the Air Force Reserve and the Air National Guard), 564,000 active-duty personnel, and 140 worldwide operational air bases.

## USAF Aircraft, 1970s

| Type | Producer | Task |
|------|----------|------|
| A-7D Corsair II | Vought | Fighter-bomber |
| A-10A Thunderbolt | Fairchild Republic | Close air support |
| A-37B Dragonfly | Cessna | Counterinsurgency |
| B-52G Stratofortress | Boeing | Strategic bomber |
| C-141B StarLifter | Lockheed | Heavy lift transport |
| E-3 Sentry | Boeing | Early warning/control |
| F-4 Phantom II | McDonnell Douglas | Defense suppression |
| F-15 Eagle | McDonnell Douglas | Fighter interceptor |
| F-16 Fighting Falcon | General Dynamics | Fighter/attack |
| F-105G Thunderchief | Republic | Fighter-bomber |
| F-111 Aardvark | General Dynamics | Fighter-bomber |
| KC-135 Stratotanker | Boeing | Air refueling tanker |
| RC-135 Rivet Joint | Boeing | Strategic reconnaissance |
| SR-71 Blackbird | Lockheed | Strategic reconnaissance |
| T-38A Talon | Northrop | Trainer |

**ABOVE: As part of the 1991 Strategic Arms Reduction Treaty (START) signed by President George H. W. Bush, hundreds of B-52s lay idle at the Aerospace Maintenance and Regeneration Center, Davis-Monthan AFB, Arizona.**

### The Iranian Hostage Crisis

The climax to Carter's presidency began on November 4, 1979, when a mob of Muslim students led by Mahmoud Ahmadinejad, Iran's present day president, stormed the U.S. embassy in Tehran and seized its employees. Several American hostages were eventually freed, but fifty-three remained in captivity for 444 days. Carter's diplomatic efforts to free the hostages failed. Five months later he authorized Operation Blue Light, a complicated rescue effort, hurriedly organized and launched on April 24, 1980, as Operation Eagle Claw The army patched together six air force C-130 transports from Egypt, eight navy helicopters from the USS *Nimitz* in the Arabian Sea, and a detachment of commandos. All were to rendezvous at a desert site 200 miles south of Tehran to perform the rescue attempt. Helicopters suffered mechanical failure blamed on cutbacks in aircraft parts, and after a collision occurred in the desert, destroying a C-130 and a helicopter, the army commander aborted the mission.

General Jones, who had become chairman of the JCS in 1978 and the third air force officer to hold that position, looked back on the sad affair in 1996 and said the greatest mistake made was

Carter's idea of dividing up the responsibility so that every service could share in the rescue effort, and then not providing any time for rehearsing the operation. When Iran's ayatollahs learned of the botched mission, they held the hostages until the day Jimmy Carter left office.

The Iran hostage crisis marked a new brand of terrorism in the Middle East, serving as an example of an epidemic that would fester, grow, and spread into the twenty-first century.

**ABOVE: In the aftermath of the aborted Iranian hostage rescue attempt, the remains of the collision between a navy RH-53D helicopter with an air force C-130 tanker/transport smolder in a desolate area called Desert One.**

### The Reagan Years (1981–1985)

Ronald Reagan won the presidential election in 1980 because he campaigned against Carter's military ineptness and promised to restore America's military supremacy. His secretary of defense, Caspar Weinberger, took the promise seriously. He revived the B-1 program, boosted the B-2 stealth bomber program, obtained approval for the MX missile, brought the armed services up to strength, and added $150 billion for strategic modernization, research, and development. Because of the huge appropriation, the JCS feared such funding could not be sustained. As soon as Reagan's negotiators reopened discussions with Russia on new strategic arms limitation talks (START), Congress began pinching back funds for the military. Relations between General Jones and Secretary of Defense Weinberger rapidly cooled over defense spending. When Jones's term as chairman of the JCS expired, Secretary of the Air Force Verne Orr and incoming air chief General Charles A. Gabriel made concessions that satisfied Weinberger and guaranteed growth and modernization of the USAF.

On October 25, 1983, General Gabriel obtained a glimpse of the sad condition of the air force during Operation Urgent Fury, the often-derided, massive, 20,000-man invasion of Grenada to protect American students at St. George's Medical School. Flyers participating in the operation faced deadly antiaircraft fire that brought down a dozen helicopters and riddled C-5A, C-130, and C-141 transports carrying troops and supplies. The outcome convinced Gabriel that, ten years after Vietnam, the air force still had command and control problems that needed attention.

Toward the mid-point of his administration as chief of staff, Gabriel worked closely with incoming Secretary of the Air Force Edward C. Aldridge, Jr., a brilliant man of science who anticipated the eventual collapse of the U.S.S.R. and the likely reduction in military budgets that would follow. In 1986 Gabriel's successor, General Larry D. Welch, worked assiduously with Aldridge to offset the expected reduction in manpower by obtaining funds while money was still available for research and development, technology, and modernization. The combined efforts of Gabriel,

Welch, and Aldridge during the Reagan administration are still manifest in today's air force.

## The USAF and Space

The development of ICBMs produced keen interest in exploring the potential of space as a resource for developing defensive countermeasures. During 1954, the first effort emanated from the massive buildup of strategic bombers by the Soviet Union, which convinced the USAF to start work on the WS 117L reconnaissance satellite project. Meanwhile, the air force implemented a defensive program in 1956 using missile-armed Convair YF-102 Delta Daggers stationed in Alaska and Canada.

The following year the Soviets pushed warfighting technology to the next level with ICBMs, which created a new American industry. With antiballistic missiles still far in the future, President Eisenhower's only recourse was to counter with General Dynamics's Atlas, America's first ICBM. The development of Atlas came on the heels of the Soviets' successful launch of the Sputnik satellite in 1957. Air planners quickly

*ABOVE: The North American X-15 rocket-powered research aircraft bridged the gap between manned flight within the atmosphere and manned flight into space. The only mother craft large enough to launch the X-15 were modified B-52As and B-52Bs.*

## The USAF Strategic Missile Program

As a matter of policy, Soviet politicians never signed arms limitation treaties unless they feared falling behind. During the Reagan years, Soviet military buildup lagged, hence the signing of START I in 1991. A few months later the U.S.S.R. unraveled, partly because of the race to build strategic missiles. That race encompassed several research programs, including the 1950s Navajo missile project, based on German V-1 and V-2 technology, and intended to carry a 7,000-pound warhead 5,500 miles, but which did not get beyond the experimental stage.

Started by the army and designed as an intermediate-range ballistic missile (IRBM), the Jupiter eventually went to the USAF and became the SM-78 Standard Missile. At the time, the USAF was already working on the PGM-17 Thor missile and in 1964 retired the Jupiter. The 60-foot-long Jupiter, however, had led to the development of the Juno-1 rocket, which launched America's first satellite into orbit. The 65-foot-long Thor had a range of only 1,976 miles and was retired in 1965.

In 1958 General Dynamics built the Atlas, the first U.S. 11,500-mile intercontinental ballistic missile. Atlas featured a two-booster propulsion system with a frameless propellant tank carrying a fuel mixture of liquid oxygen and RP-1 kerosene. Atlas was decommissioned after launching the first American astronauts into orbit, beginning with John Glenn.

On April 18, 1962, the Titan I became operational and replaced the Atlas. In 1966, Titan I gave way to the silo-launched Titan II, which could deliver a 10-megaton thermonuclear warhead more than 9,300 miles. Titan II used a new compounded fuel that increased the missile's thrust.

Launched in 1961, the Boeing Minuteman I became the first solid-fuel ICBM. Solid fuel reacted more rapidly than liquid fuel, increasing the missile's survivability in a nuclear exchange. Prior to START I, a thousand Minuteman missiles had been deployed, but by 2006 the inventory had dwindled to 500 Minuteman IIIs. This version has three solid-propellant rocket motors capable of flying 6,000 miles at 15,000 mph. The Carter administration terminated production in December 1978.

Design of the MX four-stage Peacekeeper ICBM began in 1972 as a hard-target weapon capable of destroying Soviet thermonuclear missiles shielded in underground silos. The MX carried ten independently targetable thermonuclear warheads about 7,000 miles at 15,000 mph some 500 miles above the earth. After successful tests in 1983, fifty MX missiles were placed in converted Minuteman silos. They are still there, but slated for retirement under START II.

The AGM-86B Air-Launched Cruise Missile (ALCM) became one of the most versatile intermediate-range thermonuclear weapons produced during the Reagan administration, ranging 1,500 miles at 550 mph. AGM-86Bs can be launched from B-52s and B-1Bs. During 1980–1986, Boeing produced 1,715 AGM-86Bs.

**ABOVE: A missile maintenance crew perform an electrical check on a Minuteman III intercontinental missile. The current force consists of 500 Minuteman IIIs located at F. E. Warren Air Force Base, Wyo., Malmstrom AFB, Mont., and Minot AFB, N.D.**

**ABOVE CENTER: At Vandenberg Air Force Base in California, an LGM-25C Titan II missile, with a launch weight of 330,000 pounds, soars skyward. Retired from its nuclear-deterrent task, the Titan became the boost vehicle for satellites.**

**ABOVE RIGHT: An air-to-air cruise missile (ALCM) air-launched from a B-52 Superfortress streaks across desolate terrain during trials prior to Desert Storm, during which thirty-five ALCMs were fired from Superforts.**

concluded that the USAF must command space as well as the skies. The North American Aerospace Defense Command (NORAD), created on September 12, 1957, provided a U.S.-Canadian bi-national early warning and defense program but could not contend with the space menace. The advent of ICBMs and Sputnik forced the creation of a second kind of air force.

The USAF's first approach to the problem began in February 1955 with the development of the Lockheed U-2 reconnaissance aircraft. Then, on September 7, 1956, Korean War ace Ivan Kincheloe flew an experimental Bell X-2 to a record altitude of 126,200 feet. Twenty days later Captain Milburn pushed the X-2 to a speed of 2,094 mph, but he died when his aircraft plunged out of control. North American X-15s followed and set many records, peaking at 354,200 feet altitude and 4,534 mph. The hazards of high-altitude hypersonic flight did not provide solutions for intercepting ICBMs or destroying Soviet satellites. Although Eisenhower preferred to avoid the expense and hazards of an arms race in space, he could not.

In 1958 Congress created the National Aeronautics and Space Administration (NASA), a civilian agency for "peaceful purposes for the benefit of mankind." Eisenhower stepped in and authorized Project Corona, a reconnaissance satellite program managed by the National Reconnaissance Office. Corona's camera team worked on higher resolution stereoscopic photography to provide intelligence analysts with the location of Soviet missile sites and other military targets. On August 19, 1960, Discoverer XIV launched the first successful Corona mission and put the camera into space. The first recovered satellite film capsule produced more data on Soviet targets than all the U-2 flights flown during the previous four years. Corona started out as an interim project until the Samos Atlas-Agena reconnaissance program became available, which continued to provide vital intelligence until superseded by improved photographic reconnaissance systems in 1972.

*ABOVE: The air force used a specially modified Fairchild C-119J Flying Boxcar to retrieve a Corona space capsule in mid-air by "snagging" the parachute of the satellite at 8,000 ft altitude as it reentered the atmosphere from space.*

Air Force chief of staff General Thomas D. White recognized space as a continuum of the atmosphere. With Brigadier General Bernard Schriever, USAF's space pioneer, White fought tenaciously for air force leadership in the national space program. By 1960 the USAF controlled about eighty percent of the military space budget. However, spending funds haphazardly led to confusion, and during the Kennedy administration, followed by the Johnson administration, Secretary of Defense Robert McNamara muddled the effort by revising programs.

During the 1960s the space program evolved to have twofold aims: to provide an effective deterrent to Soviet ICBMs, and to outperform the enemy in space. McNamara insisted that USAF space efforts be consistent with NASA programs, and then used those programs to cancel air force projects.

The Boeing X-20 Dyna-Soar became the first casualty. A rocket-boosted vehicle with a single pilot, the X-20 was intended to orbit the earth, and then land

**ABOVE: This 363-foot-long Saturn V launch vehicle carried Apollo 8 astronauts Frank Borman, James Lovell, and William Anders into space in December 1968 in the first manned flight utilizing a Saturn V.**

| USAF Astronauts—The First Ten Years | | |
|---|---|---|
| **Year** | **Name** | **Operation** |
| | Captain L. Gordon Cooper, Jr. | Mercury, Gemini |
| 1959 | Captain Virgil I. "Gus" Grissom | Mercury* |
| 1959 | Captain Donald K. "Deke" Slayton | Apollo |
| 1962 | Major Frank F. Borman, II | Gemini, Apollo |
| 1962 | Captain James A. McDivitt | Gemini, Apollo |
| 1962 | Captain Thomas P. Stafford | Gemini, Apollo |
| 1962 | Captain Edward P. White | Gemini* |
| 1963 | Major Edwin E. "Buzz" Aldrin, Jr. | Gemini, Apollo |
| 1963 | Captain William A. Anders | Apollo |
| 1963 | Captain Charles A. Bassett, II | Killed in aircraft |
| 1963 | Captain Michael Collins | Gemini, Apollo |
| 1963 | Captain Donn F. Eisele | Apollo |
| 1963 | Captain Theodore C. Freeman | Killed in aircraft |
| 1963 | Captain David R. Scott | Gemini, Apollo |
| 1966 | Captain Charles M. Duke, Jr. | Apollo |
| 1966 | Captain Joseph H. Engle | Shuttle |
| 1966 | Major Edward G. Givens, Jr. | Apollo |
| 1966 | Major James B. Irwin | Apollo |
| 1966 | Major William R. Pogue | Skylab |
| 1966 | Captain Stuart A. Roosa | Apollo |
| 1966 | Captain Alfred M Worden | Apollo |
| 1969 | Major Karol J. Bobko | Shuttle |
| 1969 | Major Charles G. Fullerton | Shuttle |
| 1969 | Major Henry W. Hartsfield, Jr. | Shuttle |
| 1969 | Major Donald H. Peterson | Shuttle |
| *Died in Apollo 1 fire, 1967* | | |

at a designated airfield. The vehicle actually became the forerunner of the Space Shuttle. Fitted to the nose of a Titan III, the delta-winged vehicle was to be boosted into orbit, released, and controlled thereafter by the pilot. At the time, it represented America's only manned space program. The X-20 satisfied multi-mission requirements and would be supported by a vast network of existing ground facilities.

While preparing for the first trials of the hypersonic X-20 in 1962, future senator John Glenn made the first successful manned-orbital flight in the Mercury spacecraft *Friendship 7*. Although the Dyna-Soar would have been a far more advanced vehicle than the Mercury spacecraft, McNamara believed the Mercury-Gemini-Apollo programs would accomplish more, and cancelled the X-20, wiping out the USAF's premier program to defend against ICBMs. NASA's Mercury-Gemini-Apollo programs would not have gotten off the ground, however, without the USAF's rocket boosters and facilities at Cape Canaveral, which had been designed for launching, tracking, and communicating with Dyna-Soars.

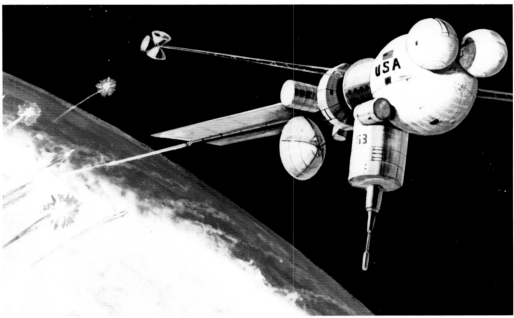

## "Star Wars"

In 1961 the USAF developed plans for a satellite system capable of infrared homing on enemy ICBM rockets and destroying them during their initial boost phase. McNamara considered the ballistic missile boost intercept weapon (Bambi) too technically demanding for consideration and squelched the program, although at the time it represented a revolutionary leap needed to move research and development forward and diminish the threat of Soviet ICBMs. Instead, McNamara opted for "technological building blocks"

and supported aircraft projects like the hapless, all-purpose, joint-service, swing-wing TFX fighter, which USAF engineers derisively referred to as the secretary's "switchblade Edsel." The Bambi concept remained on the planning table as the precursor to President Reagan's Strategic Defense Initiative (SDI).

When Reagan took office, responsibility for satellite and space technology had been scattered between NASA, service groups, and several industries. USAF Chief of Staff General Lew Allen put General James V. Hartinger, a pugnacious former fighter pilot, in charge of developing the rationale for a unified space command with the air force as the manager and operator of all assigned space assets, including spacecraft and Space Shuttle flights. Interservice rivalry created bumps in the process of unification, but every rival admitted that SDI would be completely dependent on space-based systems. The roles and controversies of SDI still bedeviled the USAF throughout the 1990s, but after 1992 the Department of Defense finally agreed to use the Space Shuttle only for SDI or research and development missions. Although the SDI program provided a major

*ABOVE: Following experiments at LTV's Aerospace and Defense Company on hypervelocity launch technology, an artist conceptualizes the interception and destruction of nuclear-armed re-entry vehicles by a space-based electromagnetic railgun.*

*LEFT: The Delta II remains the air force's sole launch platform for placing GPS IIR satellites in orbit. The program includes eighteen Delta IIs. So far there have been more than 270 successful military and civil/commercial Delta II launches.*

component in edging the USSR into bankruptcy, President William J. Clinton saw no need to continue spending money on SDI research. In 2001, President George W. Bush revived SDI, and the USAF resumed the development of intercepting missiles in response to threats in the Middle East, North Korea, and elsewhere.

## Navigation

During the 1960s the USAF became the executive for developing the Navstar Global Positioning System (GPS), operated by the 50th Space Wing at Falcon Air Force Base, Colorado. The first Navstar satellite went into service on February 22, 1978. There are now twenty-four satellites orbiting twice a day and operating twenty-four hours, sending signals to earth on longitude, latitude, altitude, and time measured to a millionth second. The 1,860-pound satellites are 5 ft wide and 17 ft 6 in long, and orbit the earth at an altitude of 10,900 miles. They are launched by Delta II medium-lift expendable vehicles at a price of roughly $50 million per launch. The system is also a component of SDI, pinpointing and tracking the

*ABOVE: During a long-range dual Minuteman II ICBM test between California and Kwajalein Atoll in the Pacific, particles and water left in the missiles' wake freeze and turn color in the upper atmosphere.*

*RIGHT: A Booster Verification Test-5 rocket launched from Vandenberg AFB tests a new three-stage booster configuration for use with the Missile Defense Agency's system for intercepting and destroying long-range ballistic missiles.*

location of military targets within thirty feet, after which fired weapons take over. Civilians also have access to a low-level "differentially corrected" use of the system for terrestrial and maritime navigation.

GPS achieved international recognition during the 1990–1991 Persian Gulf War when stealth bombers and B-52s flew the longest combat missions in history and struck discrete targets by using precise reference points upon which inertial navigation systems could be calibrated. The system worked in any kind of weather. Miniaturization and technological advances made it possible for civilians to buy GPS devices, while in Britain, for example, Jaguar fighter-bomber pilots attached hand-held units to their instrument panels.

GPS is also a component of other attack equipment such as the low-altitude navigation and targeting infrared for night (LANTIRN) system. Fighter-bombers use LANTIRN against mobile launchers and for fast-forwarding air control work. By the time of the Iraq war in 2003, targeting had become so precise that a single missile could do the work that it took ten to do during the Persian Gulf War.

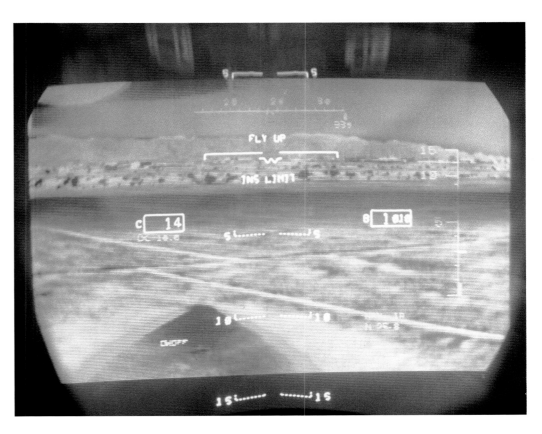

*ABOVE: Using the low-altitude navigation and targeting infrared for night (LANTIRN) system, an F-15E pilot from the 5th Fighter Interceptor Squadron scans an infrared image projected onto his heads up display monitor.*

## Libya—Operation El Dorado Canyon

During the mid-1980s, radical Muslim terrorists became suddenly bolder. On December 27, 1985, they simultaneously attacked airports in Vienna and Rome, and in April 1986 detonated a bomb on a TWA airliner and blew up a Berlin discotheque, taking American lives. The strikes led back to anti-American Libyan dictator Colonel Muammar al-Qadhafi, whose training camps produced the terrorists.

The Pentagon mounted Operation El Dorado Canyon, a joint air force/navy operation against several targets in Libya. While USAF F-111 Aardvarks based in Britain struck targets near Tripoli, navy F/A-18 Hornets, A-7E Corsair IIs, and A-6Es from the Mediterranean-based carriers *America* and *Coral Sea* struck targets near Benghazi. Few of the pilots had

*LEFT: The Delta II serves as an expendable launch vehicle used to launch GPS satellites, which are 5 ft wide, 17.5 ft long, weigh 1,860 pounds, and are produced by Rockwell International and Lockheed-Martin.*

*LEFT CENTER: The Block IIF Global Positioning System satellite with infrared under development at Boeing will be launched into orbit as required once Block IIR vehicles have been placed in the GPS constellation.*

## Women in the USAF

The authorized number of women serving in the USAF rapidly declined until 1965, and the remaining 4,700 were mostly confined to clerical, administrative, personnel, and medical fields. Rebuilding the force began in November when Colonel Jeanne M. Holm, a World War II veteran from the Women's Auxiliary Army Corps, became Director, Women in the Air Force (WAF). Holm knew the air force system and how to get things done. On July 16, 1971, she became the first WAF to wear a star, and on June 1, 1973, she became the first woman to attain the rank of major general. Holm deserved every promotion because she transformed the WAF into a multi-faceted organization of exceptional women.

ABOVE: First Lieutenant Jeannie Flynn, the first F-15E female pilot, sits in the cockpit as she performs engine start during six months of tactical training with the 555th Fighter Squadron at Luke Air Force Base, Arizona.

Holm opened doors for women to enter the collegiate Air Force Reserve Officers Training Program (AFROTC), and on March 17, 1971, Jane Lesley Holley became the first graduate officer. Holm also wanted engineers and recruited 2nd Lieutenant Susanne M. Ocobock, who became the USAF's first female civil engineer. Her most difficult task was getting women into the Air Force Academy, which she accomplished in 1975. The first class of female "doolies" entered the academy in 1976 and graduated in 1980. Holm understood that many women had no desire to work in offices and shuffle papers, so on March 18, 1971, Captain Marcelite C. Jordan took over the women's maintenance program and began training mechanics and electricians.

Holm's most difficult hurdle was getting women into flying school, but in 1975 she did. In 1977, First Lieutenant Christine Schott became the first among nine others to complete flight training in a T-38 Talon and win her silver wings. Women began moving into other aircraft. Captain Sandra M. Scott became the first to pilot a KC-135 Stratotanker, and 2nd Lieutenant Mary L. Wittick became the first woman to complete the helicopter program.

In 1993 the air force dropped the combat-exclusion clause and women became eligible for assignments in fighter, bomber, and attack squadrons. First Lieutenant Jeannie Flynn became the first woman to pilot an operational fighter, a McDonnell Douglas F-15E. Two years later Lieutenant Colonel Eileen Collins became the first woman in the USAF to serve as Space Shuttle pilot.

By 1996, the number of women in the air force had grown to 11,937 officers and 51,417 enlisted. More than 12,500 WAFs would serve in Desert Shield/Desert Storm in virtually every career field offered by the air force.

ABOVE A 48th Tactical Fighter Wing ground crew prepares an F-111F for a retaliatory strike on Libya. While one crewman extracts arming pins from GBU-10 modular guide bombs, another clears engine-clogging debris from the runway.

twenty-four two-man F-111s had to fly a fourteen-hour, 6,300-mile circuitous round-trip over the Atlantic, through the Straits of Gibraltar, and across the Mediterranean. Twenty-eight KC-10s and KC-135s kept the F-111s refueled in flight. Regular Aardvark missions took two to four hours. Despite mission radio silence, European radar spotted the F-111s, and the Maltese government reported them to Libya.

Early in the morning of April 15, the unified force struck Libya simultaneously in a thirteen-minute attack that destroyed all five targets, including airfields, missile sites, and military installations. Heavy defensive fire lit up the sky, creating a panorama much like Desert Storm six years later. Because of equipment malfunctions, navigational errors, and efforts to minimize civilian casualties, fourteen F-111s never released their payloads. Some bombs struck within fifty feet of Qadhafi's residence and gave the colonel a severe jolt. One plane was lost and two flyers were killed.

The strike against Libya produced favorable fallout. The Soviet Union did nothing, European community nations stiffened resistance to the meddling of Muslim militants, and Libyan terrorist activity subsided along with terrorist efforts sponsored by Syria and Iran.

combat experience, and they were flying into an area where 3,000 Soviet technicians operated Libya's air defense system comprised of 500 aircraft and scores of SAM sites, antiaircraft guns, and advanced radar.

After Spain and France denied overflight clearance, and Italy and Greece refused use of their airbases,

## Panama: Operation Just Cause

In 1989 Congress celebrated the end of the Cold War, symbolized by the dismantling of the Berlin Wall, and accelerated reductions in air force strength at a time when President George H. W. Bush moved to meet a new crisis developing in Panama. Relations with Panama began deteriorating in 1983 after strongman General Manuel Noriega seized power and turned the country into Latin America's drug trafficking hub. Bush strengthened U.S. military forces in the Canal Zone and began evacuating American civilians. On December 17, after General Noriega's Panama Defense Force (PDF) killed and wounded several American off-duty servicemen en route to a restaurant, Bush authorized Operation Just Cause, a military operation to remove Noriega and reestablish a democratic Panamanian government. U.S. forces were already based in Panama when on December 19 a fleet of C-5s and C-130s flew in reinforcements and supplies. C-141s dropped airborne units and army rangers on Panama City's two principal airfields, Torrijos International Airport and Tocumen Military Airfield. Tactical combat aircraft involved included AC-130H Spectre gunships and six Lockheed F-117A Nighthawk stealth fighters, which made their debut. Working with a Special Forces unit, three Lockheed AC-130E Combat Talons covered the seizure of airfields and a ranger assault on the PDF base at Rio Hatos. Nighthawks hit PDF bases with 2,000-pound bombs. Five Sikorsky MH-53J and four Sikorsky MH-60 Pave Low helicopters, all equipped with nose-mounted, forward-looking infrared (FLIR) terrain-following and terrain-avoidance radar, also aided Special Forces units. The strikes were enough to discourage most Panamanians from fighting. Noriega took refuge in the Vatican embassy and surrendered January 3, 1990.

During Just Cause, the Military Airlift Command transported more than 37,000 troops and 20,329 tons of cargo. Once again, KC-135 and KC-10A tankers from the Strategic Air Command demonstrated that far-flung air operations could not be conducted without in-flight refueling. Operation Just Cause resulted in the creation of the Special Operations Command, which separated fixed-wing gunships and special mission helicopters from the Tactical Airlift Command. These moves proved timely several months later after Saddam Hussein's Iraqi army invaded Kuwait and a massive new airlift operation ensued.

*ABOVE: The Lockheed F-117A Nighthawk stealth "fighter," which had been one of the best kept secrets in military history, made its combat debut during Operation Just Cause and performed exceptionally well during the Persian Gulf War.*

*ABOVE LEFT: The Sikorsky MH-53J helicopter of the 21st Special Operations Squadron is stacked with weapons and equipped with a Pave Low infrared system for night operations.*

**ABOVE: General Dynamics F-16 Fighting Falcons (foreground) and Lockheed C-130 Hercules transports (background) of the 157th Tactical Fighter Wing line an airfield in Saudi Arabia during Operation Desert Shield.**

**BELOW: A General Dynamics F-16 Fighting Falcon from the 614th Tactical Fighter Squadron based at Torrejon Air Base in Spain refuels from a Boeing KC-135R Stratotanker as two other F-16s fly alongside during Operation Desert Shield.**

| USAF Chiefs of Staff—1990s | |
| --- | --- |
| General Michael J. Dugan† | July 1, 1990–September 17, 1990 |
| General John H. Loh** | September 18, 1990–October 29, 1990 |
| General Merrill A. McPeak | October 29, 1990–October 25, 1994 |
| General Ronald F. Fogelman | October 26, 1994–September 1, 1997 |
| General Michael E. Ryan | November 6, 1997–September 6, 2001 |
| † Resigned after tiff with Secretary of Defense Richard Cheney<br>** Served as acting chief of staff | |

## Organizing Desert Shield

In 1990, as the former U.S.S.R. disintegrated, JCS chairman General Colin Powell turned attention away from Soviet issues and began focusing on a possible attack by Iraq on Saudi Arabia. Powell preferred sanctions over open warfare. He turned military planning over to General H. Norman Schwarzkopf, commander in chief of Central Command (CENTCOM), which had been formed in 1983 to look after the Middle East, Southeast Asia, and Northeast Africa. Lieutenant General Charles A. Horner, commanding CENTCOM air forces as well as the Tactical Air Command's Ninth Air Force based in South Carolina, drew the assignment for planning air operations. There were no sanctions in the Schwarzkopf/Horner game plan. Operations Plan 1002–90 called for massive deployments in Saudi Arabia, and Horner prepositioned more than $1 billion in fuel, bombs, and other war supplies in Oman, Diego Garcia, and on ships in the Indian Ocean. Saudi Arabia also cooperated, building airfields and military installations in event of an emergency. The crisis occurred on August 2, 1990, when Iraq invaded Kuwait.

At that time, General Horner had only two KC-135Rs on the Arabian Peninsula, and the tankers were there to participate in refueling exercises with United Arab Emirates fighters. There would be no more American planes on Arab soil until King Abdul Aziz ibn Fahd agreed, although 200,000 Iraqi troops were already massing on the Saudi border. Fahd could

alienate Arabs by allowing American military forces, including service women, into Saudi Arabia, or risk losing his country. Fahd chose survival, and on August 8 President Bush announced Operation Desert Shield. The first Lockheed C-141B landed with airlift control elements from Andrews Air Force Base. A few hours later, forty-eight F-15C and D Eagles arrived from Langley, Virginia. For several days F-15s and the Royal Saudi Arabian Air Force provided the only buffer against Saddam Hussein's 1,000-plane Iraqi air force, which consisted of 550 combat aircraft and a few state-of-the-art MiG-29s. Because Iraq had the fourth largest army in the world, the sixth largest air force, 17,000 surface-to-air missiles, and 10,000 antiaircraft guns with Soviet high-tech targeting capabilities, Hussein discounted the USAF's airpower.

While diplomats and politicians organized coalitions and the U.N. Security Council imposed trade embargoes on Iraq, air chief General Michael J. Dugan's staff worked around the clock planning "Instant Thunder," which had no similarity to the failed graduated response policies of Vietnam. With input from General Horner and Brigadier General Buster C. Glosson, director of CENTCOM air campaign plans, Instant Thunder called for massive strikes on Iraq's "centers of gravity" with precision-guided munitions to avoid civilian casualties. Strategic targets included Iraq's air force, command and control centers, communications, oil refineries, Scud missile sites, and industries producing nuclear, chemical, and biological weapons.

**ABOVE LEFT: Three General Dynamics F-111F Aardvarks and one EF-111 Raven from the 48th Tactical Fighter Wing fly in formation over Saudi Arabia during Operation Desert Shield. The USAF retired all F-111s in 1998.**

**ABOVE: A Lockheed C-130E Hercules transport from the 314th Tactical Airlift Wing located at Little Rock Air Force Base does an assault landing exercise on a desert runway during Operation Desert Shield.**

**LEFT: The front- and rear-loading Lockheed C-5 Galaxy has tremendous payload capacity, providing the Air Mobility Command with intertheater and intercontinental airlift flexibility anywhere in the world.**

Not fully aware of the massive buildup of U.N. forces in the Persian Gulf, the Iraqi army continued to dig defensive positions and emplace field fortifications in the sands along the Kuwaiti-Saudi border. On January 15, 1991, after all negotiations failed and Hussein refused to withdraw Iraqi troops from Kuwait, President Bush authorized military action. Two days later the Persian Gulf War began in earnest.

## Desert Storm

At 3:00 A.M. Baghdad time on January 17, 1991, a combination of cruise missiles, stealth fighters, and Special Operations helicopters blasted Iraqi air defenses,

communications, electrical power grids, and command bunkers with unprecedented ferocity. Special Operations USAF MH-53E and MH-53J Pave Low helicopters and army Apache helicopters blinded Iraq's air defense system by destroying radar sites. The night-vision-equipped helicopters used laser-guided Hellfire missiles, hundreds of rockets, and thousands of rounds of 30mm cannon fire from M230 chain guns. With Iraqi radar jammed, seven B-52G bombers flying a 14,000-mile, thirty-five-hour, longest-ever mission from Barksdale Air Force Base, Louisiana, and back launched AGM-86C cruise missiles with 1,000-pound conventional warheads that struck key communications and power facilities.

### Buildup in the Gulf

| Buildup: USAF Aircraft in the Gulf (1990–1991) | | | | | |
|---|---|---|---|---|---|
| | 8/7 | 8/12 | 9/11 | 1/17 | 2/24 |
| Fighters | 0 | 129 | 398 | 652 | 747 |
| Other combat aircraft† | 0 | 7 | 67 | 87 | 161 |
| Support aircraft** | 2 | 72 | 210 | 394 | 463 |
| Total | 2 | 208 | 675 | 1,133 | 1,371 |

† Bombers, tactical reconnaissance, Special Operations, etc.
** AWACs, theater airlift, tankers, etc.

The USAF built an "aluminum bridge" of 118 C-5s and 195 C-141s to move men and supplies from the U.S. to the Arabian Peninsula. During the rapid buildup of forces, long-haul transports, including Civil Reserve Air Fleet aircraft, averaged one landing every seven minutes at Dhahran. Another 140 USAF C-130s in the area performed tactical

airlift. Refueled in flight by KC-10s and KC-135s, the massive airlift brought 125,000 troops and 400 tons of cargo to the Arabian Peninsula. The "aluminum bridge" eventually reached the rate of 17 million ton-miles per day, exactly ten times that of the Berlin Airlift.

Prior to Desert Storm, KC-135s flew sixty-six sorties a day and refueled 175 aircraft.

During Desert Storm, tanker sorties jumped to 215 a day, refueling 839 mainly combat aircraft.

On September 11, 1990, the USAF had 398 fighters in the Gulf. At the outset of Desert Storm, the air force had placed 1,133 aircraft in the Gulf, with more on the way. The mix consisted of 652 fighters, 394 support aircraft (tankers,

AWACs, and airlift vehicles), and eighty-seven other combat aircraft, including bombers, special operations, reconnaissance, and electronic warfare planes. Navy and Coalition forces added another 1,481 planes to the mix, bringing the total number of fighters and attack aircraft to 1,838

*ABOVE LEFT: First flown in December 1963, the Lockheed C-141B Starlifter continues to be the workhorse of the Air Mobility Command, performing both military and humanitarian missions throughout the globe.*

**ABOVE: An Iraqi hardened aircraft shelter at Ali Al Salem Air Base in Kuwait suffers severe damage from USAF bombing strikes during the opening hours of Operation Desert Storm.**

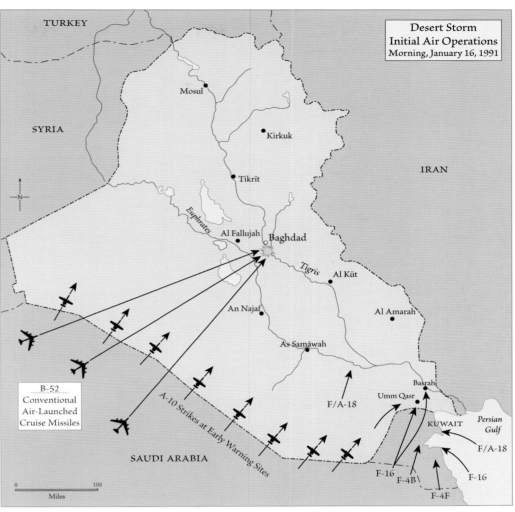

During the turmoil, 37th Tactical Fighter Wing (TFW) pilots flying Lockheed/Martin F-117A Nighthawk stealth aircraft refueled in flight from tankers, separated from airborne squadrons, and flew at different altitudes to attack specific targets deep in Iraq. Only four of the sixty-five pilots had ever been in combat. They used inertial guidance systems to get to the target area and then used forward-looking infrared (FLIR) and downward-looking infrared (DLIR) to locate and track the exact targets. The infrared/laser turret designated the target and the system released 2,000 pound GBU-10s or GBU-27 Paveway III laser-guided weapons down chimneys and through specified windows. The spectacle, later displayed on television, stunned American viewers. That night, pilots surgically destroyed thirty percent of the most difficult targets in Iraq. The Iraqis never detected one F-117 on radar. The planes remained "invisible," and the pilots registered eighty-five percent bombing accuracy. Iraqi antiaircraft fire and SAMs launched helter-skelter into the pitch-black night of Desert Storm never so much as scratched a Nighthawk.

The combination of helicopters, B-52s, F-117A Nighthawks, and cruise missiles opened the way for a second storm of 650 Coalition aircraft armed with runway-cratering bombs and laser-guided missiles to sweep into Iraq and devastate airfields, hardened shelters, and chemical-weapon storage facilities. During the first day of action, the USAF flew more sorties than the Iraqi Air Force had flown against Iran during eight years of war. Forty-one enemy planes got off the ground, engaged in combat, and were shot down with Sparrow missiles. Hundreds remained in shelters and were eventually destroyed. Iraq hastily shifted other aircraft to refuge in Iran. Of thirty-eight Coalition aircraft lost in combat during Desert Storm, fourteen belonged to the USAF.

**ABOVE: Air strikes launched Desert Storm at 6:00 A.M. on January 16, 1991. The first strikes concentrated on knocking out Iraqi early warning systems along the southern tier. Fighter-bombers flying out of Saudi Arabia struck Iraqi ground and control forces in Kuwait, Umm Qasr, and Basrah. B-52s followed, striking strategic communications and ground and air control centers in and around Baghdad. Surgical air strikes continued throughout the day and the days that followed.**

## USAF Missiles—Desert Shield/Desert Storm

| Designation | Classification | Specifications/Range (miles) |
|---|---|---|
| AGM-65 Maverick | Air-to-surface | TV, IRR, or laser-guided/10 |
| AGM-86C Cruise | Air launched | B-52G launch/1,500+ |
| AGM-88 HARM | Antiradiation | Air launched/15 |
| AGM-114 Hellfire | Antitank missile | 95-pound laser guided/10 |
| AIM-7F Sparrow | Air-to-air missile | Semi-active radar/20 |
| AIM-9L/M Sidewinder | Air-to-air missile | Heat-seeking/5+ |
| AIM-120A AMRAAM | Air-to-air missile | Fire-and-Forget/25 |
| BMG-71A/C Tow | Antitank missile | 42-pound wire-guided/2 |

## Desert Storm—The Summing Up

Before and during the ground campaign, new weapons combined with older weapons to obliterate the Iraqi army. The controversial F-111 from General Dynamics released 7.3 million tons of precision-guided munitions, wiped out 245 hardened Iraqi aircraft shelters, blasted hundreds of bunkers, and destroyed 1,500 tanks and armored vehicles. Older McDonnell Douglas F-4Gs resorted to Wild Weasel tactics of the Vietnam era and worked together with General Dynamics F-16s using cluster bombs, conventional bombs, and Maverick and HARM missiles to wipe out hundreds of Iraqi SAM sites. B-52G bombers devastated Hussein's crack Republican Guard units near Kuwait. Each B-52 carried fifty-one M-117 general-purpose 750-pound bombs, and a flight of three aircraft could upend more than a square mile of troop-occupied desert.

## Joint STARS

At General Schwarzkopf's request, and six years before the planned deployment date, two E-8As arrived in Saudi Arabia on the eve of the opening air campaign. The converted Boeing 707-320 aircraft carried a Norden multimode, side-looking, twenty-five-foot radar antenna housed in a "canoe" under the forward fuselage. Schwarzkopf wanted the synthetic aperture radar (SAR), which scanned 155-plus miles, to locate stationary and slow-moving objects such as tanks, armored vehicles, and Scud missile carriers. The instrumentation, known as Joint Surveillance Target Attack Radar System (Joint STARS or J-STARS), alternated between SAR and a Doppler mode to detect the ground targets.

The USAF's two E-8As logged more than 600 hours during Desert Storm, and flew fifty-four 10-hour missions at night. J-STARS picked up everything that moved on the ground, from troops to mobile Scud launchers, and provided air commanders with a "real-time, god's eye view of the battle." A-10s, F-15Es, F-16s, and F-111Fs operated through the night with data transmitted from E-8As, and began "plinking" tanks, armored vehicles, and artillery emplacements weeks before the ground assault. When the "100-Hour War" began on February 24, 1991, USAF aircraft had severely reduced the enemy's ability to fight.

**ABOVE: Lieutenant Greg Nahrgang (foreground) and Lieutenant Craig Osborne, both airborne weapons officers, monitor E-8C Joint Surveillance Tracking Reconnaissance System consoles during Desert Storm.**

**ABOVE: The Grumman/Boeing E-8C Joint Surveillance Target Attack Radar System (Joint STARS) is carried in flight over Iraq as a long-range, all-weather, air-to-ground surveillance system for locating, classifying, and tracking ground targets.**

Of 54,706 USAF personnel in the Persian Gulf, 12,098 were Air National Guard or Air Force Reserve personnel. Thirty-seven guard and twenty-eight reserve units flew A-10s, C-5s, C-130s, C-141s, F-16s, HH-53Es, and KC-135s. Every fourth guard or reservist was a woman. Reserve units flew 5,200 combat sorties: the guard flew 3,550 missions and dropped 3,500 tons of ordnance. KC-135 tanker pilots made 14,000 in-flight hookups and transferred 200 million pounds of fuel to combat aircraft. Much to the annoyance of Coalition Muslims, women reservists and regulars flew tankers, helicopters, and reconnaissance aircraft. They also drove trucks, repaired airplanes, and some commanded units up to brigade-size strength in combat support and combat service areas.

When two satellites covering the Iraq/Kuwait area proved insufficient to keep watch over the battleground, the air force Space Command motored-up a reserve satellite over the Pacific and restationed it in a new position 22,300 miles above the earth to carry part of the load. For the first time in a major war, space power came of age and joined with air and ground power to become an integral part of an enormously successful campaign.

On February 28, 1991, the ground war ended. Never had an army the size of Iraq's been so rapidly vanquished at so little cost to the victors. Fewer than two of the forty-two Iraqi divisions posted in the Kuwait area survived.

Although the Cold War was over, Kuwaiti independence was restored, and the Iraqi army was neutered, serious threats to world peace still existed. With another presidential election slated for 1992, air force chief of staff General McPeak began gearing his command for the possibility of another "peace dividend." The USAF had never been better prepared for war, but in 1992 there appeared to be no powerful enemy poised to provoke a world crisis.

*ABOVE LEFT: Munitions specialists from the 23rd Tactical Fighter Wing load an AGM-65 Maverick air-to-surface missile onto a Fairchild A-10A Thunderbolt II attack aircraft during Operation Desert Storm.*

*ABOVE: An F-4G Phantom II Wild Weasel of the 35th Tactical Aircraft Wing, armed with AGM-88 high-speed anti-radar air-to-surface missiles, flies on a mission during operations in the Persian Gulf.*

## The Balkan Wars

With the dissolution of the Warsaw Pact on March 31, 1991, Soviet troops began withdrawing from Eastern Europe. In Yugoslavia, between June 25 and December 23, 1991, the provinces of Slovenia, Croatia, Bosnia-Herzegovina, and Macedonia opted for pre-World War II status and declared independence. Kosovo followed in 1997. Yugoslav President Slobodan Milosevic, a Serb, attempted to retain control of the provinces by using the Serbian army to launch attacks under the banner of ethnic cleansing. On May 22, 1992, the U.N. recognized the independence of the provinces under attack and sent multinational troops to safeguard all minorities. In an attempt to end the fighting, NATO established a no-fly zone over Bosnia-Herzegovina, enforced predominantly by USAF aircraft flying out of Aviano Air Base in Italy. Most Serbian aircraft operating in Bosnia were helicopters, but on February 28, 1994, USAF F-16Cs intercepted six Bosnian Serb Super Galeb light attack aircraft and shot four down.

To stop the rampant ethnic cleansing of Muslims in Sarajevo, the U.N. on August 30, 1995, authorized Operation Deliberate Force, which involved 200 aircraft. The USAF flew more than 2,000 sorties and applied precision weapons in highly accurate strikes against Serbian command and control bunkers, air defense installations, and other military targets. The powerful air attacks stunned Milosevic, who in December signed a peace agreement but continued to create trouble in Croatia, Bosnia, and Kosovo.

On March 24, 1999, NATO responded to Milosevic's military mischief with Operation Allied Force, an air assault without a ground war. For seventy-eight days the USAF pounded Serb positions, destroyed a handful of MiG-29s, and forced Milosevic to withdraw his troops. The defeat led to Milosevic's forcible removal from power and his indictment for war crimes by an international tribunal.

During Operation Allied Force, the USAF used its best weapons, including more than 100 F-16 and 56 F-15C/E attack-fighters and a number of B-1B and B-

52H bombers, while the B-2 bomber also made its debut in combat. More than 184 KC-135s and KC-10s combined to refuel planes in the air. The stealthy B-2s made the trip non-stop from Whiteman Air Force Base, Missouri, performed forty-nine missions, and delivered highly accurate GPS-guided weapons to designated targets, marking once more the tremendous potential of aerospace. At the time, USAF Chief of Staff General Michael E. Ryan did not realize that sorties in the Balkans in 1999 would serve as a warm-up for operations in the twenty-first century.

## Afghanistan—Operation Enduring Freedom

Efforts by Islamic radical militants to drive non-Muslims out of the Middle East reached horrific new dimensions on September 11, 2001, when members of Osama bin Laden's al Qaeda organization hijacked four airliners in American airspace and flew two of them into New York's World Trade Center and another into Washington's Pentagon. The fourth plane crashed in Pennsylvania after passengers disabled the hijackers.

The surprise attack on American soil killed 3,025 American and foreign citizens and took 622 more lives than Japan's 361 carrier-plane strike on Pearl Harbor. The USAF immediately mobilized, including guard and reserve units, and began flying combat air patrols over major American, cities while AWACs searched the skies for planes off course.

President George W. Bush soon learned that the strikes had originated from bin Laden's al Qaeda terrorist camps in Taliban-controlled Afghanistan. A few days later, USAF Special Operations personnel landed in the northern mountains of Afghanistan and began organizing countermeasures with the country's anti-Taliban Northern Alliance.

As politicians built diplomatic bridges in southwest Asia, the USAF began positioning B-1Bs, B-52s, F-16s, A-10s, and KC-135 tankers for joint air operations with navy carrier planes. On October 7, B-1s and B-52s from Diego Garcia in the Indian Ocean joined navy carrier aircraft and struck al Qaeda airfields, air defense sites, command-and-control centers, troop

*ABOVE: B-2 Spirit bombers deployed during Operation Allied Force flew non-stop missions from bases in the United States, relying on in-flight fueling to strike targets in Afghanistan and Iraq and return home.*

concentrations, training camps, and the residential compound of Taliban leader Mullah Mohammad Omar in Kandahar. B-2 Spirits flew the longest sorties ever from Whiteman Air Force Base. Days later, air strikes began around the clock. None of the Taliban's twenty fighters got off the ground. By November 4, al Qaeda/Taliban fixed assets had been destroyed, and a day later the Northern Alliance took the offensive.

The ground war took shape around helicopters. During Operation Anaconda in March 2002, USAF personnel became heavily engaged in the air and on the ground. Because of scattered enemy pockets, Sikorsky HH-60 and HH-53 helicopters became the most efficient way of getting Special Operations troops to hot spots. Although the Taliban ceased to exist as a governing power, and al Qaeda disappeared into the mountains along the Pakistan-Afghan border, operations still continue in areas where al Qaeda has melded into the civilian population.

*BELOW: Members of the 16th Special Operations Wing offload a Sikorsky MH-53J Pave Low helicopter from a Lockheed C-17 Globemaster III in support of Operation Enduring Freedom during December 2001.*

Air Force Chief of Staff General T. Michael Moseley, during an interview on the global war on terror in October 2007, acknowledged that "...we've been fighting in Afghanistan [26] months longer than the United States fought World War II." By April 2003, B-1s, B-2s, B-52s, F-15Es, F-16s, A-10s, and AC-130s had flown more than seventy-five percent of all combat missions in Afghanistan, dropping more than 30,750 munitions (9,650 tons) and damaging or destroying more than seventy-five percent of the designated targets. Throughout the combat phase, the USAF flew more than 85,000 sorties, including 48,000 airlift missions that moved more than 513,000 passengers and 487,000 tons of cargo.

The USAF is still in Afghanistan and expects to be there as long as terrorists threaten the nation's newly organized democratic government.

**Operation Iraqi Freedom**

On March 19, 2003, after months of debate in Congress and much confusion over U.N. resolutions, President George W. Bush took the position that Saddam Hussein supported terrorists and possessed weapons of mass destruction (WMDs). Bush gave the order to launch Operation Iraqi Freedom and gave the job of leading it to army General Tommy Ray Franks. Part of the president's irritation emanated from Iraq shooting down some thirty-six coalition aircraft over a period of several months, using SAMs and antiaircraft artillery in no-fly zones.

General Franks' mission entailed the removal of Hussein from power, liberating the Iraqi people, ridding terrorists, and destroying Iraq's nuclear, chemical, and biological weapons. The toughest assignment proved to be political: creating the transition to representative self-government in a country rife with sectarian hatred.

General Moseley, commanding the Ninth Air Force and U.S. Central Command Air Forces, played a key role in the day-to-day planning and execution of Iraqi

Freedom air operations. The air strike opened at 5:30 A.M. March 20 with attacks by Lockheed F-117A Nighthawk and Northrop B-2 Spirit stealth aircraft, and ship-launched Tomahawk cruise missiles, targeting the residential compound where Hussein and his family often stayed. Stealth aircraft were specifically designed to make first strikes on high-priority targets such as leadership bunkers, command posts, and air and communications centers, but that night Hussein slept elsewhere. At 7:15 A.M., U.S. and British troops crossed from Kuwait and seized the border town of Umm Qasr. By March 22, more than a 1,000 air sorties and an equal number of cruise missiles had struck and surgically eliminated Iraq's most strategic targets.

To penetrate bunkers, USAF pilots deployed Guided Bomb Unit 28 (GBU-28) 5,000-pound (BLU-113) laser-guided munitions. The "Bunker Busters" were built with a 4,414-pound case filled with 647 pounds of explosives and fitted with GBU-27 laser-guidance kits to navigate the bomb.

For four days, air and missile attacks continued non-stop while 300,000 Coalition troops deployed for combat and support tasks. During early operations the USAF employed several new weapons. In central Iraq on April 2, B-52s dropped CBU-105 cluster bombs fitted with wind-corrected munitions dispenser tail kits. The armor-busting, sensor-fused weapons clobbered and turned back an Iraqi tank column attempting to intercept Coalition troops.

BLU-82 "Daisy Cutters" had been used in Vietnam to clear vegetation from landing zones, destroy minefields in Desert Storm, and suck the oxygen out of caves in Afghanistan. Now the 15,000-pound general-purpose fuel/air bomb filled with 12,600 pounds of gelled slurry explosive generated a tremendously negative psychological impact on Saddam's Republican Guard units. The BLU-82 produced a huge fiery blast without creating a crater. Being too large to hitch to a bomber, crewmen rolled the monsters out of the back of Special Operations Hercules transports.

*ABOVE: A Lockheed F-117A Nighthawk from the 37th Tactical Fighter Wing engages its target over Afghanistan and drops a GBU-28 guided bomb unit on a Taliban encampment near Jalalabad.*

**ABOVE: A weapons trailer loaded with MK-84 2,000-pound bombs fitted with Joint Direct Attack Munitions (JDAM) is transported to a waiting B-1B Lancer bomber for a strike on Iraq during Operation Enduring Freedom.**

**INSET ABOVE: An F-16C Block 30, Fighting Falcon, of the 93rd Fighter Squadron, is equipped with a Litening II navigation/targeting pod and an A1Q-131 jamming pod prior to departing on a mission.**

On April 7, a B-1B Lancer from the 34th Bomb Squadron, Ellsworth Air Force Base, South Dakota, dropped four GBU-31 satellite-guided Joint Direct Attack Munitions (JDAMs) on what was suspected as being a meeting site of senior Iraqi leaders in the Mansour section of Baghdad.

The JDAMs guided air-to-surface system—designated GBU-31, GBU-32, or GBU-38—uses as the payload the 2,000-pound BLU-109/Mk-84, the 1,000-pound BLU-110/Mk-83, or the 500-pound BLU-111/Mk-82 warhead. The GBU guidance tail kit converts existing unguided free-fall bombs into accurate all-weather "smart" munitions. Desert Storm highlighted a deficiency in air-to-surface JDAMs when delivered in adverse weather and, in particular, from medium to high altitudes. Correcting the problem occurred in 1997 with the addition of a new tail section that incorporated a GPS-enabled inertial navigation system. By the time of

Iraqi Freedom, the JDAMs performance had improved to a system reliability of ninety-five percent while achieving an accuracy rate delivered from higher altitudes through rain, clouds, and snow, of just over 30 ft. The GBU-31 JDAM has a wingspan of twenty-five-inches, a range of fifteen miles, and a ceiling of 45,000-plus feet. The warhead weighs about 2,100 pounds.

JDAMs are currently compatible with B-1B, B-2A, and B-52H bombers, and F-15E, F-14A/B/D, F/A-18E/F, F-16C/D, F/A-22, and F/A-18C/D fighter-bombers and suppression aircraft.

On April 11, also for the first time in history, a B-52 using a Litening II advanced airborne targeting and navigation pod demolished specific facilities at an airfield in northern Iraq.

Many munitions used during Iraqi Freedom air strikes contained refinements to general-purpose bombs designed in the 1980s.

## The Air Forces

During the summer of 2002, the Iraqi air force consisted of about 33,000 personnel and 800 aircraft, including 120 armed helicopters and more than ninety combat aircraft, mainly French Mirage F-1s and Russian MiGs. In addition to seven main air bases, Hussein also operated eight smaller special purpose bases where he distributed fighters and bombers. All the bases were heavily protected by antiaircraft guns, SAMs, and surveillance radar.

General Moseley, operating out of Combined Air Operations Center at Prince Sultan Airbase in Saudi Arabia, began preparing the battlefield in June 2002 by selectively destroying all Iraqi command posts and communication sites that had been pestering American and British planes in no-fly zones. By mid-March 2003, some 21,736 sorties had been flown and 345 targets destroyed. Air strikes commencing on March 19 virtually wiped out the rest of Iraq's air force and Hussein's air defense system.

ABOVE: Testifying to improvements in surgical strikes since Desert Storm, the remains of several Iraqi air force MiGs were destroyed on an Iraqi air base in Abril Province without damage to the airfield's infrastructure.

### Free-fall General-purpose Bombs

| Type | Size/lb | Explosive/lb | Aircraft |
|---|---|---|---|
| Mk-82 | 500 | 192 | AV-8Bs, B-52s, F/A-18s, F-16s |
| Mk-83 | 1,000 | 416 | AV-8Bs, F/A-18s |
| Mk-84 | 2,000 | 945 | F-15Es, F-16s, F-111Fs |
| M117 | 750 | 386 | B-52s |
| BLU-109* | 2,000 | 550 | F-117As |

*laser-guided, penetration type*

### U.S. Personnel in the Middle East—March 19, 2003

| Service Branch | Number |
|---|---|
| U.S. Army | 233,342 |
| U.S. Navy | 61,296 |
| U.S. Marine Corps | 74,405 |
| U.S. Air Force | 54,995 |
| U.S. Air National Guard | 7,207* |
| U.S. Air Force Reserve | 2,084* |

*Included in U.S. Air Force numbers*

### Coalition Aircraft Deployed in the Gulf

| | |
|---|---|
| USAF fixed-wing | 1,477 |
| USAF helicopters | 186 |
| USAF National Guard | 236 |
| USAF Air Reserve | 70 |
| U.S. Army helicopters | 700 |
| U.S. Navy aircraft | 408 |
| Marine Corps aircraft | 372 |
| British aircraft | 200 |
| Australian aircraft | 22 |

*ABOVE: A McDonnell Douglas F-15E Strike Eagle dual-role fighter aircraft prepares to refuel while flying a combat mission over Iraq on July 23, 2004. F-15s served in Desert Storm, Afghanistan, and Iraqi Freedom.*

## The Strategic Air Campaign

General Moseley focused the March 21, 2003, opening air campaign on dismantling the Iraqi government by striking Saddam Hussein's palaces, bunkers, security sites, intelligence network, and Ba'ath Party facilities. General Franks referred to the unrelenting, seventy-two-hour strike as "shock and awe," during which some 2,500 bombs and cruise missiles plastered priority targets in Baghdad. During the air strikes, suppression-of-enemy-air-defense (SEAD) planes moved into the area and dropped chaff corridors to confuse Iraqi radar and then target them with Raytheon AGM-88 high-speed anti-radiation (HARM) missiles.

Every evening, fixed-wing aircraft sortied into Baghdad's "super missile engagement zone" to clobber palaces, telephone exchanges, terrorist conclaves, and 102 sites associated with weapons of mass destruction. Iraqi forces launched 1,660 radar-guided SAMs during the "shock and awe" phase without striking one U.S., British, or Australian aircraft. Nor did the Iraqi air force get a single plane off the ground during the air strikes. Saddam fired his air defense commander and had Iraqi planes hidden in palm groves or residential areas, while some were buried in sand.

Air strikes during Iraqi Freedom were more selective, limited in intensity, and accurate compared

LEFT: *Aerial reconnaissance snaps a photograph of one of Saddam Hussein's many palaces scattered all over Iraq and financed by funds that were to have been earmarked for the oil-for-food initiative.*

with those in Desert Storm. Much of the infrastructure was left untouched. Airfields were bombed, but not hardened shelters or facilities. Fifteen hundred regime leadership targets were destroyed, 1,441 air supremacy facilities were struck, and 832 sorties were flown against suspected WMD targets. Within three days, the strategic air campaign had paralyzed the Iraqi regime from fighting back with any unified resistance.

## Supporting the Ground War

On the evening of March 20, 2003, U.S. and British ground troops advanced into southern Iraq, driving to the gates of Basrah and pushing 200 miles up the Euphrates valley towards Baghdad. USAF Special Forces in Sikorsky MH-53M Pave Low helicopters preceded the main assault by taking control of oil facilities. For air support, the USAF received assistance from Marine Corps AH-1 SuperCobras and British AH-7 Lynx helicopters during the ground assault. As the U.S. Army V Corps pressed towards Baghdad with the aim of destroying Republican Guard forces, army OH-58D Kiowa Warrior scout helicopters flew ahead of the 3rd Infantry Division and on March 22 seized Talill Airbase and Najaf. Once in Najaf, Hunter unmanned aerial vehicles began spotting for the 11th Aviation Brigade's AH-64D Longbow Apaches. As

**ABOVE: Following a USAF surgical strike on Balad Air Base, Iraq, F-16s from the 510th Expeditionary Fighter Squadron are still able to use the facility, taxiing toward the runway for a February 13, 2007, mission in Anbar Province.**

fighting intensified along the route to Baghdad, Major General Daniel Leaf ramped up aircraft support for the Third Army with four squadrons of A-10A Warthog "tank busters," several squadrons of F-16C Fighting Falcons, and F-15E Strike Eagles. Also on call were twenty-eight B-52H Stratofortresses and eleven B-1B Lancers armed with conventional bombs and satellite-guided JDAMs.

During the ground war, General Moseley applied tried and tested tactics. He established kill boxes over and beyond the moving front lines. Air controllers in E-3 Sentry AWACS circled overhead for hours, relaying minute-by-minute fire-control messages to ensure that maximum damage was inflicted on Iraqi ground troops. Once Moseley established a kill box, the combination of jet air support, artillery, rockets, and Apache gunships systematically and thoroughly worked the area. Every pilot flying into a kill box knew the location of his target, whether stationary or moving, and never returned to base without hitting

either a primary or a secondary target with the entire payload. After a few days, pilots began returning to base with bombs because there were no longer any targets.

Despite a sand storm that interrupted operations, U.S. troops entered the center of Baghdad on April 9 and began mopping up the city. Four days later marine armored vehicles entered Tikrit. Air support for ground troops, the top priority for the combined air forces, made up about fifty percent of the sorties.

Although President Bush declared on May 1, 2003, that major combat operations in Iraq had ended, a new war against insurgents, terrorists from other Muslim nations, and disaffected religious and political groups continues. The USAF is still flying support missions over Iraq and will probably continue to do so for years to come.

As the war on terror continues across the globe, the USAF now has the task of quelling a new enemy that has no country, no boundaries, no government, and the goal of "Islamizing" the world.

**ABOVE: A Boeing E-3B/C AWACS (Airborne Warning and Control System) aircraft from the 965th Airborne Air Control Squadron and deployed to the 363rd Air Expeditionary Wing takes off on a mission in support of Iraqi Freedom.**

# CHAPTER 9

# INTO THE FUTURE

To achieve the air force's mission, Secretary of the Air Force Michael W. Wynne and Air Force Chief of Staff General T. Michael Moseley have projected a strategic vision—*Global Vigilance, Reach and Power*. The three core competencies involve the development of airmen; the advancement and transfer of technology to warfighting; and the integration of operations within the air force and with the other services. *Global Vigilance* requires the acquisition of new observation, reconnaissance, and surveillance aircraft, such as Northrop Grumman Global Hawks and MQ-1 and MQ-9 Reaper "Predators" equipped with pods for every shooter; and also an upgraded and modernized global network and information grid. *Global Reach* entails upgraded and modernized cargo and precision-drop aircraft such as C-17s, C-130Js, and new joint cargo aircraft. *Global Power* requires upgraded and modernized legacy fighters and bombers such as Lockheed-Martin's F-35 Joint Strike Fighter (JSF) and the F-22A Raptor. To upgrade *Global Power*, the air force also wants to enhance special operations capabilities using a combination of CV-22 Osprey tilt-rotor aircraft, Fairchild Republic A-10 Thunderbolt IIs for close air support, platforms for counter-insurgency operations, and unmanned aerial vehicle (UAV) squadrons.

**RIGHT: The Northrop Grumman Global Hawk, an unmanned aerial vehicle (UAV) with a 4,000-mile range, awaits refueling at Langley Air Force Base, Virginia, after completing a non-stop flight from Edwards Air Force Base, California.**

## The USAF Mission

The mission of the United States Air Force is to deliver sovereign options for the defense of the United States of America and its global interests—to fly and fight in the Air, Space, and Cyberspace. To leverage asymmetric advantages across the "Commons" to provide desired kinetic and non-kinetic effects as part of the Joint Team. To develop, sustain, and always sharpen our warfighting edge. To continue to provide the most highly motivated, trained, and respected Airman in the world to accomplish our missions with integrity and leadership.

The air force mission involves a comprehensive strategy of divestiture, procurement, and modernization that eliminates the most expensive, least effective systems, and replaces them with new platforms and systems that will result in a more lethal, agile force. The outcome will be a reduction in manpower in exchange for improvements in technology, but also an integration of active, guard, and reserve components into a seamless global force.

To implement the USAF mission in the twenty-first century, General Moseley's staff prepared *Air Force Roadmap 2006–2025.* The guidelines take into account the assets of today's air force, and after considering their effectiveness in today's military environment, projects the needs for a capability-based force structured over the next two decades.

*BELOW: Lockheed Martin's F-35 Joint Strike Fighter (JSF) will replace most of the aging fighter inventory in the air force, navy, and Marine Corps and will serve as a supersonic, multi-role stealth fighter.*

*ABOVE: Boeing C-17 Globemaster III cargo aircraft fly in formation through the early-morning gloom prior to an air drop exercise over North Field, South Carolina. Globemasters form an integral part in the air force's plans for rapid strategic delivery of troops and supplies.*

### USAF Based Commands

| |
|---|
| Air Combat Command, Langley AFB, Virginia |
| Air Education and Training Command, Randolph AFB, Texas |
| Air Force Material Command, Wright-Patterson AFB, Ohio |
| Air Force Reserve Command, Robins AFB, Georgia |
| Air Force Space Command, Peterson AFB, Colorado |
| Air Force Special Operations Command, Hurlburt Field, Florida |
| Air Mobility Command, Scott AFB, Illinois |
| Pacific Air Forces, Hickam AFB, Hawaii |
| U.S. Air Forces in Europe, Ramstein AFB, Germany |

## General T. Michael Moseley

In September 2005, fifty-six-year-old General T. Michael Moseley became the eighteenth chief of staff of an air force consisting of 710,000 active-duty, guard, reserve, and civilian forces serving in the United States and overseas. His immediate mission was to prepare air force strategy for the next twenty years, hence the *Air Force Roadmap 2006-2025*.

Unlike most air chiefs, Moseley began his career with bachelors (1971) and masters (1972) degrees in political science from Texas A&M University. After graduating, he decided to become an air force pilot and began undergraduate training at Webb AFB, Texas. Since 1973, his career and promotions have moved him steadily forward, from piloting F-15s to commanding the Ninth Air Force and CENTCOM air forces in 2001-2003. Moseley also served for two years as vice chief of staff under his predecessor, General John P. Jumper.

Moseley's *Roadmap* brings together not only the needs of the present air force but makes a sharp assessment of the assets and organization required during the next two decades to maintain air supremacy in a world of constantly evolving threats. Having been trained in political science, Moseley is acutely aware of congressional gyrations with funding. "While there is a degree of uncertainty associated with planning twenty years into the future," Moseley cautioned, "such an effort charts a course, which allows all affected parties to work towards a common goal. But uncertainty does exist, not only in the strategic environment, but in the fiscal environment as well."

**RIGHT: General T. Michael Moseley, USAF chief of staff, conducts a briefing with air officers regarding the future plans and strategies that will guide the air force through the changing threats of the next decade.**

### Air and Space Superiority

The *Roadmap* for air and space superiority entails the ability to control everything vertically from the surface of the earth to the highest orbiting satellite. Such control provides freedom to attack as well as freedom from attack. The USAF considers gaining air and space superiority the vital first step in military operations essential to winning in combat. The concept is not new and has been the goal of military commanders ever since the invention of aircraft.

Existing aircraft are continuously being upgraded with new avionics, electronics, and enhanced battlespace situational awareness. Older assets, such as the F-16 Fighting Falcons, will be aged-out because of increased support costs.

Air superiority cannot be achieved and maintained without domination of space. Without space superiority and counterspace capability, land, sea, air, and special operations forces cannot be effectively conducted and coordinated without interference by opposing forces. Counterspace missions include defensive and offensive countermeasures and space situation awareness. Defensive capabilities deter adversaries from attacking space assets, defend them if attacked, and recover lost capability following an attack. Offensive countermeasures are designed to deceive, degrade, or destroy enemy space capabilities. Space situation awareness systems provide "find, fix, and track capabilities" through a series of ground-based radars and optical sensors, space-based sensors, and the Space Control Center, which passes data and intelligence to several command centers.

Space superiority is an essential component in enabling the USAF to develop and maintain information superiority.

> Military leaders will resist any temptation to assume the force needed for the future will be a cookie-cutter version of today's needs.
> *General Richard B. Myers, July 25, 2005.*

## Information Superiority

Achieving *Global Vigilance, Reach, and Power* relies on information superiority, which occurs when deployed assets can dominate the strategic intelligence-gathering domain and provide friendly forces with the ability to collect, control, exploit, and defend information without effective opposition, while preventing the enemy from doing the same. The process melds together into C4ISR, which is composed of command, control, communications, and computers (C4) with intelligence, surveillance, and reconnaissance (ISR). Information superiority provides joint force commanders with predictive battlespace awareness to facilitate and conduct precise and persistent attack and to compress the sensor-to-shooter kill chain. The most recent demonstration of effective C4ISR occurred during the 2003 invasion of Iraq, but the overall purpose of the system is to provide the joint force commander with the flexibility to anticipate and assure, dissuade, deter, or defeat threats to the United States and its worldwide interests.

To perform effectively, C4ISR must dominate in four crucial domains—space, air, ground, and cyberspace—and integrate and disperse the gathered information to where it is essentially needed. Space systems enhance crucial warfighting decision-making and situation awareness by providing timely communications that monitor the status of foreign forces worldwide, develop courses of action, and engage targets. Air systems find, fix, track, and assess air and ground targets and disseminate gathered information through command and control (C2) to joint forces. Ground systems are the centerpiece of joint command and control and battle management. They are also a never-ending work-in-process to improve operational integration systems to further facilitate precise, persistent attack and reduce the sensor-to-shooter kill chain. Cyberspace, the fourth domain, is the electronic medium of net-centric operations that brings

ABOVE: Staff Sergeant Jessica Diem, serving with the 140th Communications Flight, Colorado Air National Guard, prepares to install a remote satellite dish used for secure and non-secure communications.

communications and computers together with command and control to build the complete C4ISR information network.

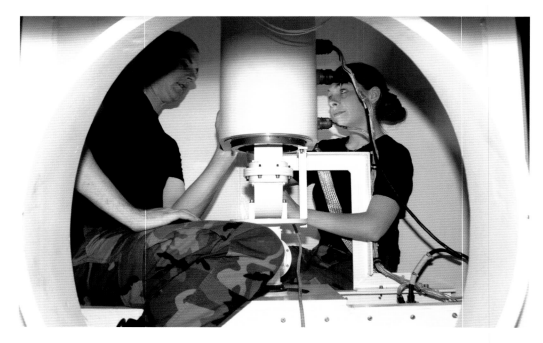

ABOVE: USAF Airman 1st Class Eric Hanes (left) and Airman 1st Class Janina Kowalski of the 30th Space Communications Squadron adjust the azimuth housing on an antenna pedestal for the Next Generation Weather Radar.

RIGHT: In the distance a Titan 4B lifts off from Vandenberg Air Force Base, California, with a new CRYSTAL imaging satellite to be placed in orbit for the National Reconnaissance Office's fleet of Earth Imaging System Satellites.

## Information: The Space Domain

Space domain systems consist of satellite communications, positioning, navigation, and timing data, and include surveillance and reconnaissance information. The role of these systems is to maximize the effectiveness of military air, land, sea, space, and cyber operations from space. Since the Vietnam War, military operations have become increasingly dependent on space capabilities for enhancing crucial warfighter decision-making and situation awareness by providing timely communications and information dissemination. The USAF is currently exploring the development of "near-space" systems, which are between the 65,000-foot flyable altitude and the 325,000-foot orbital level.

Looking into the future, many of the satellites performing today's C4SIR operations are scheduled for replacement in Moseley's *Roadmap*.

## Information: The Air Domain

The air domain finds, fixes, tracks, targets, and assesses air and ground targets and disseminates this information through the command and control constellation to joint forces. The current system worked well during Desert Storm but became exceptionally effective during Iraqi Freedom.

| C4ISR Space Domain Force Structure: SATCOM | | | |
|---|---|---|---|
| **Satellite Purpose** | **Satellite Designation** | | |
| | **Today** | **2017** | **2025** |
| Global Positioning | GPS II | GPS III | GPSIII |
| Defense Communications | DSCS | WGS | TSAT |
| Communications | Milstar | AEHF | TSAT |
| Transformational Communications | | TSAT | TSAT |
| Defense Support | DSP | SBIRS | SBIRS |
| Defense Meteorology | DMSP | NPOESS | NPOESS |
| Wideband Gapfiller | WGS | TSAT | |
| Advanced High Frequency | AEHF | TSAT | |
| Space Radar | SR | SR | |

*RIGHT: A single-seat, single-engined, high-altitude Lockheed U-2 Dragon Lady assigned to the 99th Reconnaissance Squadron takes off from an undisclosed location in southwest Asia in support of Operation Iraqi Freedom.*

The program began in the 1950s with the Lockheed U-2 high-altitude reconnaissance spyplane. The newer U-2 Dragon Lady still performs the same function. The aircraft roams between 70,000 and 90,000 feet altitude in all weather conditions and is capable of collecting a variety of digital imagery using a "wet film" optical bar camera. Intelligence collected can be transferred almost real-time anywhere in the world through air-to-ground or air-to-satellite data links. The USAF intends to replace U-2s with the RQ-4 Global Hawk, a high-altitude, long-endurance, remotely piloted aircraft serving the same reconnaissance and surveillance purpose. The RQ-4 will provide unrelenting warfighting intelligence day, night, and in any weather.

The General Atomics Aeronautical Systems MQ-1 Predator unmanned aerial vehicle (UAV) became part of C4SIR in 1996. MQ-1 was used extensively during Iraqi Freedom for interdicting and conducting armed reconnaissance against perishable targets. When not performing its primary mission, MQ-1 performs theater reconnaissance, surveillance, and target acquisition for joint forces commanders. The Predator is more than an aircraft. Although remotely flown by a pilot stationed on the ground and two sensor operators for information gathering, the Predator carries two AGM-114 laser-guided Hellfire anti-tank missiles. When not in use, the aircraft can be disassembled and loaded into a "coffin" for transportation elsewhere.

Both the Boeing E-3 Sentry and the Northrop Grumman E-8C Joint Stars were deployed in Desert Storm, Afghanistan, and Iraqi Freedom. They each perform a different but complementary function. The E-3 is an airborne warning and control system (AWACS)

*BELOW: A General Atomics Aeronautical Systems remotely piloted MQ-1 Predator assigned to the 46th Expeditionary Reconnaissance Squadron in Iraq provides real-time surveillance imagery to air and ground control units.*

aircraft that provides all-weather surveillance, command, control, and communications needed by commanders of air defense and other forces. A large rotating radar dome held by two struts provides 250 miles of surveillance from the earth's surface (land or water) and into the stratosphere, enabling the E-3 to direct fighter-interceptor aircraft to airborne targets. The E-8C adds another equation to the information cycle by providing a platform for airborne battle management, command and control, intelligence, surveillance, and reconnaissance. Unlike the dome on an AWAC, the E-8C carries a canoe-shaped radome under the forward fuselage that houses a twenty-four-foot, side-looking phased array antenna. Both aircraft continue to be part of the long-range plan for air domain control.

Boeing RC-135 variants, derived from the C-135, date back to 1964. The 55th Wing RC-135 fleet recently included two RC-135S Cobra Bells, one RC-135X Cobra Eye, two RC-135U Combat Sents, fourteen RC-135V/W Rivet Joints, and two RC-135 trainers. Each aircraft performs a slightly different mission, but their main task is to provide strategic electronic reconnaissance information to the president, secretary of defense, the JCS, and theater commanders with near real-time on-scene intelligence collection, analysis, and dissemination capabilities. For information gathering, the large aircraft are crucial for locating and identifying foreign military land, naval, and airborne radar signals.

With the exception of the U-2, which is being replaced by the RQ-4 Global Hawk, every plane in the air domain for information gathering will remain active through 2025.

## Information: The Ground Domain

The C4ISR ground domain consists of several networked warfighting headquarters responsible for command and control and the battle management of aircraft, satellites, and weapons, all of which collectively facilitate joint warfare.

Air and Space Operations Center (AOC) provides the weapon systems through which the air force

commander exercises command and control of air and space forces. The AOC is the governing element of the Theater Air Control System and has the capacity to automatically display current air, surface, and space situations. The operation center then collects, analyzes, evaluates, and disseminates the information in a manner that plans and tasks joint operations assets consistent with guidance from the theater commander.

The Distributed Common Ground System (DCGS) is a multi-service and powerful network-centric global enterprise. The air force portion is the AN/GSQ-272 Sentinel ISR weapon system that drives off the entire information collection system across the globe in peace and in combat. The air force DCGS is scalable and serves as the USAF's primary tasking network for warfighting.

The Battlefield Control System (BCS) is the front line weapons system that provides theater battle management to forces on the ground and in the air from satellites, sensors, and surveillance aircraft. The BCS is also a component of the North American Air Defense (NORAD) system, which is linked to the president, secretary of defense, and the National Military Command Center.

The ground domain contains several other niches. Combat commanders have access to an Integrated Command and Control System that provides near real-time warning of threats against North America from missiles, aircraft, and space. The system includes six early/long-range warning radars in northern hemisphere polar regions. The USAF also operates Space Situation Awareness Systems (SSA) to detect, track, catalog, and identify every object in space, specifically monitoring those satellites having adversarial space capabilities. Information from SSA and other sources will feed into a new Rapid Attack Identification, Direction, and Reporting System (RAIDRS) and have the capability to detect electromagnetic interference and identify the geolocation of the source. The ground domain depends heavily on the space domain for data, and new satellites are being constantly designed to meet the defensive/offensive needs of the future.

**ABOVE: Satellite tracking and control range management are conducted through the headquarters of the Air Force Space Command's 2nd and 3rd Space Wings and the Consolidated Space Operations Center.**

*ABOVE: In preparation for being called to duty, the 193rd Special Operations Wing of the Pennsylvania Air National Guard continues training on EC-130J Commando Solo psychological and information operations aircraft.*

## Information: Cyberspace

Cyberspace is the electronic medium of net-centric operations, communication systems, and computers in which on-line communication takes place. Net-Centric Warfare (NCW) exploits information superiority. It creates increased combat power by networking sensors, decision makers, and shooters to achieve shared awareness, increased speed of command, greater tempo of operations, greater lethality, increased survivability, and a degree of self-synchronization. NCW operations are conducted through a dynamic combination of hardware, software, data, and human components in the cyberspace domain of information.

Net-centric C4ISR operations are built around the command and control (C2) constellation, which is a component of C4ISR sharing horizontally and vertically integrated information through computer-to-computer conversations enabled by peer-based sensors, command centers, and shooters. The constellation net covers air, space, and terrestrial communications that facilitate a rapid free flow of information to warfighters.

## Global Attack

Global attack teams up with *Global Reach and Power* and provides the ability to engage adversary targets rapidly and persistently with a wide range of munitions, anywhere at any time. Military attributes require air and space power—speed, range, flexibility, precision, and persistence—to give the strike force the ability to locate and attack targets of choice anywhere within the battlespace. The USAF continues to develop the ability to engage globally and apply force using a variety of weapon systems producing both lethal and non-lethal effects. Flexibility includes the support of joint forces in both traditional and irregular threat conditions. The Global Attack system relies on manned and remotely piloted aircraft, ICBMs, and current and future attack systems with both regional and deep strike capabilities.

Part of the system, the Lockheed F-117A Nighthawk, designed around now-dated low-observable stealth technology, is now more than twenty-five years old and scheduled to be replaced by the Lockheed-Martin F-22A Raptor, which in 2005 received approval for full production. The Raptor's combination of stealth, supercruise, maneuverability, and integrated avionics, combined with its ability to carry JDAMs, small bombs, and other munitions, represent an exponential leap in warfighting capabilities.

Another new entry, the F-35A Joint Strike Fighter (JSF), will be a stealthy, multi-role, strike aircraft with high lethality, survivability, and maintainability. The aircraft will be capable of performing air-to-air and air-to-ground missions for the air force, navy and Marine Corps. F-35As will replace the aging F-16 Fighting Falcons, which have been around since 1979, and eventually the A-10 Thunderbolts, which debuted in 1975.

The current bomber force, consisting of North American B-1B Lancers, Northrop Grumman B-2 Spirits, and Boeing's B-52H Stratofortresses, will be around for at least another two decades, although the

ABOVE: Two Lockheed F-22 Raptors out of Tyndall Air Force Base, Florida, trail behind a KC-135R Stratotanker after in-flight refueling during a preparedness exercise over the Atlantic on April 2, 2007.

ABOVE: The General Atomics Aeronautical Systems MQ-9 Reaper unmanned aerial vehicle (UAV) with a hunter/killer weapon system is flown remotely by a two-man crew and has a combat radius if 1,878 miles.

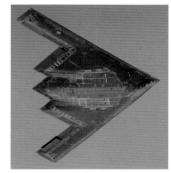

ABOVE: This Northrop Grumman B-2 Spirit out of Whiteman Air Force Base, Missouri, has low-observable stealth characteristics and massive firepower, and is capable of delivering conventional and nuclear weapons anywhere in the world.

USAF is looking at new bomber designs for fielding by 2018. The new bomber will have the range, persistence, payload, and survivability to operate in present and future threat environments. The design will include leap-ahead technology now in development.

The Predator family of UAVs includes the MQ-9 Reaper, a medium-to-high altitude, long endurance, remotely piloted hunter-killer weapon system built by General Atomics Aeronautical Systems. The Predator's primary mission is to destroy emerging targets with Hellfire missiles and JDAM bombs. Its secondary mission is to provide real-time intelligence through surveillance and reconnaissance to theater commanders.

The Boeing LGM-30 Minuteman III intercontinental ballistic missile is still a part of the nation's strategic deterrent force. Fired from a hardened silo, the 79,432-pound ICBM has a range of 6,000-plus miles. Production stopped in December 1978, and the USAF feels that a replacement or modernization for the Minuteman should be considered sometime during the early 2020s, though no designs have been announced.

## Rapid Global Mobility

To achieve *Global Reach* requires rapid global mobility, which includes air refueling, airlift, spacelift, and other capabilities that together enable and sustain joint force operations around the world. The system must be agile enough to deploy U.S. military power anywhere at a speed and tempo adversaries cannot match, and be

LEFT: December 15, 2006, marked the initial, full-fledged capability test of Lockheed Martin's F-35 Joint Strike Fighter, which is a multi-national, multi-service family of next-generation strike fighters that will replace the air force's F-16s and A-10s.

capable of operating effectively across the entire battlespace.

The backbone of U.S. global mobility today depends on Boeing C-17 Globemaster IIIs, Lockheed C-141 Starlifters, Lockheed C-130 Hercules, and Lockheed-Georgia C-5 Galaxies. While the C-141s (now all assigned to the Air Force Reserve) are scheduled for replacement, the huge C-5 has gone through several modifications and is scheduled for more, variants of the C-130 (including E/H/J models now in service) have been steadily modernized with better engines, avionics, and capabilities, and the C-17 is the USAF's newest and most flexible cargo aircraft. The Pentagon is currently studying designs for a new Joint Cargo Aircraft (JCA) that will offer a light airlift solution to requirements for supply of combat forces for all the services.

Essential components of rapid global mobility are the air refueling tankers that increase the range, payload, and ultimately the flexibility and versatility of combat and combat support aircraft. Air refueling is the in-flight transfer of fuel between McDonnell Douglas KC-10 Extenders or Boeing KC-135 Stratotankers and receiving aircraft.

The KC-10, built around the DC-10 airliner, entered service in 1981, has a speed of 619 mph, and can carry 356,000 pounds of fuel or 170,000 pounds of cargo 4,400 miles. There are currently fifty-nine KC-10s active in the air force. The KC-135 Stratotanker has been the USAF's aerial refueling and airlift workhorse since 1965. It has a range of 1,500 miles when loaded with 200,000 pounds of fuel or 83,000 pounds of cargo and thirty-seven passengers. Although the current tankers are not scheduled for retirement, the air force is studying plans for a new KC-X, which will fill the perceived requirements for future tankers and transports in support of rapid global mobility.

## Precision Engagement

Providing precision engagement has been demonstrated during Desert Storm and with new refinements a decade later during Iraqi Freedom. As a component of *Global Reach and Power*, precision engagement is the ability to apply discriminate lethal or non-lethal force exactly where required to achieve control of the battlespace. One of the perceived key objectives in future conflicts, especially during irregular operations during the global war on terror, is to develop, in addition to more precise kinetic weapons, non-lethal weapons that disable the target without destroying infrastructure and non-combatants. Although today's precision weapons attempt to reduce collateral damage, the development of non-lethal weapons is still forthcoming.

Today's air-to-ground munitions will remain about the same over the next two decades. The JDAM guidance tail kit attached to GBU bombs has already turned conventional ordnance into "smart" munitions. The High Speed Anti-radiation Missile (HARM) will continue to destroy enemy radar-equipped air defense systems. The Joint Air-to-Surface Standoff Missile-Extended Range (JASSM-ER) will continue to function as the USAF's precision, low observable, cruise missile to kill hardened and soft fixed and relocatable targets at ranges well beyond enemy air defenses.

Meanwhile, the USAF is working on a small, 250 pound-class air-to-ground weapon with a precision munition capable of striking fixed and relocatable targets from a standoff range with explosive technology designed to minimize collateral damage. The SDB, planned for implementation during the next decade, carries its own mission planning system for taking out a discrete target.

The USAF is also studying a conceptual High Speed/Hypersonic Standoff Weapon (HSSW) with rapid all-weather response capability against time sensitive targets. The weapon will be compatible with all modern global attack platforms during the 2020s.

ABOVE: While piloting an F/A-22 Raptor, Lieutenant Colonel Wade Tolliver, director of operations, 27th Fighter Squadron, releases a 1,000-pound GBU-32 Joint Direct Attack Munition (JDAM) on a practice target.

BELOW: A weapons crew from the 157th Aircraft Maintenance Unit loads a GBU-31A 1,000-pound Joint Direct Attack Munition (JDAM) guided bomb onto an F-16C Fighting Falcon during Operation Iraqi Freedom.

## Specialized Air Power

*Global Vigilance, Reach and Power* cannot be achieved without the specialized air power required to combat irregular operations and pursue the global war on terror. Ingredients require an Air Force Special Operations Command (AFSOC) and an Air Combat Command with specialized airpower. The duties are different but mesh. AFSOC provides special operations strike, ISR/information, and airmobility forces. Air Combat Command provides combat search and rescue (CSAR) operations.

Special operations strike forces rely on the primary missions of Lockheed/Boeing AC-130H/U gunships—close air support, air interdiction, and force protection. The AC-130H's call sign is "Spectre," while the AC-130U's is "Spooky." The gunships' psychological impact on the enemy makes both names appropriate. AC-130s have a long combat history, dating back to Vietnam. The heavily gunned aircraft provide armed reconnaissance and direct support of ground troops engaged with enemy forces. AC-130s will continue as part of AFSOC into the 2020s, although a next generation gunship (NGG) with better survivability

**ABOVE: An F-15C Eagle assigned to the 28th Test Squadron from Elgin Air Force Base, Florida. powers into a vertical climb during a mission to evaluate the AIM-9X Sidewinder short-range, heat-seeking, air intercept missile.**

The current mix of air-to-air munitions is constantly being upgraded and improved with better guidance systems. The AIM-7 radar-guided Sparrow will eventually be replaced. The AIM-9X Sidewinder will replace AIM-9M short-range, infrared-seeking, fire-and-forget missiles. The all-weather Advanced Medium Range Air-to-Air Missile (AMRAAM) will be upgraded to be compatible with the latest combat aircraft, including F-22A Raptors and F-35A JSFs. A fourth air-to-air missile, the Joint Dual Air Role Dominance Missile (JDRADM) is under consideration for the 2020s. It will be a single missile for both air-to-air and air-to-ground combat. It has a highly classified guidance system to address anticipated changes in evolving threats.

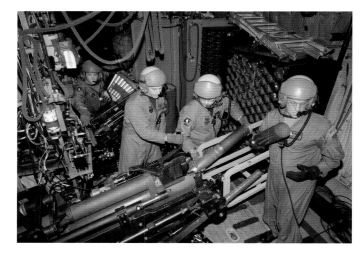

**ABOVE: The aircrew on board a Lockheed/Boeing AC-130U Hercules "Spooky" gunship, 4th Special Operations Squadron, load the 40mm Bofors gun (to the rear) and 105mm howitzer for close air support during the surge in Iraq.**

*LEFT: Three air force CV-22 tiltrotor Ospreys from the 58th Special Operations Wing perform vertical take off during a training mission that replicates the landing capabilities of helicopters and the flight characteristics of turboprop aircraft.*

*BELOW: During Operation Northern Watch, personnel from the 129th Expeditionary Rescue Squadron board a Lockheed MC-130P Combat Shadow for a nighttime training exercise prior to deployment in the Middle East.*

and armed with a combination of more lethal and less-than-lethal weapons is on the drawing board for 2025.

AFSOC information gathering operations have been uniquely adapted to Special Forces needs. The EC-130J Commando Solo aircraft is a Hercules transport that conducts psychological operations and civil affairs broadcasts in addition to gathering information. The aircraft carries extra armor, air refueling capability, and an enhanced navigation system.

Another part of AFSOCs system uses MQ-1 Predator remotely piloted UAVs for air interdiction and conducting armed reconnaissance against critical and perishable targets. When not performing Special Forces missions, the MQ-1 provides airborne surveillance and target acquisition for joint forces in the battlespace.

During the next decade, the MQ-1 will be augmented by the MQ-9 Reaper, which will be a more powerful, multi-mission, and scaled-up derivative from the Predator.

A Special Forces mobility unit is a combination of highly specialized MC-130E/H Combat Talons and MC-130P Combat Shadows working with Sikorsky MH-53 Pave Low helicopters and CV-22 tilt-rotor Ospreys. The missing element is the Joint Cargo Aircraft (JCA), which the air force hopes to make available before 2017.

The MC-130E/H, with a J version planned for the near future, provides infiltration, extraction, and resupply of special operations in hostile territory. The Combat Talon can also air-refuel helicopters, provide electronic warfare, and carry up to seventy-seven troops or fifty-seven litter patients. The MC-130P flies clandestine or low-visibility operations, often at night, intruding hostile areas and providing air refueling for MH-53 special operations helicopters. The heavy-lift MH-53 Pave Lows fly low-level, long-range, undetected penetration missions into denied areas, day or night, for infiltration, extraction, and resupply of embedded Special Forces operations. Pave Lows are the largest, most powerful and technologically advanced helicopters in the air force inventory. The MH-53 is gradually being replaced by the CV-22 tilt-rotor Osprey, which can fly all-weather long-rage missions with greater fuel efficiency and twice the speed of helicopters.

Air Combat Command provides combat search and rescue (CSAR) as part of Specialized Air Power. Today's force consists of Sikorsky HH-60G Pave Hawk helicopters and HC-130P/N transports. The primary mission of the HH-60 is to conduct long-range missions, day or night, into hostile environments to recover downed aircrew or other isolated personnel. The HH-60s, derivatives of Black Hawks, are currently wearing out and during the next decade will be replaced by the CSAR-X, a faster helicopter with greater range, increased payload, all-weather penetration, and state-of-the-art defensive systems. It is specifically designed for special operations in chemical, biological, and nuclear environments.

The HC-130P/N is also an older aircraft that has extended range for CSAR operations at night. Its primary mission is to extend the range of recovery force helicopters by in-flight refueling. The HC-130 is also headed toward replacement during the next decade by the CRT-X, a combat refueling tanker specifically designed for deeper penetration and search and rescue operations.

## Flight Training

One of the foremost requirements in achieving *Global Vigilance, Reach and Power* is the air force's tradition of producing the world's most proficient pilots. Undergraduate training today annually turns out about 1,500 pilots and 550 combat systems operators for the air force, Air National Guard, Air Force Reserve Command, and sister services. Every man and woman also receives joint operations and survival training.

The current undergraduate flying training structure contains five types of aircraft, many of which are already operating on extended life cycles. The Raytheon Beech T-1A Jayhawk, used for training airlift and tanker pilots, went into service in 1992. The Cessna T-37 Tweet, used for joint specialized training, made its first flight in 1955. The Northrop T-38 Talon, an advanced jet pilot trainer, first flew in 1959. The Boeing T-43A, a navigator version of the 737, began flying in 1973. The Raytheon T-6A Texan II became operational in May 2000 as a basic, single-engined, two-seat primary trainer to start future pilots on the learning curve. All of the aircraft are routinely upgraded and modernized to keep pace with technology. Both the T-37B and the T-43 are scheduled for discontinuation or replacement, partly to

satisfy the needs of the USAF and partly to meet the requirements of joint forces.

## Sustaining the Future Force

Chief of Staff Moseley expects science and technology to compensate for a smaller but significantly more capable force through developments in advanced energetics, directed energy, hypersonics, and nanotechnology, along with improved aircraft, operational support, expeditionary logistics, and training techniques. Over the next decade, efforts will be concentrated on agile combat support.

Moseley looks ahead to the *Air Force Roadmap* creating a force structure that "will not only revolutionize traditional, high-intensity combat operations, but also help enable the United States to face new irregular, potentially catastrophic, and disruptive challenges."

As world threats change, so must the air force.

*ABOVE: Lieutenant Colonel Dave Wright taxis his Raytheon T-6 Texan II into Randolph Air Force Base after completing a certification flight on February 10, 2005, which qualifies him to demonstrate the trainer's performance at air shows.*

# BIBLIOGRAPHY

*Air Force Roadmap 2006-2025*. http://www.af.mil/roadmap

Ambrose, Stephen E. *Eisenhower: President and Elder Statesman*. Vol. 2. New York: Simon & Schuster, 1984.

Anderton, David A. *History of the U.S. Air Force*. New York: Military Press, 1989.

Arnold, Henry H. *Global Mission*. New York: Harper & Bros., 1949.

Axelrod, Alan. *Encyclopedia of the U.S. Air Force*. New York: Checkmark Books, 2006.

Baudot, Marcel, and Henri Bernard, et al, eds. *The Historical Encyclopedia of World War II*. New York: Greenwich House, 1977.

Benson, James, and Holmes, Tony. *USAF for the 21st Century: Super Wing Total Force Integration*. London: Osprey Aerospace, 1996.

Boyne, Walter J. *Beyond the Wild Blue: A History of the U.S. Air Force 1947-1997*. New York: St. Martin's Press, 1997.

_____. *Silver Wings: A History of the United States Air Force*. New York: Simon & Schuster, 1993.

Berman, Larry. *Lyndon Johnson's War: The Road to Stalemate in Vietnam*. New York: W. W. Norton, 1989.

Brereton, Lewis H. *The Brereton Diaries*. New York: William Morrow & Company, 1946.

Carter, Kit C., and Mueller, Robert. *The Army Air Forces in World War II: Combat Chronology 1941-1945*. Washington, D.C.: Office of Air force History, 1973.

Coyne, James P. *Air Power in the Gulf*. Arlington, Va.: Aerospace Education Foundation, 1992.

Curtiss, Glenn, and Post ,Augustus. *The Curtiss Aviation Book*. New York: Frederick A. Stokes, 1912.

Daso, Dik Alan. *Hap Arnold and the Evolution of American Air Power*. Washington, D.C.: Smithsonian Institution Press, 2000.

Fall, Bernard B. *Last Reflections on a War*. New York: Doubleday, 1967.

Freeman, Roger A. *The Mighty Eighth: A History of the U.S. 8th Army Air Force*. Garden City, NY: Doubleday, 1970.

Friedman, Norman. *Desert Victory: The War for Kuwait*. Annapolis, Md.: Naval Institute Press, 1991.

Frisbee, John L., ed. *Makers of the United States Air Force*. Washington, D.C.: Office of Air Force History, 1987.

Futrell, Frank. *The United States Air Force in Korea, 1950-1953*. Washington, D.C.: Office of Air Force History, 1983.

Gauvreau, Emile. *The Wild Blue Yonder: Sons of the Prophet Carry On*. New York: E. P. Dutton & Company, 1944.

Glines, C. V. *From the Wright Brothers to the Astronauts: The Memoirs of Major General Benjamin D. Foulis*. New York: McGraw-Hill, 1968.

Gurney, Gene. *Vietnam: The War in the Air*. New York: Crown Publishers, Inc., 1985.

Halberstadt, Hans. *The Wild Weasels: History of U.S. Air Force SAM Killers, 1965-Today*. Osceola, Wis.: Motorbooks International, 1992.

Huie, William Bradford. *The Fight for Air Power*. New York: L. B. Fischer, 1942.

Jablonski, Edward. *Airwar*. Garden City, N.Y.: Doubleday & Company, 1971.

Jackson, Robert, and Jim Winchester. *Military Aircraft: 1914 to the Present Day*. Edison, N.J.: Chartwell Books, 2004.

Kutler, Stanley I. *Encyclopedia of the Vietnam War*. New York: Charles Scribner's Sons, 1996.

Lambeth, Benjamin S. *The Transformation of American Air Power*. Cornell University Press, 2000.

Lopez, C. Todd. "Air Force focused on three priorities," www.af.mil/news/story_print.asp?id=123027010

Marcy, Sam. "The general blows it: Fired for leaking Pentagon plan to terror-bomb Iraq civilians," www.workers,org/marcy/cd/sam90/1990html/s900927b.htm

McCarthy, James P. and DeBerry, Drue L., eds. *The Air Force.* Andrews AFB, Md.: Air Force Historical Foundation, 2002.

Mets, David R. *Master of Air Power: General Carl a Spaatz.* Novatny, Ca.: Presidio Press, 1988.

Mitchell, William. *Memoirs of World War I: From Start to Finish of Our Greatest War.* New York: Random House, 1960.

Momyer, William W. *Air Power in Three Wars (WWII, Korea, Vietnam).* Washington, D.C.: Office of Air Force History, 1985.

Murray, Williamson. *Air War in the Persian Gulf.* Baltimore: Nautical & Aviation Publishing Company, 1991.

*New World Vistas: Air and Space Power for the 21st Century (Summary Volume).* Washington, D.C.: Department of the Air Force, 1995.

*Peterson, Harold L.,* ed. *Encyclopedia of Firearms.* New York: E. P. Dutton, 1964.

Ripley, Tim. *Air War Iraq.* Barnsley, UK: Pen & Sword. 2004.

Roberts, Michael. *The Illustrated Directory of the United States Air Force.* New York: Crescent Books, 1989.

Rust, Kenn C. *The 9th Air Force in World War II.* Fallbrook, Ca.: Aero Publishers, 1967.

Schwartz, Richard Alan. *Encyclopedia of the Persian Gulf War.* Jefferson, N.C.: McFarland & Company, 1998.

Seversky, Alexander P. *Victory Through Air Power.* New York: Simon & Schuster, 1942.

Shulman, Seth. *Unlocking the Sky: Glenn Hammond Curtis and the Race to Invent the Airplane.* New York: HarperCollins Publishers, 2002.

Speer, Albert. *Inside the Third Reich.* New York: The Macmillan Company, 1970.

Sunderman, James F. *World War II in the Air: Europe.* New York: Franklin Watts, 1963.

_____. *World War II in the Air: The Pacific.* New York: Franklin Watts, 1962.

Swanborough, F. G., and Bowers, Peter M.. *United States Military Aircraft Since 1909.* New York: Putnam, 1963.

Tillman, Barrett. *Above and Beyond: The Aviation Medals of Honor.* Washington, D.C.: Smithsonian Institution Press, 2002.

Tillman, Barrett, with Boyne, Walter J., ed. *The U.S. Air Force.* New York: Alpha Books, 2003.

Tucker, Spencer C., ed. *Encyclopedia of the Korean War: A Political, Social and Military History.* New York: Checkmark Books, 2002.

_____. Encyclopedia of the Vietnam War: *A Political, Social and Military History.* New York: Oxford University Press, 1998.

Veronica, Nicholas A., and Dunn, Jim. *21st Century U.S. Air Power.* St. Paul, Minn.: MBI Publishing Company, 2004.

Whitehouse, Arch. *The Years of the Sky Kings.* New York: Doubleday & Company, 1959.

# INDEX